Wise Up to Teens

Insights into Marketing and Advertising to Teenagers

2nd Edition

Wise Up to Teens

Insights into Marketing and Advertising to Teenagers

2nd Edition

by Peter Zollo

New Strategist Publications, Inc.
Ithaca, New York

New Strategist Publications, Inc.
P.O. Box 242, Ithaca, New York 14851
607/273-0913
www.newstrategist.com

ISBN 1-88507020-9

Printed in the United States of America

To Debbie, Ben, Nini, and Jimmy

Table of Contents

Tables

Chapter 1. Why Teens Are Important Consumers

Chapter 2. Teens, Products, and Brands

Chapter 3. Teens and Media

Chapter 4. Teen Activities and Interests

Chapter 5. Teen Trends and Social Hierarchy

Chapter 6. Teens and Music

Chapter 7. The Power of Celebrity

Chapter 8. Teen Values

Chapter 9. The Essence of Being Teen

Chapter 10. Teen Life: Home, Play, School

Chapter 11. Advertising and Promoting to Teens

The children now love luxury. They have bad manners, contempt for authority, they show disrespect for adults, and love to talk rather than work or exercise. They no longer rise when adults enter the room. They contradict their parents, chatter in front of company, gobble down food at the table, and intimidate their teachers.

—SOCRATES (469–399 B.C.)

Acknowledgments

I agree with the teens we study, who (perhaps to their parents' pleasant surprise) place family first and foremost in their lives. So—thank you Debbie for being my best sounding board and, of course, for just putting up with me. Ben, Nini, Jimmy—you guys are the best! Thanks for always understanding your dad's crazy travel schedule. Dad and Mom, thank you for your unbridled pride and never-ending interest.

TRU's success is really due to the incredible people I'm fortunate enough to work with and learn from on a daily basis. Since this book mostly emanates from our syndicated division, let me start there. Michael Wood, your unparalleled enthusiasm for what we do, who we are, and where we're going is completely contagious. I thank you for it and so much more. Jill Kilcoyne, let me simply say that I don't know (and I hope not to find out) what I'd do without you. Kate Danaj, you've already brought so much to TRU, and I know, there's much more to come. Dan Drath, I'm still trying to figure out what you can't do—thank you for your wisdom that belies your years. Gary Rudman, I thank you for cutting down on my travel schedule by being probably the researcher who talks to more teens face to face than anyone, anywhere. The insights you bring cut to the essence of what we do. What can I possibly say to Chris Efken, who's now the senior TRU staffer. . .but thank you for your continuing commitment to TRU and the pride and love you always show for your work. Thanks, too, to the people who make TRU really work—our wonderful field, administrative, and junior staff: Jackie Stierwalt, Shannon McLowry, Danielle Craven, and Mary Robbins.

Though some staff inevitably moves on, they've left their mark and will always be appreciated. Thank you especially to Marla Grossberg, Jackie Orenstein, John Baker, and Jason Frankena.

Paul and Ann Krouse, without you, there simply would be no TRU. Thank you for your continuing support and friendship. Burleigh Gardner's vision and brilliance will forever inspire me.

Research and marketing are collaborative processes. I've benefited greatly from my clients' experiences, ideas, and challenges. (Fortunately) you're too many to name, so I thank you all for what you've brought to each study and to each new day.

Thank you to those who helped in the publishing, editing, and design of this book—Penelope Wickham and Cheryl Russell of New Strategist Publications, and Bill Ewing of Ewing Davison Group for the great book jacket.

Lastly (and perhaps most important), let me thank all of TRU's teen respondents through the years, whose numbers (at last count) exceed 250,000. You've informed me, inspired me, and constantly interest, amaze, and surprise me. How lucky I am to have a career at which you're the center.

Introduction

Our company, Teenage Research Unlimited, is fortunate to specialize in what's arguably the most fascinating, challenging, and quickly changing age segment: teenagers.

The challenge for anyone who studies teenagers is that all of us were once teens ourselves. Because of this experience, we carry with us certain expectations, beliefs, perceptions (and misperceptions) rooted in our memory. Studying teenagers is unlike studying ethnic groups of which you are not a member, because we've all been teenagers. This makes it inherently more difficult to view teenagers as a market segment in an objective, unbiased manner.

We used to advise our clients to forget everything they remembered about their teen years and start with a clean slate. These days, we guide our clients in employing "selective memory." We ask them to remember their experiences while growing up and (most important) the *feelings* associated with those experiences. It is the feelings associated with the tumultuous developmental transition from adolescence to adulthood that remain the same from generation to generation. These are the life-stage truths and motivations that are fundamental and timeless.

In contrast to the timeless motivations and emotions of teenage life, the external trappings—fashion, music, social concerns, lifestyle choices, and related behaviors and attitudes—change with each teenage cohort. This book examines both areas: teenage as a life stage and teenagers as a cohort.

This book is based upon my more than 15 years of experience as a researcher and marketing consultant with Teenage Research Unlimited (TRU), which is located in Northbrook, Illinois. Most of the data included in these pages come from TRU's syndicated study of teenagers, titled the

Teenage Marketing & Lifestyle Study. This is the largest and most frequently published study of its type. More than 100 of the top youth-oriented brands rely on it to assure that their products, marketing, and advertising efforts are compelling and relevant to teens. The study is based on the responses of a nationally representative sample of more than 2,000 12-to-19-year-olds, with results released every six months. This large sample allows the data to be analyzed in many different ways, including by demographics, product and brand usage, activities, attitudes, and TRU's segmentation system, known as Teen/Types. TRU has been conducting this semiannual multiclient study since 1983, giving us a considerable amount of historical data with which we can show where teens are headed across a great variety of areas and issues.

Many of the insights in this book come from my experience as a research moderator and consultant. Over the years, I've moderated countless focus groups, minigroups, triads, buddy pairs, and one-on-ones in almost every configuration and venue and on almost every subject imaginable—from athletic shoes to anti-tobacco, cars to condoms, sneakers to soda, peer pressure to partying. Fortunately—and by design—these quantitative and qualitative experiences overlap and provide a fuller, synergistic experience. Therefore, this book features not only data but also the insights behind the numbers.

Finally, it's imperative to recognize that understanding teens is a continuing process. At TRU, we like to say that trying to understand teens doesn't have to be trying. We're committed to uncovering new methods to more effectively (and more enjoyably) research teens—digging deeper and deeper into who teens are, what they do, what they think, how they feel, and why they feel the way they do. If I had to choose a single word to describe teens, it would be "change." Teens are personally evolving as human beings emotionally, intellectually, and physically. And each generation of teens has its own set of characteristics, many of which are results of the events and the environment of that cohort's teen years.

So, teens are at times a volatile and fickle audience. If anything, it is this constant change that is their most consistent characteristic. It is also their most challenging and endearing quality.

Marketers, too, must be ready for change to stay truly attuned to teenagers. At TRU, we're constantly examining and changing not only what we say to teens, but how and where we observe them, talk to them, and listen to them.

The moral is, if you're serious about marketing to teens, you need to be in it for the long run. Taking an occasional "snapshot" view of teens can dangerously mislead you. Only by committing yourself to an ongoing program of talking to, listening to, and systematically monitoring this age group can you hope to profit from the teen market.

Chapter 1.

Why Teens Are Important Consumers

Coca-Cola, McDonald's, adidas, Dr. Pepper/7-Up, Revlon, Jordache, Converse, TDK, Columbia Pictures. Although this list sounds like a veritable *Who's Who* of teen marketers, when I approached these companies about marketing to teens when TRU began in 1982, teenagers were not their primary target.

Most of these companies have wised up to teens since then. In fact, Coca-Cola has to be on anyone's short list of today's most effective teen marketers.

What convinced most of these companies, and many others, to change their strategy? For some, it was the recognition that their business could profit from teens today. For others, it was a long-term commitment to develop a relationship with teens now for future payoff. And for some, it was simply the coming of Generation Y, the biggest population cohort since the boomers. Over the past 10 years, many marketers have come to the same conclusion: teens are a consumer segment too powerful and a marketing opportunity too profitable to ignore.

There are two keys to success in this market: first, acknowledge the importance of teenage consumers; and second, recognize their uniqueness. Advertising and marketing that work with adults often will not work with teens. And certainly, advertising and marketing that are geared to children are almost always inappropriate for teens. Teenagers not only like ownership, they demand it. They want media and products they can call their own. This characteristic, which is uniquely teenage, dictates the strategies and tactics needed to communicate with teens. But there's a fine line between what works and what doesn't in marketing to teens. If teens regard marketing messages as blatantly teenlike or trying too hard to be cool, they can quickly reject not only the message but also the messenger. In fact, teens in the late 1990s have become particularly savvy about marketing. In focus groups we conduct, teen respondents use terms like "target marketing" and "product attributes" in discussing the advertising or product issues at hand. And no wonder. Teens are the targets of more marketing efforts today than ever before. So although many companies are wising up to the potential of what teens can mean for their business, teens are wising up to marketing tactics.

This scenario strikes fear in the hearts of some of the bravest marketers. It is a major reason why many companies shy away from the teen market. Clearly, teens are a high-risk proposition. But they also promise high reward. If you can reach and communicate with them effectively, the payoff will be worth the effort. And if you steer clear of Gen Y, you risk stopping the growth of your business for many years.

Over the past few years, two misconceptions about marketing to teens have finally been erased, and rightfully so: one, teens are too elusive to reach because, as a target, they move too fast to hit them with any precision; and two, they are simply too fickle. As media vehicles for youth proliferated in the 1980s and 1990s, from MTV to Channel One and from *Teen People* to countless Web sites and 'zines, and from countless local radio stations to a plethora of "lifestyle" special events and venues, teens have become easier to reach than ever before. When companies realize that teens can be a viable target, they systematically work to understand teens so they can profit from this market, creating advertising, promotions, events, and new products specifically for teens.

Marketers are rethinking their teen positioning for reasons that range from demographic to sociological. There are six key reasons why teens are such an important segment, and why more companies are jumping on the teen bandwagon every day.

1. Teens are important because of their discretionary spending power. How much teens spend continues to be the subject of more media stories about the teen market than all other topics combined. Their spending—more than $140 billion a year—is staggering, astounding reporters and marketers alike. Our firm probably gets at least 10 calls a week from

Teen Spending

Teenagers spend more than $50 a week of their own money, plus another $28 a week of family money.

(average weekly spending of teenagers by gender, age, and source of funds, 1998)

	Total money	Own money	Family money
Total	**$84**	**$56**	**$28**
Boys	84	59	25
Girls	83	53	30
Aged 12 to 15	53	27	26
Aged 16 to 17	103	65	38
Aged 18 to 19	125	105	20

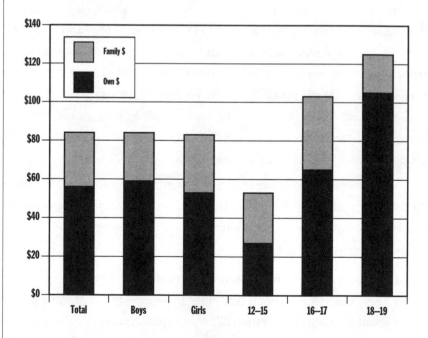

Source: TRU *Teenage Marketing & Lifestyle Study*

reporters with questions ranging from teen vegetarianism to what's hot in fashion. But probably half the questions concern what we've come to refer to as "the teen market story."

I must admit that we enjoy these interviews least of all because the reporters want to know only the basics: how much money teens spend and earn. We've recited these figures more times than any of us cares to admit, but there's no escaping just how compelling they are. Combined with population trends, the numbers have convinced quite a few marketers to get serious about teens.

In the 1980s, we called teens "skippies" (School Kids with Income and Purchasing Power) to help open marketers' eyes to the vast potential teens represent. Back then, we at TRU spent as much time trying to convince companies of the viability of the teen market as helping them understand teens. These days, companies are coming out of the woodwork to market to teens, saving researchers from having to invent any more lame acronyms and allowing us instead to concentrate on the business of researching teens. So, on with the numbers.

Teens spent $94 billion of their own (earned) money in 1998, according to projections by TRU. Combine that with the family money they spend, and teens spend more than several states put together—an amount equivalent to half the U.S. defense budget! Teens still spend their money on typical teen products such as music, snack foods, cosmetics, and clothes. They also spend it on family groceries, pagers, cell phones, and Internet service providers. (The next chapter discusses in detail the many things teens buy.)

Teenage boys spend an average of $59 a week of their own money, while girls spend $53. Although boys have more of their own money to spend, girls spend more of their family's money. Consequently, the difference in total spending between teenage boys and girls narrows to just $1 a week.

Boys have more of their own money to spend than girls because their incomes are greater. That boys work at paying jobs about an hour per week more than girls only partially explains this disparity. Boys either work for higher wages than girls or they receive more money from their parents for their own spending than girls. Overall, teen boys have a weekly income of $84 compared to $71 for girls.

Teens get their money from a variety of sources. In fact, we like to think of teens as having a more diversified income portfolio than most adults. Because of this spread, their income is more stable than that of adults (although not entirely protected).

In 1998, American teens had a combined income of $121 billion, up from $86 billion in 1993. Although teens think they are insulated from national economic trends, teen income rises and falls with the economy. Many parents say that if they're suffering financially, their children will be the last to feel it. But when the economy dips, teen income also drops because much of it comes from parents. Similarly, when the economy is on the upswing, so is teen income.

The older a teen, the more likely he or she is to have a regular job. Younger teens are more dependent on the allowance and as-needed money their parents give them. Not surprisingly, older teens earn and spend dramatically more money than younger teens.

Not only are today's teens earning and spending significant sums of money, they are gaining experience in handling money. More than 9 out of 10 are involved in a financial transaction (spending or earning) every week. Over two-thirds (69 percent) have savings accounts; almost one-third of 18- and 19-year-olds hold a credit card in their name; 17 percent of teens own stocks or bonds. Additionally, nearly 21 percent of teens have checking accounts and 12 percent have certificates of deposit. Nine percent have access to a credit card in their parents' name, and 35 percent say they would like to have a credit card in their own name.

2. Teens are important because they spend family money. Because most teens live in families with two working parents or a single parent,

Teen Income

The weekly income of older teens is four times that of younger teens, on average.

(average weekly income of teenagers by gender and age, 1998)

	average weekly income
Total	$78
Boys	84
Girls	71
Aged 12 to 15	32
Aged 16 and 17	95
Aged 18 and 19	151

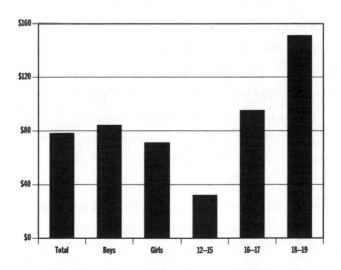

Source: TRU *Teenage Marketing & Lifestyle Study*

they are assuming greater responsibility for household shopping than did teens in the past. Simply put, teens are sometimes the only family members who have time to stand in line at the grocery store.

More than one-half of teenage girls and more than one-third of teen boys do some food shopping each week for their family. Most just do fill-in buying, but some are responsible for major household shopping. And, of course, most teens at times accompany parents to the food store.

When teens stroll the grocery aisles, they're not only being exposed to hundreds of products and thousands of brands, they are also sorting out those brands and products in their minds and in their hearts. When they do the shopping themselves (typically funded by parents), they make household brand decisions. In doing so, they begin to develop buying habits, patterns, and loyalties. Most teen food shoppers go to the store with a list prepared by mom, but typically the list is generic. Instead of specifying "Hellmann's," for example, it simply says "mayonnaise." In this scenario, most teens choose the same brand they are used to seeing in their refrigerator or cupboard. But for a smaller segment of teens, a more rebellious nature emerges even in the mundane setting of a grocery store. These teens seem to say, "Mom buys Hellmann's. . .hell if I'm going to!"

TRU projects that teens spent a total of $47 billion of family money in 1998. Notably, this figure does not include the family spending that is influenced by teenagers. Consequently, the total economic impact of teenagers far exceeds the $141 billion of their own and family money teens spent in 1998.

3. Teens are important because they influence their parents' spending. Teens influence their parents' purchases in four all-too-familiar ways. First, when teenagers (or children) accompany their parents to the store, their parents often let them add some "gimmes" to the cart: either the teen convinces the parent to buy something, or the teen grabs something from the shelf without much protest from mom or dad. (In focus groups, teens have told us about a variety of seemingly devious tactics they use to get what they want, such as sneaking items into the grocery cart or handing an item directly to the cashier, quickly bypassing their parent's eyes.) Most parents understand that when their teenage children volunteer to keep them company during a grocery-store excursion, it is not because the teen is seizing the opportunity to spend quality time with them. Instead, teens know that there is something in it for them. As much as they may request that mom or dad buy them a certain product or brand, teens know the odds of getting exactly what they want increase if they make the trip themselves. They also recognize that—like adults—they often don't know what they want until they see it on the shelves or sample it in the aisles.

Second, as alluded to above, teenagers influence their parents even when they are not with them by encouraging them to buy a preferred brand. Either the teen specifically requests a brand or parents know that the purchase might go to waste if they don't buy exactly what the teen wants. In fact, most teens tell us that their moms "just know" what they want—the products and the brands they prefer. There is something in it for mom here: she doesn't want to spend money on a family food item she knows her teens don't like. And unlike with younger children, parents of teens typically have thrown in the towel when it comes to trying to change teen eating habits and preferences.

Third, teens influence adult purchases when parents actively seek their counsel. Teens often know more about certain products than their parents do, such as computers, stereos, or the latest brand of designer jeans. Many parents consult with their in-house expert before buying these and other items. Parents have told us in focus groups that part of the deal for paying for their teen's clothes is that she (this seems to apply to daughters only) must accompany them to the store to lend advice on parent clothing purchases. Don't forget that today's parents—although not younger in years than those of a generation ago—are younger in attitude. They want to dress accordingly. Who better to keep them in fashion than their own teenager?

Where Teens Get Their Money

**While 30 percent of teens receive money from an allowance,
a larger share get their money from gifts, odd jobs,
and as-needed handouts from parents.**

(percent of teens receiving income from source, 1997)

As needed	52%
Odd jobs	48
Gifts	39
Part-time job	31
Allowance	30
Full-time job	10
Own business	3

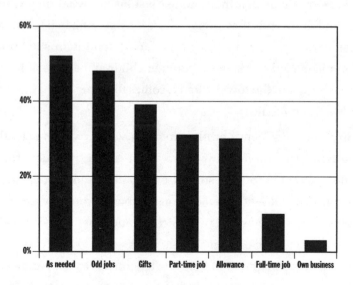

Source: TRU *Teenage Marketing & Lifestyle Study*

Fourth, teens influence parent purchasing when they ask for gifts, since teens are rarely shy about letting their parents know what they want for their birthday or other special day. From clothes to consumer electronics and gift certificates (typically the lowest-risk, most appreciated teen gift), teens trigger large amounts of spending on gifts.

4. Teens are important because they are trendsetters. Our youth-obsessed culture is oriented toward always being on the lookout for the next trend. And who's at the forefront? Teens. In fact, probably no age group is more involved with trends than teens. Wearing the "latest and greatest," after all, is a big thing in high school. Not only are teens trendsetters for one another, they also set trends for the population at large. Blue jeans, rock music, and hip-hop are just three examples of what can happen when teens embrace an idea. The importance of teens—rather than young adults—as trendsetters was driven home to me during a college project we did a few years ago. After talking to college students we discovered that fashion was far less important to them than to high school students. College students are less stratified socially and less affected by peer pressure, two factors that produce teens' perceived need to be fashionably in vogue. Further, when we asked college students how they find out about the latest fashions, several said they learn about what's current when they see their teenaged siblings during a school break.

Younger children, being aspirational, look up to teens and often adopt the latest in teen fashion. Even adults who are not parents of teens look to teenagers to see what's "in." Of course, as soon as teens see little kids or adults sport their look, they quickly discard it. Teens prefer things that are uniquely their own.

Realize, too, that teen influence extends beyond fashion and popular culture, affecting the nation's economy in a big way. A few years ago, a reporter for a leading financial newsletter called our office. Assuming it was another case of looking for "the teen market story," I was prepared to give the reporter the latest figures on teen earnings and spending. Then the writer explained his different, innovative angle. Recognizing the enormous economic power of the teen market and teens' trendsetting ability, he asked me to predict what products or brands would be popular among teens in the coming year, so he could advise his readers to buy the stocks of those companies. (TRU's Teen Market Opportunity Index, which allows us to make these kinds of predictions, is described in Chapter 2.) I've also heard from more than a few of our clients that they closely watch TRU's Coolest Brand Meter, which measures the "coolness" of hundreds of brands, to get stock-purchase ideas of their own.

5. Teens are important because of the money they will spend in the future. The most forward-thinking companies actively market adult brands to teens. If you sell acne medicine, video games, jeans, or soft drinks, marketing to teens is mandatory. But if you sell credit cards, automobiles, or newspapers, targeting teens is a less obvious and bolder move.

In discussing non-youth brands that were successfully marketed to teens, I would be remiss not to include those in the tobacco business. Camel is probably the most notorious example of an adult brand that has actively courted teenagers—and successfully so. It's been accused of developing a character, Joe Camel, that distinctly appeals to youths. Cigarette companies, which are in many ways among the most savvy of marketers, recognize the importance of teens as a future market better than most other package-good companies. Other brands can learn from their example. They understand how to effectively integrate all aspects of marketing to teens—coordinating relevant, image-oriented advertising with promotion, product placement (especially in movies), point-of-purchase displays, sampling, distribution, and merchandising (Marlboro and Camel gear, in particular). Perhaps the only good thing that has come of this marketing is that teens get really "pissed off"—to use their own vernacular—about the idea when it is presented to them in a compelling way. In anti-tobacco advertising work TRU has done, we've found it is possible to leverage the natural re-

Teen Income Tied to Economy

Teen income has surged in the past few years, along with the economy.

(total teen income, 1990–98; in billions of current dollars)

1998	$121
1997	111
1996	105
1995	102
1994	96
1993	86
1992	88
1991	95
1990	94

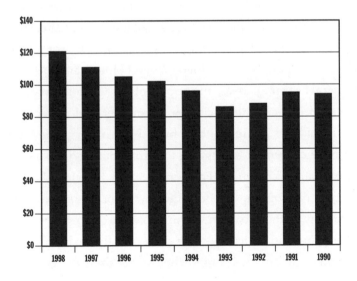

Source: TRU *Teenage Marketing & Lifestyle Study*

17

belliousness of some teens against the tobacco companies. Using tobacco-settlement funds, the state of Florida is currently waging a teen-targeting campaign, titled "Truth," based on this idea by attacking the tobacco industry and its supporters. This general positioning, known as "industry manipulation," can be effective because teens hate the thought of being manipulated by anyone. Of course, industry manipulation works only for some teens and clearly not for those whom the tobacco companies have already won over.

Although Camel and other tobacco brands have denied—despite documentation to the contrary—having gone directly after an underage market, other adult brands are openly and actively developing relationships with teens, convinced that this effort will pay off as teens enter adulthood. We have worked with a number of companies in building brand awareness and positive attitudes among teens. For example, we conducted research to assist Discover Card in developing and monitoring its youth marketing programs, which include a magazine about personal finance distributed in schools as well as college scholarships and special events. These programs have created a strong, positive, and relevant relationship with young consumers. We also helped General Motors and its publishing partner, General Learning, assess the appeal of a magazine GM distributes in high school driver-education classes. In another GM project, we conducted a series of focus groups with teens and parents to gauge the appeal and enhance the concept of a program to form a parent–teen partnership in driver's education, known as "Partners in Safety." Designed to promote safety, this type of program can build goodwill for a brand among both teens and parents. Both Discover Card and GM are betting that once teens enter the age groups in which they are prone to buy such products, they will be more likely to buy their brands because of these efforts.

TRU's Kids Research Unlimited division worked with the *Chicago Tribune* in developing *KidNews*, a weekly newspaper within the newspaper for "tweens" (8-to-14-year-olds). It has become the prototype for children's newspaper supplements nationwide. Former *Tribune* senior editor Cokie Dishon, who developed the editorial concept and has since developed *react*, a teen paper from the publishers of *Parade*, was not only committed to developing a quality newspaper for this age group but is also a brand marketer who thinks in the long term. Cokie was determined to get children and young teens accustomed to reading a real newspaper. To accomplish this, she insisted that hard news constitute a major section in each issue. She also decided not to shrink the paper to fit smaller hands, believing that by familiarizing young readers with a full-sized newspaper, they would more naturally graduate to the adult version once they were ready.

6. Teens are important because there will be more of them in the years ahead. When TRU's founders Paul Krouse, Dr. Burleigh Gardner, my father, Burt Zollo, and I first contemplated launching a teen-research firm in 1982, like all reasonably intelligent marketers, we checked out the associated demographics. When we looked at trends in the U.S. teen population, we discovered that the segment was projected to decline until 1992. Heeding the notion that it is all in how you interpret the data, we figured that if we could survive the first 10 years, it would be smooth sailing thereafter. Fortunately, we were right. Corporate America is now recognizing the huge opportunity teens present. We no longer need to sell the merits of the market and can concentrate instead on helping our clients profit from it.

The teen population began to decline in 1976, after the last of the baby boomers had aged out of their teen years. After 16 years of continuous decline (the baby bust, Generation X), a turnaround occurred in the early 1990s, as demographers had projected. Today, there are 31 million people aged 12 to 19 in the United States, about 7 million more than in 1991. This teen growth spurt is still in full force as Gen Y exerts its strength: the teen population should continue to expand until 2010 as the children of baby boomers swell the ranks of 12-to-19-year-olds. Because of teens' increased

Teen Population Is Expanding

The teen population will expand steadily during the next few years and reach 34 million by 2010.

(number of people aged 12 to 19, 1998–2010; in millions)

1998	31.0
2000	31.6
2005	33.7
2010	34.0

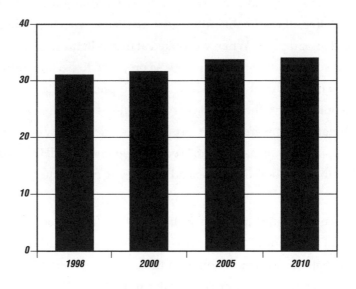

Source: U.S. Bureau of the Census

spending, the teen population boom creates a powerful synergy: more teens spending more money. No wonder so many marketers are now vying for teenage attention and favor.

We view the teen years as beginning at age 12, because that is the marketing world's definition of when teenage begins. We didn't always think this way. The youngest respondents in our first syndicated studies were aged 13, but we soon discovered that marketers and the media define the teen target as aged 12 to 17 or sometimes 12 to 19. We soon changed the age range of our sample and have been tracking 12-year-olds ever since.

At its youngest end, the 12-to-19 target includes prepubescent children who are just entering middle school. At the older end are young adults attending college or holding full-time jobs. So it is critical to keep in mind the size and diversity of this age group. Teens are not a homogeneous group. They differ by gender, ethnicity, household income, and geography. And they are segmented by attitudes and lifestyles. Clearly, the teen market is not an easy one to target, but the rewards for doing so successfully are well worth the effort.

Chapter 2.

Teens, Products, and Brands

The stereotype of today's teen is that of a brand-obsessed, label-driven, mall-congregating, free-spending, compulsive shopper. There is often some truth to stereotypes.

Teens love to shop. It is an experience rather than an errand, an event rather than a chore. What teens buy reflects what they think of themselves and how they wish others to perceive them. The act of buying can be one of independence or conformity, self-expression or socialization. Understanding the wants and needs behind teen buying is important for marketers of all kinds of consumer products.

Today's teens have the means to move brand sales in a big way. Although most adults earn more money than teens, a larger share of teen income is discretionary. Teens aren't saddled with mortgage or utility bills. They can spend their funds freely. This fact, coupled with their rising incomes, makes teens an increasingly attractive consumer segment. If you sell traditional teen products, you already know this. Marketers of adult brands are just beginning to realize it.

Teens are unique consumers. Unlike children, they have the financial resources to make big-ticket purchases such as cars, computers, or jewelry. But unlike adults, they often need the permission of a parent before they can make such a purchase. Adults play an important role in the teen buying experience, a role that needs to be recognized and addressed.

Teens are more brand conscious today than ever before. By understanding what teens look for in a brand, and by knowing when brand choice is important, you can begin to assess your opportunities and get a better picture of what and why teens buy.

What Makes a Brand Cool?

Years ago, we began conducting regular, exploratory focus groups with teens to uncover how they differentiate between brands. We learned that teens don't categorize products the way marketers do. A candy marketer

What Makes a Brand a Cool Brand?

"Quality" is the single biggest attribute of cool, cited by more than twice as many teens as the second-ranked attribute, "for people my age."

(percent of teens citing characteristic as making a brand cool, 1996)

Quality	63%
If it's for people my age	30
Advertising	23
Uniqueness	23
If cool friends or peers use it	20
If everyone uses it	18
If it's a brand that's been around a long time	15
If it's sold at a cool store	11
If it's a new brand	10
If it's expensive	10
If a celebrity I admire uses it	9
Packaging	7
If it's for people older than me	2

Source: TRU *Teenage Marketing & Lifestyle Study*

might think that its competitive set (i.e., the alternatives to its candy bar) is other chocolate candy bars, for example, or even something more specific such as "enrobed" chocolate candy bars with peanuts. To teens, the competitive set might include salty snacks, cookies, ice cream, or even pizza.

We discovered that teens have a unique way of evaluating brands and products. Brand research that works with adults may not be relevant in researching teen brand preferences. This finding helped us develop several quantitative measures for assessing teen brand perceptions.

When we began to explore the process of brand evaluation among teens, we discovered that the quality of "coolness" is of paramount importance. Teens can quickly label a brand as either cool or uncool. One of the wonderful things about qualitative research is the ability to probe as deeply as possible—which is exactly what we did, exploring the meaning behind the word cool as it applies to branding. In doing so across a variety of product categories, we uncovered the factors that mark a brand as cool. By understanding what makes a brand cool to teens, you can develop and communicate the important cues that create a relevant, desirable image for your brands among teens.

In our syndicated study we asked, "Thinking about brands of products, what makes a brand a cool brand?" The one attribute most teens associate with a cool brand is quality: two-thirds of teens associate quality with being cool. Among 18- and 19-year-olds the figure is an even higher 80 percent. That teens select quality as the number-one criterion of coolness says much about their level of consumer sophistication. Some marketers think that if they package their products in hot teen colors, use a popular celebrity, or shoot an MTV-style commercial, teens will buy. They are mistaken. Teens appreciate and seek quality. This does not mean that quality in and of itself will sell a product, but it is the fundamental criterion of a cool brand. The brands teens consider to be the coolest—such as Nike, Sony, adidas, and Tommy Hilfiger—all carry the perception of high quality among teens.

Quality means different things in different product categories. For athletic shoes, quality can mean durability or ankle support. For chewing gum, quality can mean taste or long-lasting flavor. These very different attributes have one thing in common: they separate brands within a category based on perceived product superiority—or quality.

After quality, the most common description of what makes a brand cool to teens is that it is "for people my age." Teens prefer things that are specifically for them, whether it's language, fashion, advertising, or brands.

Advertising performs strongly on this measure, cited by 23 percent of teens. The fact that so many teens name advertising as something that makes a brand cool reveals just how involved teens are with advertising and the importance it has in their lives.

Interestingly, the attributes of being a new brand and being an established brand are equally important in teens' minds. Nearly 10 percent of teens associate newness with making a brand cool, underscoring the fact that the teen market is a fertile ground for new products.

Note that cool celebrities by themselves do not do much for a brand. Celebrities can be effective in gaining teen attention, in positioning a product to teens (or a teen segment), and in furthering a brand image, but celebrities alone will not carry your brand. More on celebrities later.

So, examining the data on how teens define coolness clearly shows that for a brand to be successful among teens, it must have two fundamental factors in its favor: it must be perceived to be of superior quality *and* it must convey an image that is relevant, desirable, and aspirational to teens. Each of the coolest brands wins among teens because it delivers on both these factors—the rational/product side and the emotional/image side. Imagery alone will gain you trial, but if the brand doesn't deliver on product quality, there will be no repeat business from teens.

The Coolest Brands

Companies traditionally measured the strength of their brands based on behavior: which brands consumers buy and use. Now that marketers have widely embraced the concept of brand equity and it is firmly rooted in their minds, researchers are measuring what consumers think and feel about brands. To gauge teens' attitudes toward brands, marketers need to consider teens' special perspective.

We've developed a unique measure, known as TRU's Coolest Brand Meter, which over the past five years has become widely accepted by youth marketers as being the ultimate barometer for evaluating the current state of their own and their competitors' brands in the teen market. In our syndicated study, we ask teens to write in (with no list provided) the names of the three brands from *any* product category, service, or retailer that they think are currently the coolest.

Overall, teens list more than 200 brands in response to this question, mentioning brands from Nike to Bath & Body Shop, Chevy to BMW, and (unfortunately, but revealingly) Bud Ice to Marlboro. The five brands most frequently mentioned as the coolest in the most recent study (fielded during the summer of 1998) were Nike (38 percent), adidas (19 percent), Tommy Hilfiger (18 percent), Sony (11 percent), and Gap (10 percent).

Reflecting the emotional importance to teens of wearing the right clothes and shoes, four out of the top five responses are apparel and shoe brands. These are the brands that teens literally wrap themselves in. Because of this teen bias, brands within other categories are at an inherent disadvantage on this measure—but revealingly so. There's no way toothpaste could be as cool as a pair of jeans. Still, this measure distinguishes the brands that have been most successful at winning teen favor.

Advertising is a key criterion of what constitutes a cool brand to teens. It's no surprise, then, that teens' favorite television commercials correlate to their favorite brands. When we ask teens in qualitative research about

The Coolest Brands to Teens

**Apparel brands are most likely to rank among the cool,
and Nike is still the coolest brand to teens.**

(percent of teens citing brand as one of top three cool brands, 1998)

Brand	Percent
Nike	38%
adidas	19
Tommy Hilfiger	18
Sony	11
Gap	10
Pepsi	9
Coca-Cola	8
Levi's	7
Ralph Lauren	7
Nintendo	6
Old Navy	5
JNCO	5
Abercrombie & Fitch	4
Cover Girl	4
Calvin Klein	4
Dr. Pepper	3
Nautica	3
Mountain Dew	3
Ford	3
Reebok	3
Sprite	3
Fila	3

Source: TRU *Teenage Marketing & Lifestyle Study*

Other Brands Teens Think Are Cool

While not the coolest of brands, these names
at least earned an honorable mention from teens.

(brands mentioned by fewer than 3 percent of respondents, 1998)

Acclaim	EA Sports	Pioneer
Airwalks	Eddie Bauer	Pizza Hut
Aiwa	Express	Quick Silver
American Eagle	Fubu	Revlon
Anchor Blue	Gatorade	Roxy
Bath & Body Works	Guess	Sega
Billabong	Honda	Skechers
Blue Asphalt	J. Crew	Snapple
BMW	Lee	Sony PlayStation
Boss	Lei	Structure
Burger King	Lexus	Surge
Chevy (non-specific)	Lucky Brand	Taco Bell
CK	McDonald's	The Limited
Clinique	Microsoft	Union Bay
Converse	Mitsubishi	Vans
DKNY	Mudd Jeans	Viper
Doc Martens	Mustang	Volkswagen
Dodge	Nine West	Wet-N-Wild
Doritos	Nintendo 64	

Source: TRU *Teenage Marketing & Lifestyle Study*

their favorite ads, they typically mention ads from companies at or near the top of the cool brand list—Nike, Levi's, Sprite, Taco Bell, Coke, Pepsi, and Nintendo. Nike's standing is particularly impressive, mentioned twice as frequently as the number-two brand. But Nike has lost ground on this measure recently, after having peaked at 52 percent during the summer of 1997. Because teens are so attracted to newness and like the idea of discovering brands, it's difficult for a brand of Nike's size to maintain such a high level on this measure. But Nike's performance positioning, coupled with its product offering, has clearly appealed to teens in an unprecedented way. To teens, Nike *is* sports. Nike communicates desire, grittiness, empowerment, and even humor. And no brand has ever better leveraged celebrity than Nike.

Many brands in the second tier of coolness (after the top five) are also apparel or shoe brands, with top brands in soft drinks, electronics, automobiles, fast food, and cosmetics mixed in.

The Coolest Brand Meter is one of the most volatile measures in TRU's study, reflecting just how tenuous a position a brand (particularly a fashion brand) holds in teens' mindsets and heartsets. For example, in recent years, we've seen Calvin Klein shoot up meteorically in the rankings and then fall back almost as quickly. Interestingly, CK's rise corresponded to its controversial campaign of employing teenage-looking models in what adult media protested as being overly sexy. Teens, however, appeared to love the edginess and, in turn, the brand benefited. But, the brand's advertising didn't change, and teens grew tired of the same images. Similarly, five years ago the Guess? brand was riding high on the Meter, second only to Nike. Now, the brand ranks fairly low, again due to producing nothing really new and different in terms of advertising or products that teens find exciting or particularly relevant. Another example of the fickleness of fashion branding among teens is the stalwart Levi's brand. Although more teens (and parents) continue to buy Levi's jeans than any other brand, Levi's' coolness rating has notably dropped, which prompted the company to fire

Brand Preferences of Teen Boys and Girls

Boys are more likely than girls to think Nike, Sony, and Nintendo are cool, while girls favor Gap, Calvin Klein, and adidas more than boys.

(percent of teens citing brand as one of top three cool brands by gender, for brands favored significantly more by one gender than the other, 1998; ranked by difference)

	boys	girls	difference
Sony	17%	5%	12
Nike	42	33	9
Nintendo	11	2	9
JNCO	7	4	3
Coca-Cola	9	7	2
Abercrombie & Fitch	3	5	–2
Old Navy	3	7	–4
Calvin Klein	1	6	–5
adidas	15	23	–8
Cover Girl	0	8	–8
Gap	5	14	–9

Source: TRU *Teenage Marketing & Lifestyle Study*

its ad agency of some 60 years and develop a new ad campaign built on the strategy of regaining cool among teens.

Brand Loyalty

Because today's teens are tomorrow's adults, more companies than ever are reaching out to teens, hoping to develop a long-lasting relationship. But do teens return the favor? Just how loyal are they as consumers?

Several times during the past few years, we've been asked to submit proposals for research studies that would determine the brand loyalty of teens. Unfortunately, the optimum design for this kind of study is complex and expensive. (To date, no client has been willing to sponsor the research.) The study would need to be longitudinal, carefully tracking the same group of people from their early teens into adulthood. The study would monitor whether current purchases and brand perceptions influence future purchase behavior and attitudes, and whether and how brand choices and preferences change and evolve over time. Although we have yet to execute this type of longitudinal study, the fact that every year or two a client requests such a proposal shows how important the issue of brand loyalty is to businesses in the teen market.

Among consumers of all ages, major brands are losing market share to private-label and store brands, particularly in the grocery category. For example, Bakeline, a private-label cookie marketer (which was acquired by Keebler a few years ago) holds an impressive 7.6 percent share (in pounds sold) in the total cookie category, up about 10 percent from just two years ago. Because of the threat of private-label competitors, many marketers are intensifying their efforts to develop brand relationships with young consumers.

Even among brand-conscious teens, private-label products are making inroads. JC Penney's store-brand jeans, Arizona, are highly successful in the teen market, being purchased by 22 percent of teens in the past year.

Brand Loyalty of Teens

Teens are much more brand loyal when buying personal-hygiene products than when buying food or apparel.

(among teens who use category, percent who bought, or their parents bought for them, the same brand in the category at least two of the last three times, 1997)

	2 or 3 times	3 times	2 times
Tampons/sanitary pads*	93%	73%	20%
Contact-lens solution	86	68	17
Shampoo	86	49	38
Antiperspirant/deodorant	85	59	27
Toothpaste	84	55	29
Bar soap	84	53	31
Conditioner	83	46	37
Acne medication	81	52	29
Camera film	80	53	27
Styling gel/mousse/spritz	73	43	30
Soft drinks	66	34	31
Jeans	62	28	35
Tortilla chips	61	32	29
Gum	60	32	28
Athletic shoes	56	28	28
Nail polish*	55	29	26
Potato chips	55	22	33
Fast food	54	18	36
Cereal	51	24	28
Cookies	48	20	28
Candy	34	15	19

* Girls only.
Source: TRU *Teenage Marketing & Lifestyle Study*

Penney's has been smart in not tying the brand too closely to its own corporate image, which may be less than relevant to some teens. In fact, when we've asked teens in qualitative research where they can buy Arizona jeans, they typically not only answer JC Penney, but also list other popular retailers. Sears' Canyon River Blues brand is following the Arizona example, using its retail muscle and lower-than-premium price points to attract teens.

Contributing to the erosion of brand loyalty is the fact that today's teens have far more product and brand choices available to them than generations before them. Teenagers are willing to experiment with products rather than buy a brand because that's what their parents buy. The jeans category is perhaps the best example of the erosion of brand loyalty as jeans brands proliferate not only in store brands, but also in small, regional brands. Behemoths like Levi's are hurting because so many competitors are fragmenting the jeans market. It used to be that Levi's and maybe one or two other brands of jeans virtually owned the teen market. Now, with brand choice in this category growing so rapidly, many teens are choosing smaller brands with which they can make a statement about their own personal style. Because of intensifying competition in nearly every product category, developing a positive relationship with teens is more important for brands than ever before.

To determine the product categories with the greatest teen loyalty (i.e., the categories in which teens repeatedly purchase the same brand) we gave respondents to our *Teenage Marketing & Lifestyle Study* a list of 20 categories and asked: "Thinking about the last three times you bought (or your parents bought for you) this product, how many times was it the same brand?"

With the exception of camera film, the 10 categories eliciting the most loyalty are all health and beauty aids. The more intimate the category, the less willing are teens to risk trying a new brand if they are satisfied with the brand they are using. Experimentation in some of these categories (i.e., feminine-hygiene products, shampoo, acne medication, antiperspirant/deodorant) is risky. Teens fear that switching brands might jeopardize their appearance or social acceptability. And although teens enjoy a modicum of risk, when it comes to such high-stakes criteria as appearance and social status, they are risk-adverse.

Feminine-hygiene products enjoy the greatest loyalty among teens. Girls typically are introduced to brands in this category by their mothers, and experiment little after that.

In some of the other health and beauty aid categories (e.g., bar soap, toothpaste), teens use the same brand over and over in part because a parent is making the brand choice. Teens understand trade-offs. Campaigning for specific brands within these categories is less important to them than getting their way in other categories.

By the time children reach their teens, they have experimented with a tremendous number of brands that either they or a family member brought into their household or that they tried at a friend's home. Teenagers have a sense of which brands work best for them, based on efficacy, comfort, or a variety of social and psychological needs of which they may be unaware. So, when teens feel secure with how a brand performs, particularly a health or beauty aid, they regard changing brands as risky or unnecessary. This was our hypothesis about teen brand choice. Intrigued, we decided to investigate it further.

What always struck us about our brand-loyalty data (which, incidentally, have been extremely stable over the years) is that fashion categories rank relatively low in loyalty. On the surface, this finding appears to contradict our qualitative research, which shows that jeans, shoes, and other clothes are the categories in which brand choice is most important to teens.

We call them "badge" items—products that offer signals to the peer group about their users/wearers. Brand loyalty in badge categories typically is low because of a few key factors, such as the fluctuating popularity

Brand Choice Can Be Important to Teens

While teens are not brand loyal when buying apparel or shoes, brand choice is important to them in these categories.

(percent of teens saying, "Getting the brand of my choice is most important to me when buying [or when someone buys for me]," based on category users, 1997)

Tampons/sanitary pads*	49%
Antiperspirant/deodorant	48
Athletic shoes	40
Jeans	40
Shampoo	33
Contact-lens solution	28
Acne remedy	23
Toothpaste	20
Conditioner	19
Fast food	18
Soft drinks	17
Styling gel/mousse/spritz	13
Bar soap	13
Gum	10
Nail polish*	10
Candy	8
Cereal	8
Camera film	6
Potato chips	5
Cookies	4
Tortilla chips	3

* Girls only.
Source: TRU *Teenage Marketing & Lifestyle Study*

When Brand Choice Is Most Important

Four of the five products for which teen girls say brand choice is most important are health and beauty aids.

(the five categories in which brand choice is most important to teens, percent citing category by gender, 1997)

Boys

Antiperspirant/deodorant	52%
Athletic shoes	50
Jeans	46
Shampoo	27
Fast food	23

Girls

Tampons/sanitary pads	49
Antiperspirant/deodorant	43
Shampoo	40
Contact-lens solution	37
Jeans	33

Source: TRU *Teenage Marketing & Lifestyle Study*

of "in" brands, current styles/colors, availability, and price. This is not to say that brand name is less important in these categories. In fact, we believe it's more important. Supporting this notion is our quantitative Coolest Brands Measure, which shows that four of the top five coolest brands are fashion brands.

So, we have an apparent contradiction. Some of the categories in which teens are the most loyal behaviorally (i.e., buy the same brand repeatedly) are those in which brand choice (i.e., caring about which brand is purchased) is relatively unimportant. Therefore, investigating the importance of brand choice, both independently and in combination with brand loyalty, is a prerequisite to more fully understanding the teen–brand relationship.

The Importance of Brand Choice

Based on our research over the years, we believe that teens' willingness to buy or campaign for certain brands is directly related to the importance of brand choice in those categories. But there are categories in which brand choice is extremely important to teens, yet the brands enjoy less loyalty because the set of cool or teen-relevant brands within these categories is constantly changing.

To test the relationship between brand choice and brand importance, we added a brand-importance measure to TRU's syndicated study. We presented respondents with the same 21 categories listed in the brand-loyalty question and asked them to choose those that best fit the statement: "Getting the brand of my choice is most important when buying (or when someone buys for me)." This question examines brand relationships on an attitudinal basis, while the previous measure was behavioral. The findings identify the product categories in which getting the brand of choice is most important to teens, regardless of their loyalty to any particular brand.

The rank order of this list is rather different from that of the behavioral brand-loyalty measure. That two of the top three are fashion categories supports our hypothesis about the distinction between brand loyalty and brand choice. Our finding that teens regard brands within the fashion category as the coolest also supports this distinction. As I said before, these are the brands that teens literally wrap themselves in. Athletic shoes and jeans are badge items. Their importance to teens transcends their status as consumer products. They tell others how the teen sees himself or herself and how he or she wishes to be perceived. Expensive items signal affluence, for example, and some teens want to be perceived as affluent—or, at least, as having the means to purchase such items.

Tampons/sanitary pads rank first in brand loyalty, and four of the top five items on the list for girls are health and beauty aids. In comparison, only two health and beauty aids (antiperspirant/deodorant and shampoo) appear on the top-five list for boys. This reflects the different purchasing priorities of teen boys and girls.

Brand Loyalty and Importance: Mapping the Findings

How do brand loyalty (buying the same brand within a given category at least two of the last three times) and brand choice (the importance of brand choice within a category) interact? To find out, we ranked the 21 categories in each of these two measures and plotted them on a quadrant map.

Quadrant I contains the product categories toward which teens feel most brand loyal and for which brand choice is most important to them. Teens care about buying certain brands within these categories and repeatedly purchase the same brands.

Quadrant II contains the product categories toward which teens do not feel brand loyal but brand selective. Although teens find it important to buy specific brands within these categories, their brand of choice frequently changes.

Quadrant III contains the product categories toward which teens do not feel brand loyal or brand selective. Teens do not purchase the same

Brand Loyalty and Brand Importance

The quadrant map shows at a glance how brand loyalty and brand importance interact for teens.

(Loyalty & Importance: Combinging the Findings, 1997)

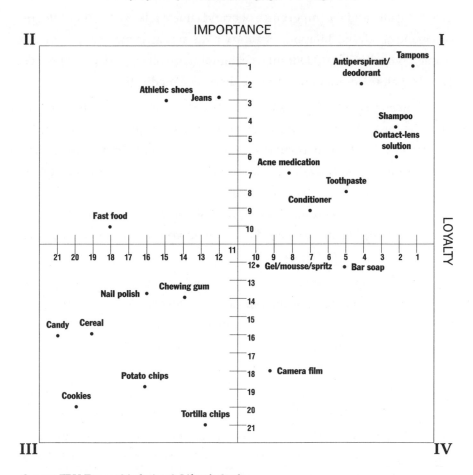

IMPORTANCE

II   I

Tampons

Antiperspirant/deodorant

Athletic shoes   Jeans

Shampoo

Contact-lens solution

Acne medication

Toothpaste

Conditioner

Fast food

LOYALTY

21 20 19 18 17 16 15 14 13 12   11   10 9 8 7 6 5 4 3 2 1

Gel/mousse/spritz   Bar soap

Chewing gum

Nail polish

Candy   Cereal

Camera film

Potato chips

Cookies

Tortilla chips

III   IV

Source: TRU *Teenage Marketing & Lifestyle Study*

41

brands nor do they consider it important to purchase specific brands in these categories.

Quadrant IV contains the product categories toward which teens are brand loyal but brand indifferent. Teens repeatedly use the same brands within these categories, yet the choice of brand is not particularly important to them.

Note not only which quadrant a product category falls into but also where in the quadrant it lies. Location within a quadrant signifies the degree of loyalty and the importance of brand choice relative to other categories in the quadrant. Tampons/sanitary pads and acne medication, for example, both fall within Quadrant I, yet tampons/sanitary pads enjoy greater brand loyalty and brand importance than acne medication.

Categories in Quadrants I and II offer marketers the greatest opportunity to develop a long-lasting relationship with teens. A brand-switching strategy would be particularly challenging for Quadrant I categories, while gaining brand loyalty is the challenge for Quadrant II categories. The big implication for marketers of Quadrant I products is to grab consumers early, understanding their "point of entry" (i.e., at what age they enter the category) and reaching them then. If you're late, you may be too late.

Notably, all the categories in Quadrant I are health and beauty aids (tampons/sanitary pads, antiperspirant/deodorant, shampoo, and acne remedies). These are all products for which brand switching could present a social risk. Once teens feel comfortable with a certain brand in one of these categories, they don't want to risk switching brands.

Quadrant II categories are composed of relatively large sets of acceptable brands. Teens rotate their brand of choice depending on price, availability, and advertising. Because brand choice is important to teens when buying products in Quadrant II, marketers of these products have an opportunity to convert less-loyal category enthusiasts to loyal brand users. To exploit this opportunity, they should explore the unique attributes of and perceptions associated with their brands and develop strategies to encourage loyalty.

Quadrant II categories are image-oriented and heavily advertised. Several are badge items that teens use to make a statement about themselves. If a similar analysis were performed among adults, beer and automobiles would almost certainly fall into this quadrant. Cigarettes, while not shown, provide an example of how products can change quadrants over time, especially considering that the average age of initiation is approximately 12 years.Undoubtedly, cigarettes as a category begin in Quadrant II—as imagery creating a distinct brand personality, which so effectively targets young people. Think about the Marlboro Man as independent, Joe Camel as the partier, and Newport as preppy all-American. There's an image for every teen to emulate. Not coincidentally, these happen to be teens' three biggest cigarette brands. But because of the unique physical properties of tobacco—namely, nicotine's addictiveness—once teens get hooked, cigarettes as a category move over to Quadrant I.

Product categories plotted in Quadrant III (low loyalty and low importance) face the most difficult challenge of all. Teens neither care strongly about brand choice in these categories nor do they, even out of habit, use the same brand frequently. Six of the seven products plotted in this quadrant are foods, each with many competitive brands vying for teen attention: candy, chewing gum, tortilla chips, potato chips, cereal, and cookies. Teens are less loyal in these categories because there are so many interchangeable brands and because low price points make it less risky to experiment. Further, purchase cycles are particularly short for these categories. Still, it is important to remember that teens have favorite brands in snack and candy categories. Most likely, their favorite sets include several brands, suggesting that pricing and value strategies may be particularly effective in these categories. Doritos is an example of a brand that may be shifting Quadrants. Though the dynamics of the category into which Doritos falls place it in Quadrant III, the brand seems to be pushing its way into Quadrants II and I. Through carefully crafted advertising, promotion, and packaging, as well as its inherent product appeal to teens, Doritos has defined itself as the teen-appropriate, fun, party snack brand.

Three product categories fall into Quadrant IV: gel/mousse/spritz, bar soap, and camera film. Teens use the same brands repeatedly in these categories, but they do not regard brand as particularlyimportant. Most likely, mom is choosing the brand and the teen is content to use whatever brand is available. Marketers of these products need to appeal to teens directly, so that teens begin to request certain brands. Another, more long-term, approach would be to develop a strong relationship with young consumers, recognizing that they typically are neither the purchasers nor active requesters now but will be when they are adults.

Teen-Specific Brands

Once a company decides to target teens, it must consider whether to develop a teen-specific product or line in addition to teen-directed advertising and promotions. Since one of the key attributes of a cool brand is that it is for "somebody my age," developing products specifically for this age group can offer some advantages. Many businesses are mining these opportunities today. In the past few years, TRU has been testing more teen-specific product concepts than ever before.

If you create a teen-specific brand, an important consideration is whether to include the word "teen" or "teenage" in the product name, to communicate to teens that this is something especially for them. Why not leverage the word "teen," since we know teens want products they can call their own?

A few years ago we went to the experts—teens themselves—and asked them what words or phrases they like to be called. We found that teens prefer to be called "young" rather than "teen" or "teenager."

What Teenagers Want to Be Called

Fewer than half the people aged 12 to 19 prefer being called a "teen" or "teenager."

(percent of teens citing label preferences, 1992)

Young men/women	62%
Young adults	59
Teenagers	43
Teens	42
Students	31
Boys/girls	14

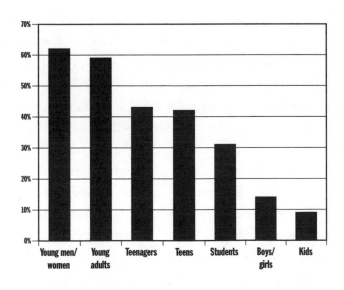

Source: TRU *Teenage Marketing & Lifestyle Study*

Not surprisingly, label preference is age-related. The oldest teens almost unanimously reject the terms "teen" or "teenager," but the youngest teens embrace these words. Twelve-to-15-year-olds have waited years to be teenagers. Now they want somebody to notice. To them, "teen" and "teenage" are aspirational. In contrast, older teens feel the "teen" label refers to someone much younger than themselves.

"Teen implies you're young, like you're 13!" a 16-year-old boy told us in a focus group.

"I don't like to be called a teen because the word makes you feel stupid. Teenagers have a stereotype stuck to them that all we care about is hair and makeup and getting dates and we don't have brains. That isn't true," said a 17-year-old girl.

We've also found that teens distinguish between the terms "teen" and "teenage," preferring the latter. They associate "teen" with being a young teenybopper, while "teenage" is more accepted because it is an age descriptor.

Perhaps because the word "teen" is shorter and punchier than "teenage," it has been the choice of marketers. A few years ago, Mennen introduced an antiperspirant/deodorant under the name Teen Spirit, originally targeted at a teen audience. The brand found its franchise more "tween" than teen, since its buyers are younger (aged 9 to 15) than originally intended, whereas many older teens are turned off by the name. Commented one 17-year-old girl about the product: "The biggest turnoff is when they [advertisers] try to relate to you. Like Teen Spirit. Their ads show teens leaping in school. It's so ridiculous a name and picture that I just flip the page. You don't want to have anything to do with them when they start relating to you." Obviously this teenager is neither chronologically nor attitudinally within the Teen Spirit target market.

Teen Spirit achieves some success with its younger audience, extending its brand into a hair-care line. Carter Wallace was less successful in

Likelihood of Buying "Teen" Products

Teens are much more likely to buy products made for people their age than products with the word "teen" in their name.

(attitudes of teens toward buying a product made for people their age or with the words "teen" or "teenage" in its name, 1993)

	likelihood of buying products	
	made specifically for people your age	with the word "teen" or "teenage" in name
Total, more likely	**57%**	**31%**
A lot more likely	25	11
Somewhat more likely	32	20
Neither more nor less likely	**35**	**45**
Total, less likely	**6**	**21**
Somewhat less likely	3	10
A lot less likely	3	11

Source: TRU *Teenage Marketing & Lifestyle Study*

Likelihood of Buying
"Teen" Products, by Age

Even among the youngest teens, a minority favor products with the word "teen" or "teenage" in the name.

(percent of teens saying they would be a lot or somewhat more likely to buy a product made for people their age or with the word "teen" or "teenage" in its name, 1993)

	likelihood of buying products	
	made specifically for people your age	with the word "teen" or "teenage" in name
Aged 12 to 15	65%	43%
Aged 16 to 17	54	22
Aged 18 to 19	40	15

Source: TRU *Teenage Marketing & Lifestyle Study*

introducing a competitive brand, Teen Image, which was an extension of its Arrid line.

Because teens want products for themselves, and because naming those products "teen" or "teenage" is the clearest way to communicate this, we asked teenagers how they felt about it. In our syndicated study we asked: "How likely would you be to buy products such as personal grooming items, snack foods, etc., made specifically for people your age?" We also asked: "How likely would you be to buy products with the word 'teen' or 'teenage' in their name?"

The results supported our earlier findings. Teens prefer products made specifically for them, but they are lukewarm at best when it comes to buying brands with the word "teen" or "teenage" in their name.

Although more than one-third of teens are neutral toward buying products for people their age, only 6 percent are negative and a 57 percent majority are positive. When it comes to including "teen" or "teenage" in a brand's name, however, the neutral figure jumps to almost one-half (45 percent) of the sample, the negative rises to 21 percent, and the positive drops to 31 percent.

Boys and girls are equally interested in products made specifically for their age group, but significantly more girls (37 percent) than boys (25 percent) are interested in products that incorporate the words "teen" or "teenage" in their name. Older teens are much less positive on both measures. Nevertheless, only 36 percent of the 18- and 19-year-olds and 25 percent of the 16- and 17-year-olds totally reject the idea of a "teen"-named product.

As expected, those teens who are most interested in products for their age group are also more interested in products with the word "teen" or "teenage" in their names.

Teens look for and appreciate products that are made specifically for them. The challenge to marketers, however, is in the name. Calling a prod-

Products Purchased
by Teens, by Gender

Fast food, compact discs, and movie tickets are the items purchased by the largest share of teen boys in the past three months, while teen girls are most likely to have purchased movie tickets, nail polish, and chocolate candy.

*(products personally purchased by at least 19 percent of teens
in the past three months, by gender, 1998)*

Boys personally buying:

Compact disc	58%	Thirst-quenching sports drink	34%
Fast food at hamburger chain	57	Breath mints	33
Movie ticket	52	Hard candy in a roll	33
Chocolate candy	44	Potato chips	31
Chewing gum	41	Gummy candy	30
Cola	41	Non-chocolate candy	26
Bubble gum	41	Fast food at Mexican chain	26
T-shirt	41	Antiperspirant/deodorant	25
Fast food at pizza chain	36	Fast Food: chicken chain	23
Magazine	34		

Source: TRU *Teenage Marketing & Lifestyle Study*

(continued from previous page)

Girls personally buying:

Movie ticket	60%	Book	32%
Nail polish	54	Casual shoes	32
Chocolate candy	53	Eyeliner	31
Compact disc	53	Eye shadow	31
Fast food at hamburger chain	50	CD single	31
Lip gloss	49	Antiperspirant/deodorant	30
Chewing gum	48	School supplies	30
T-shirt	46	Nail polish remover	30
Bubble gum	45	Potato chips	30
Lipstick	43	Poster	30
Greeting card	42	Non-carbonated bottled water	30
Magazine	42	Camera film	30
Breath mints	40	Foundation	29
Hard candy in a roll	40	Fragrance	28
Lip balm	38	Body wash/gel	26
Fast food at pizza chain	37	Fast food: chicken chain	26
Non-chocolate candy	36	Facial cleanser	24
Gummy candy	36	Pre-recorded audiocassette	23
Mascara	35	Designer jeans	23
Cola	35	Eyebrow pencil	23
Moisturizer/lotion/cream	32	Non-designer jeans	22
Cookie	32	Sweatshirt	19

Source: TRU *Teenage Marketing & Lifestyle Study*

uct "teen" or "teenage" is a turnoff to older teens, though it can increase the appeal of products targeting "tweens" and the youngest teens. If your brand's target includes teens aged 16 or older, you should communicate that the product is for them visually or verbally without labeling the brand "teen" or "teenage." Plenty of names communicate youth not by explicitly including words like "teen" or "young," but by sounding youthful, edgy, fun, and un*adult*erated.

What Do Teens Buy?

The first question reporters typically ask us at TRU is, "Why is the teen market important?" Invariably, the second question is, "What do teens buy?" The answer is less surprising and more predictable than most people might expect. Teens buy many of the same things they always have bought, but they also buy products from new and emerging categories, from low-fat to high-tech. The products teens buy segment them and reveal their priorities and lifestyles.

For girls, fashion rules. Apparel is the most important product category to teen girls, consuming both the greatest proportion of their disposable income and their greatest parent-campaigning efforts. Next to fashion, girls spend the most on personal-grooming items, from mousse to mascara. With the no-makeup look becoming popular among teens, girls are using as many cosmetics as ever to achieve the minimal look.

Boys also care about fashion, but they spend less of their own money on it, preferring to convince their parents to buy clothes and shoes for them. Boys spend more than girls on food, gas, and entertainment. This includes everything from pizza, chips, candy, and burgers to video games, movies, concerts, sports events, and video rentals. Although boys spend less on health and beauty aids than girls do, they are a ripe market for everything from hair gel to shaving cream.

In addition to buying consumables (small-ticket items), teens are serious purchasers and proud owners of a variety of big-ticket items, from

Big-Ticket Items
Owned by Teens

Most teens have their own television and telephone, and nearly half own a computer.

(percent of teens owning, 1998)

Home stereo/stereo component	79%
Wristwatch	71
Portable stereo	68
TV set	64
Bicycle	61
School yearbook (hardcover)	60
Telephone	58
Home video-game system	55
Camera	48
Computer	46

Source: TRU *Teenage Marketing & Lifestyle Study*

Big-Ticket Items
Teens Plan to Buy

Many teens plan to buy electronic equipment in the next year, including 13 percent who plan to buy a cellular phone.

(percent of teens planning to buy item in the next 12 months, 1998)

School yearbook (hardcover)	15%
Car stereo/car stereo component	14
Class ring	14
Pager/beeper	14
Used car	13
Cellular phone	13
Contact lenses	12
Sports/recreational equipment	12
Portable stereo	10
Computer	10

Source: TRU *Teenage Marketing & Lifestyle Study*

automobiles to all kinds of consumer electronics. With the exception of wristwatches and jewelry, all of teens' favorite big-ticket products provide entertainment. Teens' overriding motivation is to have fun, and they spend much of their income in this pursuit. That they are able to do so is a key difference between teens and adults, who must make sure their bills are paid before they can spend on entertainment. How often have you heard the adult complaint: "I can't believe I just spent $800 on a hot-water heater, and I get absolutely no enjoyment out of it." In contrast, if teens spend $800, they're spending it on stereos, TV sets, bicycles, and other fun things.

When we ask teens which products they plan to buy in the next year, they choose consumer electronics more than any other type of product. Many of the electronic products they plan to buy are more sophisticated versions of what they already own.

To provide marketers of durable goods with a measure of how a certain product category's sales may change in the coming year, we developed the Teen Market Opportunity Index (TMO). TMO measures the increase or decrease in the percentage of teens who say they plan to purchase a certain durable good within the next year. We calculate TMOs for each big-ticket item by dividing the percentage of teens who plan to purchase the item within the next year (current data) by the percentage who said they planned to purchase the item during the previous year (using data from the earlier year). An index of more than 100 suggests that a product's sales to teens are likely to grow in the coming year, while an index below 100 indicates sales may shrink.

The highest TMO Index in our fall 1998 study was 132 for home video game systems. To translate, this means that 32 percent more teens in 1998 than in 1997 planned to buy home video-game system within the next year. While this index does not correlate directly with sales, it indicates potential growth categories. In TRU's fall 1998 study, 41 percent of big-ticket categories scored at or above 100.

Teen Market Opportunity (TMO) Index

Home video-game system had the highest TMO Index in 1998, followed by yearbook and bicycle.

(the TMO Index is calculated by dividing the percentage of teens in 1998 who plan to purchase an item in the next 12 months by the percentage who said they planned to purchase the item in the next 12 months in 1997)

	TMO Index		TMO Index
Potential growth categories		**Potential decline categories**	
Home video game system	132	Wristwatch	99
Yearbook	122	Car stereo	97
Bicycle	117	Cellular phone	96
Camera	112	Pager	94
Class ring	111	New car	92
Backpack	107	TV set	91
Portable stereo	105	CD club membership	90
Prom dress*	104	Makeup organizer	90
Contact lenses	103	Telephone	84
		Computer	79
		Motorcycle	79
		Home stereo	67

* Girls only.
Source: TRU *Teenage Marketing & Lifestyle Study*

The TMO also identifies categories that face potential decline, either because an economic slowdown is limiting teen spending or because an item is no longer hot. If you want to portray teens in advertising, this index can tell you what's hot and what's not.

The Target: Teen, Parents, or Both?

Some purchases teens make for themselves; others their parents make for them. This distinction is critical and should guide you in determining whether to target teens, parents, or both.

Many companies are surprised to learn what teens buy for themselves and what their parents buy for them. A hair-care marketer, for example, was shocked at how involved boys are in buying or influencing the purchase of its products. Conversely, a leading acne marketer was surprised at how little involvement teens had in the purchase of acne remedies compared to their parents. Before you can decide how to position your products, you must understand the teen–parent dynamic.

To quantify this dynamic, John Baker, a former TRU researcher now an account planning director with the Richards Group in Dallas, developed the Teen Buying Control Index (TBC) from data we had been collecting for several years. The index is defined as the percentage that teens purchase by themselves of the total purchases by or for teens of a product category. The higher the TBC Index, the more the teen does the purchasing and the more important the teen is in positioning and advertising.

The categories we measure fall into six general classifications: health and beauty aids, food products, audio and video products, apparel and shoes, beverages, and miscellaneous items. For each of these classifications except miscellaneous, we calculate a norm—an average TBC—for males and females. We then compare individual product categories to the norm. For example, the health and beauty aid norm for girls is 42, meaning that 42 percent of the time that a health and beauty aid is purchased for a teen girl, it is purchased by the girl herself.

Teen Buying Control
(TBC) Index: Example

**Teen girls have more purchase control over hairstyling aids
than over shampoos and conditioners.**

*(Teen Buying Control Index among girls for hair cleansers and hairstyling aids;
the Teen Buying Control Index is the percentage of each product category that
teens personally buy themselves; health and beauty aid norm for teen girls is 42; 1998)*

	TBC Index
Cleansers	
Hair spray	39
Hair conditioner	30
2-in-1 shampoo	27
Regular shampoo	27
Dandruff shampoo	22
Styling aids	
Hair coloring	61
Styling gel	51
Hairstyling mousse	49
Hair spritz	44

Source: TRU *Teenage Marketing & Lifestyle Study*

TBC scores for hairstyling aids are at or above the norm, while the scores for hair cleansers are below the norm. So, teen girls have more purchase control over hairstyling aids than over shampoos and conditioners, which suggests that girls care more about brand choice for styling products than for cleansers. Since we know that the brand of shampoo teen girls use is very important to them, these data indicate that the brand of styling aid they use is probably even more important to them. Perhaps parents are willing to buy the more basic cleansers teens prefer than the styling aids. Therefore, teen girls must buy styling aids themselves to get their brand of choice.

The difference in TBC scores for these two product categories suggests that firms marketing shampoo and conditioner should consider targeting the parents of teens (since they are more likely to be the actual purchasers of these products) in addition to the teens themselves. But companies marketing hairstyling aids should target teens exclusively, since they are the likely to purchasers of these products.

By knowing how involved teens are in purchasing specific products, you can better position your ads, make the right choice of talent, and buy the right media. The higher the TBC Index, the more likely is it that consumer promotions directed at teens, such as free samples and in-store displays, will be more effective than mass-media advertising to an adult audience.

Teen Influence in Purchase Decisions

We find the TBC Index useful because it is a measure of the teen–parent purchase dynamic that marketers can really sink their teeth into. It quantifies how involved each party is in the purchase of specific consumer products. But if a product scores low on the TBC measure, you should not automatically write it off as having no potential for a teen-targeting effort. Before doing so, you should examine the issue of purchase influence. Often, although a parent is doing the buying, a teen is directing the purchase.

Teen Purchase Influence:
Consumables

Most teens think they influence their parents' brand choice when buying fast food, pizza, soft drinks, shampoo, toothpaste, ice cream, and cereal.

(percent of teens saying they influence their parents' purchase of selected items, 1994)

	total	boys	girls
Fast food	65%	65%	65%
Pizza	63	64	62
Soft drinks	60	61	59
Shampoo	59	49	69
Toothpaste	54	48	60
Ice cream	53	51	55
Cereal	52	52	53
Antiperspirant/deodorant	49	42	56
Potato chips	45	45	44
Chewing gum	45	39	52
Telephone	44	37	51
Juice	43	39	48
Hair conditioner	41	21	61
Toothbrush	40	36	45
Bar soap	38	31	45
Camera film	38	26	49
Chocolate candy	31	29	34
Acne remedy	31	29	33
Tortilla chips	28	30	26

Source: TRU *Teenage Marketing & Lifestyle Study*

This dynamic is difficult to measure. Can teens judge the influence they wield over their parents' purchases? Do parents acknowledge this influence? To find out, we talk to both teens and their mothers (mothers are still much more involved in buying for their families than fathers). Typically, we first spend a few minutes talking to both the teen and his or her mother, then we have a one-on-one discussion with each separately. In this way, we learn how each assesses the teen's influence and describes the parent–teen purchase-decision dynamic. We end the session by bringing both parties together again to discuss any perceptual gap (which there often is) and trying to resolve it if possible. This gap is quite different for consumables than for durable products.

Teens, and girls more so than boys, see themselves as being influential in the purchase decision and brand choice of many consumable products. But do teens think they have more influence over their parents' purchases than they actually do? In fact, just the opposite is the case. When teens think about their purchase influence, they think of how often and forcefully they ask, beg, plead, campaign for, or simply request that their parents buy them certain items. But that's not how their mothers see it. Mothers say their teenaged children are more influential than they realize. Even without their teens' urging or requesting, most mothers already know what their kids want. Most want to get them what they want for two reasons: first, moms are nice (!), and second, they don't want to see their purchases go to waste. Without so much as a "gimme," mom often buys the brand of teen choice. Consequently, the numbers in the consumables table are conservative.

Teens also perceive themselves as highly influential in their family's decisions to purchase durable goods, with about half claiming to influence the purchase of a variety of big-ticket items. In contrast to teens' understated influence over the purchase of consumable goods, qualitative research we have conducted suggests that teens overstate their influence on some big-ticket item purchases. While half the teens think they influence

Teen Purchase Influence:
Durables

Most teens think they influence their parents' choices
when buying a range of durable goods.

(percent of teens saying they influence their parents' purchase of selected items, 1994)

Vacation/travel	80%
Sports equipment	78
Magazine subscription	64
Computer software	64
Personal computer	63
Home stereo	57
Car/truck/van	51
TV set	51
VCR	50

Source: TRU *Teenage Marketing & Lifestyle Study*

the make of car their parents buy, our interviews with parents show that a smaller percentage of parents agree.

Teens do wield considerable influence over the purchase of consumer electronics. Many teens know more about these products—from CD players to computers—than their parents (particularly parents who don't use computers at work), and many parents rely on their teenage children for guidance in directing these purchase decisions. Teen influence in the purchase of computers transcends even their role as family expert. Many parents buy multimedia computers primarily because they think their children will benefit.

The 1995 IBM Aptiva advertising campaign featuring actor Paul Reiser effectively sold computers to parents through their children, while getting teens and younger kids involved in the process. The ads showed how computers really are for both kids and their parents. In other words, they are for the whole family. This message plays well for parents who feel a responsibility to give their children the educational benefits of a computer. It also motivates kids by showcasing the components that are entertainment-oriented (graphics, sound, games, etc.).

As families continue to change and the roles of family members shift, teen influence in the purchasing of durable goods is growing. Marketers of many durable goods should view teens as a primary rather than secondary market. Whenever possible, marketing efforts should reflect teens' pronounced role in decision-making. Not only will immediate benefits result from direct teen purchases and teen-influenced family purchases, but longer-term payoffs in brand loyalty may lie in the wings.

Chapter 3.

Teens and Media

Teens are not only big media users, they're also big media fans. And their avid consumption of media helps to nationalize the teen experience, connecting teens through common images and expressions. But teens use media differently than adults or children. Therefore it's important to understand their media preferences and behaviors.

There's a common misconception about teens and the media. One of the first questions many a reporter has asked our staff is, "How can advertisers reach teens given that teens are such an elusive media target?" The assumption is that teens are difficult to reach, and reporters rarely ask whether this is true. It isn't. There are many media outlets that reach teens effectively, but this misconception keeps some companies from actively targeting teens, even though pursuing them would make strategic sense.

As the teen population continues to grow to record levels and more marketers recognize teenage consumer clout, media vehicles with which to reach teens proliferate, ranging from the traditional to the innovative. From new teen magazines to branded TV network dayparts for teens and from school-based media to those based in cyberspace, there are more and more methods for reaching this audience. What's important to recognize is that teens have their own personal networks, and often interact with hundreds of peers each day. In fact, media frequency in the teen market could be judged by the amount of word of mouth generated within schools and other teen communities.

Because teens take cues not only from each other but also from the media, it's important to stay attuned to the media that most influence them. We advise our clients to watch, read, and listen to the same things teens watch, read, and listen to. For example, our company subscribes to or gets almost every magazine that influences teens, from *Seventeen, YM, Teen, Teen People, Jump,* and *Teen Beat* to *Transworld Skateboarding, Warp, Vibe, Scholastic, react, Rolling Stone, Electronic Gaming Monthly, Nintendo Power,* and *GamePro.* We also produce a document for our clients, titled (what else?)

Advertising Media to Which Teens Pay Most Attention

Most teens name cable TV, magazines, and radio as the advertising media to which they pay the most attention.

(percent of teens citing advertising source when asked, "Which advertising do you personally pay the most attention to?" 1998)

Cable TV	54%
Magazines	53
Radio	50
Before movies	48
Broadcast TV	35
Before rented videos	28
Billboards, scoreboards	28
Newspapers	26
Through mail	20
In school	15
At sponsored events	13
Internet/online service	12

Source: TRU *Teenage Marketing & Lifestyle Study*

Teen-Recommended Media

**Radio is the number-one medium teens recommend for reaching them.
One in five recommends using the Internet.**

(percent of teens recommending medium as effective in reaching teens, 1996)

Radio	55%
Cable TV	50
Magazines	39
Before movies at theater	29
In school	26
Broadcast TV	24
Through the mail	23
Internet/online services	21
Billboards, scoreboards	15
Sponsored events	15
Before rented videos	12
Newspapers	9

Source: TRU *Teenage Marketing & Lifestyle Study*

"Wise Up to Teens: A Primer in Getting Immersed in Teen Culture." This document, which is continually updated, lists media and activities clients can check out and in which they can participate to keep up with teen popular culture.

When we talk to teens about marketing, we continually are reminded of just how savvy they are, particularly when it comes to discussing and analyzing advertising. In a recent study, we gave teenagers an opportunity to point advertisers toward the media that grab their attention the most. Three choices stood out: cable TV, magazines (number one for girls), and radio. These findings are fairly consistent with a previous measure, in which we asked teens to recommend media that companies can use to reach people their age. In that study, radio came out on top (again, number one for girls), followed by cable and magazines.

Teens and Radio

Teens invest a lot of time in listening to the radio; about 95 percent of the nation's teens listen to FM radio, averaging more than ten hours each week. When asked which media companies should use to reach them, teens heartily recommend radio. This finding may surprise some advertisers, but it makes sense when you consider what radio offers teens.

To teens, radio means music. Teens' love of music is well documented. Music both separates teens and unites them, providing a soundtrack for their busy lives. Radio programming is almost exclusively comprised, then, of what teens love best. Radio also offers teens a selectivity in music they can't get elsewhere, including even MTV. If a researcher had asked my peers and I what type of music we liked when we were teenagers in the late 1960s, we all would have said "rock," or maybe "soul." Today, teen taste in music is extremely fragmented. Teens might say their favorite music is "trip hop," "rap," "alternative," "metal," "techno," "house," "punk," "reggae," or "R&B." A few would even say "country," "classic rock," or "swing." Radio allows teens to instantly select whatever music they prefer.

Favorite Radio Formats
of Teens

Alternative music is the favorite radio format
of the largest share of teen boys and girls.

(percent of teens mentioning format as one of their top two favorites, 1998)

Boys

Alternative	40%
Rap	39
R&B	24
Hard Rock	22
Classic Rock	16

Girls

Alternative	40
R&B	37
Rap	31
Country	15
Soft Rock	11

Source: TRU *Teenage Marketing & Lifestyle Study*

When we ask teens about local radio, whether in Chicago, Los Angeles, Atlanta, or Tucson, the discussion often becomes heated. Teens are extremely loyal to particular stations. Especially in small towns, radio connects local teenagers, informing them of coming events such as concerts, sports, school events, and so on. Radio also makes celebrities out of local disc jockeys. And, in most markets, there are typically a few strong teen stations, allowing advertisers to efficiently reach large numbers of teens.

Because of the selectivity of radio, it offers efficiency for reaching different teen segments according to ethnic, gender, and geographic characteristics. Because teens are differentiated by their taste in music, the selectivity of radio allows marketers to use different executions for different radio formats.

A teenager who likes rap probably isn't a metal fan and vice versa. A preference for one type of music often excludes other styles. This difference goes far beyond musical preference. Teen language, fashion, style, activities, friends, and attitudes often correlate with taste in music. Understanding this psychographic segmentation, you can communicate in a relevant and appealing way to teen listeners.

African-American teens are the most efficiently targeted teen segment with radio, as they gravitate to two formats: rap and R&B (often programmed together on a single urban station). Whereas white teens, in smaller numbers, also listen to these formats, they greatly prefer alternative and also listen to classic rock and country. Latino teens are the most musically adventurous, liking all of the above-mentioned formats. Those who aren't bilingual often prefer Spanish-language radio.

The other important thing to remember about this medium is that radio accompanies teenagers. It's with them at home, in their cars, on their ways, forging a relationship which is the basis of why teens rate radio so highly.

For marketers who need help navigating the world of teen radio, an organization called Next Generation Radio can point the way. One of its founders, Deb Esayian, who now sits on its Board of Directors and manages a local station in Connecticut, believes that most brand managers, agency account executives, and even media supervisors understand little about radio and its unique role in a young person's life, nor do they know much about the medium, which she admits is fairly confusing and complicated. So, Next Generation Radio, which is funded by teen and young-adult radio stations across the country, guides advertisers through the process of planning, budgeting, and executing youth-targeted radio campaigns. Specifically, what Deb believes is the single most important fact that brand managers, agencies and even people in radio don't seem to "get" about teen radio is that it's a reach, not a frequency, vehicle. Radio is highly efficient for reaching teens in big numbers. It's not surprising, then, that teens themselves, in large numbers, advise advertisers to get on the airwaves to reach people their age.

Teens and Magazines

No medium is more intimate or directly relevant to teenage girls than magazines. In fact, to learn about trends, girls rely more on magazines than on any other information source—including friends, peers, and other media or entertainment outlets. Girls bond with their favorite magazines, depending upon them for critical information about the key questions and issues of their lives—from boys, beauty, and fashion to parents, school, and community. Magazines are an intimate part of growing up for American girls, and advertisers who appear on the pages of their favorite magazines benefit from such a welcomed environment.

Magazines are far more important to teen girls than to teen boys. Girls view many teen magazines, like Se*venteen*, *YM*, and *Teen*, as big sisters on whom they can rely for advice about what matters to them. Boys have an altogether different relationship with magazines. Spending less time read-

Top 15 Magazines Read by Teens

It's easier to reach teen girls through magazines than teen boys.

(percent of teens who read a typical issue of each magazine, by gender, 1998)

Boys		Girls	
Sports Illustrated	28%	Seventeen	49%
TV Guide	22	YM	39
Scholastic Network (gross measurement)*	21	Teen	38
Scholastic Senior Edition	16	TV Guide	26
Game Pro	15	Scholastic Network (gross measurement)*	24
Nintendo Power	13	People	22
Cable Guide	12	Scholastic Senior Edition	16
Sport	11	Glamour	15
Inside Sports	11	Cosmopolitan	13
Newsweek	11	Cable Guide	12
Electronic Gaming Monthly	10	Parade	12
Rolling Stone	10	Teen Beat	10
People	10	Vibe	10
Sports Illustrated for Kids	10	Vogue	9
Time	9	Time	9
		16	9
		All About You	9
		Newsweek	9
		Mademoiselle	8
		Sports Illustrated	8

* Includes *Science World, Scope, Update, Choices, Jr. Scholastic.*
Source: TRU *Teenage Marketing & Lifestyle Study*

ing than girls do and not having the same type of "horizontal" magazines written just for them, boys use magazines for information and entertainment. They seek and read magazines that focus on their particular interests, from TV and sports to video games, music, and celebrities. Specifically, the magazines most read by teen boys are *Sports Illustrated, TV Guide, Scholastic, GamePro, Cable Guide, Nintendo Power, Electronic Gaming Monthly, Rolling Stone, Newsweek,* and *People.*

Girls rate magazines highly on several levels, and they advise marketers to use magazines to reach them. Perhaps they are savvy enough to realize that magazines are a cost-effective way to target their particular demographic.

With the exception of friends, magazines are the medium by which most teen girls say they find out about the latest trends. Girls depend on magazines for more than leisure reading. They rely on them to learn about the latest fashions and lifestyle choices and to connect with other girls their age across the country. Girls also "shop" print ads and editorial fashion photos as if they were catalogs.

Seventeen and *YM* are probably the strongest magazines in the field. *Teen* is especially strong with slightly younger girls, and *Teen People,* which debuted concurrently in print and online in 1998, has made a big splash with advertisers and girls, leveraging the equity of *People,* which has always done well with teen readers, particularly girls. *Teen People* is edited by Christina Ferrari, formerly of *YM* magazine, and has the muscle of Time Inc. behind it.

Nevertheless, *Seventeen* remains the stalwart book of the field and has been the category leader in circulation and ad pages for years. *YM,* formerly titled *Young Miss,* has been gaining ground in its competition with *Seventeen,* however.

Though its audience is slightly younger than *Seventeen*'s and *YM*'s, *Teen* has noticeably improved its editorial product over the past few years.

Its keener understanding of its readership is reflected in a more contemporary look. And, aiming at a slightly younger audience helps *Teen* differentiate itself from its competitors, giving advertisers an opportunity to reach younger girls at the "point of entry" of their product categories.

Not all magazines, of course, can survive in such a heady environment. *Sassy* magazine was the American relative of the Australian magazine *Dolly*. *Sassy* was actually a tame version of *Dolly*, reflecting more conservative American attitudes. Even so, *Sassy* made a big splash during its launch in 1987, when Jerry Falwell's Moral Majority criticized it for its frank talk about sex. One article included an illustration of a boy's body, with an arrow pointing to each part and describing its function. Although *Sassy* lost a few advertisers temporarily because of the controversy, Falwell created enough media attention to reach parents and teens. As soon as teens were told to stay away from *Sassy*, they flocked to it. Falwell turned out to be a great *Sassy* circulation marketer. From a profitability perspective, *Sassy* was a disappointment to its former publishers, however. Its third owner, Petersen Publications, which already published *Teen*, eventually folded *Sassy* into *Teen* as a 16-page insert called "The Sassy Slant." The section has subsequently disappeared, as Petersen found that *Sassy* no longer had any special equity with the current crop of teens.

In addition to these strong magazines, there are several others written for teen girls. *Teen Beat*, from MacFadden Sterlings Partnership, is widely read. The same company publishes *Tiger Beat, 16, Teen Machine, SuperTeen, Metal Edge, Black Beat, Sisters in Style,* and *Right On!* It has developed a strong niche and thrives when there's a current teen heart throb. Leonardo DiCaprio, in fact, is just what they had been waiting for. Now they're looking for the next Leo. Though the star of *Titanic* appeared concurrently on the May 1998 issues of *Teen, Seventeen, YM* and *Teen People*, it's MacFadden Sterlings' magazines that probably have benefited the most from DiCaprio's phenomenal appeal to teen girls.

In addition *to Teen People*, two other teen-targeted magazines debuted in 1998: *Jump* from Wieder Publications and *Twist* from Bauer Publisher. With the cover line "for girls who dare to be real," *Jump* has a sports and fitness slant, which is not surprising since it comes from a company which also publishes a number of muscle and fitness titles. *Jump* understands that teen girls not only care more about fitness and health than boys do, they're also more involved in sports than any previous generation of teen girls. *Twist* has shown patience, allowing its audience to develop slowly. Although the publisher did not seriously promote the magazine or mount a subscription effort, girls found it at the newsstand. Editor-in-chief Lisa Lombardi, another former *YM* editor, says what sets *Twist* apart is that it is more interactive. Graphically, *Twist* has a busy look; Lombardi calls it "Web-inspired." Editorially, the magazine benefits from reader involvement. Not only are girls e-mailing their suggestions, they're also writing articles. TRU's experience is that you always benefit by getting teens directly involved—whether you're a magazine or a brand. The more you hear from teens in the development stage and keep listening to them as you grow, the more successful you'll be.

Another new magazine launched in late 1998 is *Latingirl*. It's aimed at the fastest-growing U.S. teen segment—Hispanics.

It is doubtful that all these magazines can survive, but the odds are with *Teen People*. Certainly, the danger in publishing a magazine for teens is the perception of being a teen magazine. Teens are aspirational, always looking to the *next* level. So, magazines such as *Teen, Seventeen* and *Teen People*, which carry the t-word in their title, are at risk of attracting a younger teen and tween audience. Clearly, *16*'s readers are younger than *Seventeen*'s (and, based on editorial content, probably by more than one year). Because their reading is aspirational, older teen girls are moving from teen magazines into magazines like *Cosmopolitan, Glamour, Mademoiselle,* and *Vogue*. This older audience is the one *Jane* is going after.

If you want to reach an audience of both teen boys and girls, magazines distributed in high schools can be especially effective. The most successful publisher in this arena is Scholastic Publications, which currently distributes *Science World, Scope, Update, Choices, Literary Cavalcade*, and (for younger students) *Junior Scholastic* in the nation's schools. These magazines reach about 9 million teens. *Careers & Colleges*, from E. M. Guild, is also distributed in schools. It targets college-bound students twice a year. *Fast Times*, from a California entrepreneur and former high school teacher, is a high-quality publication distributed in history classes. At www.fast-times.com, the magazine also hosts a great-looking, detailed web site. *react*, from Parade, is distributed in schools and as an insert in daily newspapers. About 3.6 million teens read each issue. *react* also has a strong online presence, developed side-by-side with the print version.

A rising print category targeting teen girls is the catalog. The editorial content typically is limited to pictures and descriptions of merchandise—mostly apparel and accessories. Still, this subject is near and dear to teens, and that's why *delia's*, in particular, is finding huge success. A relaunched entry is *mXg* (formerly *Moxie Girl*), which is more of a "magalog," surrounding the merchandise with typical teen girl editorial. What's unique about *mXg* is that it allows outside advertising. Along with *delia's*, this catalog has a strong online presence.

In fact, we often hear girls in qualitative research refer to some of these catalogs as "magazines." Clearly, the line between the two is blurring, as catalogs are bringing more editorial into their pages. Still, the jury is out on whether—as a genre—fashion catalogs will achieve long-term success with teen girls. Although girls love to peruse their pages, catalog buying requires a credit card or a check, two methods of payment few girls have of their own. Instead, girls are forced to try to cut deals with parents for using parents' credit cards or checkbooks. Also, girls are leery of buying clothes which may not fit—particularly pants—through a catalog. They (and their parents) don't want to hassle with returning the merchandise.

Already, two of the better-known catalogs targeting girls—*Zoe* and *Just Nikki*—have called it a day. Although they created a lot of buzz among girls, they simply didn't produce enough sales. Other catalogs targeting teen girls include *Wet Seal* and *Alloy*. *Droog* is the first apparel catalog we've seen that targets teen boys.

Not all teen magazine launches are successful, of course. Prospective publishers can learn from the failures. Reflecting advertisers' increasing interest in the teen market, more publishers are giving teens a try. In the last few years, two major publishers launched teen magazines, without great success. *Tell*, from Hachette, and *Mouth2Mouth*, from Time Publishing Ventures, were slick magazines. Like *Scholastic*, they were designed for both boys and girls. *Tell*, which was a joint venture between Hachette and NBC, was an example of a cross-media partnership forged so as to reach more teens. *Tell* looked like a younger version of *US* and found a significant female audience. Unfortunately, it didn't find enough readers and never reached its first birthday.

Mouth2Mouth was the vision of its editor-in-chief, Angela Jankow Harrington, whose Hollywood connections and exuberant style fueled the magazine's celebrity focus. Despite keeping its promise to deliver an in-your-face information- and celebrity-packed magazine, *Mouth2Mouth* was unable to attract enough teen newsstand buyers or subscribers in its two test issues to convince Time to proceed. This was unfortunate, because the magazine found advertising support and high reader interest. Delivering on its editorial promise, however, made it an extremely expensive magazine to publish and that much more of a financial risk.

No one has yet created a magazine that is specifically aimed at and appeals to teen boys. We can't even begin to count the number of calls we've received in the past 15 years from major publishers and entrepreneurs who, noting the absence of a general lifestyle magazine for teen boys, wanted to explore the market. But they all face the same problem: the kind of magazine that a lot of boys would buy is often the kind they cannot sell to an underage audience. *Sassy's* previous publisher experimented with seven issues of a male version, titled *Dirt*, distributing it with *Sassy* and in a polyethylene bag with *Marvel* comic books. Without a more direct means of targeting its readers and a greater financial commitment from its publisher, *Dirt* was swept under the rug.

The most effective way of targeting boys through print is by tapping into the vertical or niche publications that reflect their special interests, such as sports, video games, or music. The magazine that enjoys the highest teen male readership is *Sports Illustrated*. Because this is a magazine targeting adults, it is an extremely expensive and inefficient vehicle for reaching teen boys. Magazines such as *GamePro, Electronic Gaming Monthly, Transworld Skateboarding, Heckler* (which combines skateboarding, snowboarding, and music), and *Nintendo Power* draw niche audiences of highly interested teenage boys.

Teens and Broadcast Television

With the exception of radio, teens spend more time watching TV than they do with any other medium. Although there is often much waste in targeting teens through network television, certain programs and smaller networks deliver not only large numbers of teens but also a disproportionately large teenaged audience. Fox, in particular, has been successful in programming for teens, hosting several teen favorites over the past few years. The WB network has also aggressively courted the teen market with shows like "Dawson's Creek," "7th Heaven," "Buffy the Vampire Slayer," and "Felicity." In fact, when asked for their favorite non-cable TV networks, twice as many teens named the WB than CBS, one of the big three networks. What a lesson in teen marketing—when you craft relevant products and messages to teens, they *will* come.

With few exceptions, teens' favorite programs are situation comedies. Humor is a key ingredient in programming success with teens. Humor is also key to creating advertising that appeals to this age group. When humor is combined with family situations involving teens, the appeal is even greater.

From "Ozzie & Harriet," "Leave It to Beaver," and "Dobie Gillis," to "The Partridge Family" and "The Brady Bunch," teens historically have gravitated toward programming centered on people their own age in family situations. Most of teens' favorite TV shows today focus on families with teenaged children. Regardless of what teens think about their own families, family is the core of teen life. Teens like to watch other families—real or fictional—to gain a perspective on their own experience.

The single most important network program for teens in the past 10 years was not a sitcom, however. Yet it does incorporate family situations. "Beverly Hills, 90210" has been among the favorite programs of teen girls since its debut. It's rare for one television show to sustain this level of popularity for so long. At one time, nearly half the teen girls said that "90210" was one of their three favorite programs. Its popularity has since declined by more than half, but it still ranks as one of girls' favorite shows. TV seems to be an exception to the rule that teens are most attracted to whatever is the newest. Although a number of new shows are launched and promoted each season, teens hold onto their favorites from years past. During their runs (some of which continue), teens remained extremely loyal to "The Simpsons," "Home Improvement," "Seinfeld," and "Friends."

Other programs that rank among teens' favorites are "South Park," "The X-Files," "King of the Hill," "Party of Five," "ER," "Boy Meets World," "7th Heaven," "Sabrina, the Teenage Witch," "Moesha," and "USA High."

Teens and Cable Television

MTV remains teens' most-watched cable network. Although it is not as cutting-edge as it was when it debuted in the early 1980s, MTV remains

Teens' Favorite
Cable Networks

MTV continues to be the most popular cable channel among teens.

(average hours teens view weekly, by gender, 1998)

	hours
Boys	
MTV	5.4
ESPN	4.4
USA	3.7
Girls	
MTV	6.1
VH-1	3.2
USA	2.8

Source: TRU *Teenage Marketing & Lifestyle Study*

hugely important to teenage popular culture. These days, there is not as much "M" in MTV, as the network has vacillated in its programming strategy to arrive at the ideal balance of music videos and non-music programming. Nevertheless, MTV continues to innovate, probably launching more new programs than any other network. MTV's influence transcends music and pervades all of youth culture, from fashion and sports to celebrities and advertising.

Among other reasons, MTV backed away from its originally heavy focus on music because of teens' musical tastes. Any music-based cable network geared toward teens or young adults faces the programming challenge of appealing to increasingly fragmented musical tastes. While radio can target its programming to distinctive musical preferences, MTV must rotate between alternative, rap, R&B, and other genres. Someday, if we ever have 500 cable channels, maybe there will be an MTV Rap, MTV Metal, and so on.

Hispanic teens are the biggest MTV viewers. TRU data have consistently shown that Latino teens have the most diverse tastes in music. It can polarize black or white teen audiences when MTV rotates between musical genres, but it rarely does so to Hispanics.

As influential as MTV is on the overall teen market, African-American teens spend more time viewing BET (Black Entertainment Television), whose programming mix is similar to MTV's. Because African-American teens are on the forefront of teen trends, BET's influence is considerable.

ESPN is another important vehicle for reaching teens. Teen boys spend almost as much time watching ESPN as MTV, and just as many turn on ESPN in a given week as MTV. As ESPN took a leadership role in sports programming and included more non-game programs, teen boys have become bigger fans of this network. "SportsCenter," in fact, is one of teen boys' favorite TV shows.

Although its audience is small compared to MTV's, The Box is another influential cable network. A sort of pay-per-view jukebox, this net-

Newspaper Section Readership

Sports and comics are the most popular newspaper sections among teen boys, while comics and advertising rank first and second among girls.

(percent of teens who have read newspaper section in the last seven days, 1998)

Boys

Sports	64%
Comics	56
Entertainment	45
Local/community news	42
National news	35
TV and radio listings	35

Girls

Comics	54
Advertising	50
Horoscopes	49
Local/community news	49
Entertainment	48

Source: TRU *Teenage Marketing & Lifestyle Study*

work is closely monitored by record labels for cues as to who's hot. Rap and hip-hop dominate airplay on The Box, and consequently its audience is primarily African-American.

Through syndicated sitcoms, reruns, movies, sports events, and even cartoons and animated features, other cable networks, including USA, TBS, TNT, Nick at Nite, Comedy Central, and HBO, offer teens wide programming choices that appeal to their different tastes. In fact, USA is girls' third-most watched network. Currently, Comedy Central's "South Park" ranks fourth among favorite TV programs (network or cable) for teen boys.

Teens and Newspapers

Considering all the talk about the weakness of newsprint in the face of the increasing number of electronic and interactive media, it may surprise many marketers to discover that 77 percent of teen boys and 73 percent of teen girls look at a newspaper each week. That newspaper readership is slightly higher among teen boys than girls can be explained in part by the fact that many boys are simply glancing at the box score of yesterday's game. Nevertheless, many teens spend a considerable amount of time reading newspapers—boys average 2.8 hours per week, and girls, 2.3 hours.

Newspapers can be a viable medium by which to reach teens for several reasons. First, school newspapers enjoy a special bond with their readers. Second, many major dailies have regular teen sections. *Parade's* teen newspaper, *react*, has a two-tiered distribution: in school and—in many markets—as an insert in the weekly magazine. Cokie Dishon, who premiered the *Chicago Tribune's Kid News*, was responsible for the editorial vision of *react*. The third reason why newspapers are an important medium for reaching teens is that they provide a convenient daily source of entertainment and information. Teens prefer comics, sports, entertainment, horoscopes, and even the classifieds over national news, and fortunately for teens, newspapers contain more than just the news.

Teen Use of Online Services

Most teens have used online services, and 53 percent use them at home.

(percent of teens using online services by type of service and location of use, 1998)

	used anywhere	used at school/ someplace else	used at home
Total, used any service	**81%**	**61%**	**53%**
Internet/World Wide Web	66	49	36
America Online	55	32	31
Microsoft Network	36	25	18
Prodigy	11	7	5
CompuServe	10	7	4

Source: TRU *Teenage Marketing & Lifestyle Study*

What Teens Do
in Cyberspace

**Two out of three teen boys and girls surf the Net
when online, checking out Web sites.**

(percent of teens saying they do activity while online, 1998)

	boys	girls
Check out Web sites	66%	62%
Do research for school	53	69
Chat	50	58
E-mail	47	58
Play games	37	33
Download pictures	41	29
Check out sites on AOL/Prodigy	22	25
Buy stuff	4	4

Source: TRU *Teenage Marketing & Lifestyle Study*

Online and the Internet

Computers are hugely important to teens today. They rely on them for everything from schoolwork to entertainment. Seventy-two percent of teens use a computer at home, and nearly three-fourths of the computer users have a modem. Teens are traveling in cyberspace at ever-faster speeds, and advertisers are taking notice. Although teens say that online advertising doesn't particularly grab their attention, they're probably unaware of its impact or don't think of it as advertising.

As shown on the previous page, 53 percent of teens have used an online service or the Internet at home, and 61 percent have been online at school or at someone else's home. Overall, 81 percent of teens have ever been online. At home, 36 percent have been on the Internet. America Online appears to be the biggest gateway to the Web from home, and 31 percent of teens use AOL at home, compared to 18 percent who use the Microsoft Network and only 5 and 4 percent, respectively, who use Prodigy or Compuserve. Many more teens get on the Web at school or elsewhere other than at their own home (61 percent versus 53 percent). Slightly more teens use one of the online services away from home than at home, reflecting the fact that these dial-up services have become entertainment for teens when they go to friends' homes.

As many girls as boys are going online, as are teens of all ages. But significantly fewer minority teens have access: 39 percent of both African-American and Latino teens have ever gone online at home, compared to 59 percent of white teens. The margin is narrower at school because many schools in financially strapped school districts are receiving state funding to get wired.

Most of our clients are developing a Web presence for their teenage consumers. After all, nearly 90 percent of teens say the Internet is "in." This is an astonishing figure, higher than the percentage of those who say partying, dating, or shopping is "in." Because attitudes toward the Internet are so positive, the only factor holding back more rapid growth in Internet use is lack of access. Marketers need to recognize that economically disadvantaged teens do not have the ready access to the Internet that their more affluent counterparts have. Computers and the Internet may be cool, but still only the bare majority of teens are fortunate enough to have access to the online world from their home.

Teens fortunate enough to have access to the Internet are quite active in their cyberadventures. They are surfing, chatting, researching, downloading, e-mailing, and gaming. The only major cyberactivity in which few teens participate is the buying of products and services, primarily because few teens have their own credit cards, and partly because of parents' uncertainty both about online commerce and the safety of their children online. We do believe, based on more parents shopping online and more online commerce sites developed with teens and kids in mind, that we will soon begin to see a sharp increase in teen cyberpurchases. As with mail order, though, teens will need to "cut deals" with parents for paying with credit cards.

Teens who go online are fairly fluent in navigating the Web. Online marketers have a variety of means at their disposal to reach and interact with teens—from setting up cool but appropriate sites of their own to bringing celebrities into chatrooms to promote a brand and buying banner ads at popular teen destinations.

What's most important is to keep a site fun, intriguing, interactive, and ever-evolving. Give teens something to do. Their attention span is short. They're most attracted to whatever is new. And, to ensure that teens find you on the Web, promote and advertise your URL address along with a benefit or reason why teens should check out your site. In addition to providing another way to promote and increase awareness of your brand, your site could be a valuable way to get feedback from teens who are interested enough to check you out.

Teens and Alternative Media

While most teens have seen a variety of alterative media, most like only free product samples, ads before movies in theaters, and billboards.

(percent of teens who have seen and who like advertising medium, 1993)

	alternative media	
	seen	like
Before movie (video)	99%	45%
Before movie (theater)	92	56
Billboards	88	56
Mail	86	38
Free product samples	82	68
Grocery cart/shelf	77	32
Sponsored events	75	49
Scoreboards	67	42
Posters at school	63	38
School newspaper	52	36
TV news at school	46	35
Classroom materials	42	24

Source: TRU *Teenage Marketing & Lifestyle Study*

Other Media Outlets

In addition to traditional and online media, you can reach teens through place-based media. TRU's *Teenage Marketing & Lifestyle Study* asks teens which alternative media they have seen and which they like.

The results of this measure are revealing. Exposure to alternative media and actually liking them can vary, although there is some correlation. Advertising before movies (in-theater) ranks second in exposure and second in likability. While many adults find advertising at theaters annoying, or even an infringement on their time (after all, they paid to be there), teens view it as bonus entertainment. The ads shown at theaters often are highly original, because advertisers understand that, to be effective, theater ads must have greater production and entertainment value than television ads.

More than 80 percent of teens have received advertising through the mail, but only 38 percent like it. In our syndicated study, only 23 percent of teens recommend direct mail as one of the two best ways to reach them. We believe, however, that this number doesn't truly reflect the potential of direct mail. First, teens don't get the volume of mail that adults do; therefore, they're more attentive to offers and promotions sent through the mail than adults are. From our own syndicated study, which is fielded through the mail, we know that teens are great respondents. Certainly, the recent proliferation of teen-targeted catalogs is testament to the power of this medium for reaching teens.

One potential setback for direct-mail advertising is misdirected privacy legislation. Positioned as a protective measure for children, this legislation could, if ever passed, end the use of direct mail to reach teens. Proposed legislation would eliminate many beneficial services that provide information to parents and children, protect children, and recognize the achievements of young people. But unless and until such legislation is passed, marketers should consider using direct mail to reach teens. One of our clients, Nintendo of America, has had great success in mailing a video of highlights from upcoming games to a list of video game–buying boys.

Spring break is a marketing bonanza for many companies, a chance to have a presence and distribute samples of their products to throngs of vacationing, partying, happy students. College students embrace what's free. A few years ago we conducted a spring-break research project among college students at two of their favorite destinations: South Padre Island in Texas and Lake Havasu in Arizona. At Padre Island, we discovered that a common spring-break chant was, "Free shit! Free shit! Free shit!" Clearly, these students didn't object to being marketed to while on vacation. Similarly, teens' favorite alternative advertising is product sampling. They love getting something for nothing, yet only about one in five teens has ever received a free product sample.

Probably the best-known place-based advertising vehicle directed at teens is Channel One, a daily news program sent by satellite into many of the nation's middle and high schools. Channel One launched several years ago amid much controversy over the inclusion of two minutes of advertising in the 12-minute daily programs. Those who object to Channel One argue that advertising does not belong in schools, especially not being shown to a captive audience. But advertising has long been in schools, from space advertising in *Scholastic* or school newspapers to corporate-sponsored promotions such as the Campbell Soup label program in elementary school. Channel One set off critics because of the high impact of television advertising and the belief that students would be force-fed commercials as part of their classroom lessons.

Our position is that Channel One is sound programming. It makes news relevant to kids. Its coverage of the fall of the Berlin Wall, in Channel One's early days, opened the eyes of thousands of American teens. Furthermore, teens are bombarded with hundreds of advertising messages every day. Because advertising has become so much a part of their lives, they are quite adept at tuning it in or out. To some, this point alone might not justify in-school TV advertising, but in combination with the quality of the program, we feel comfortable recommending Channel One to advertisers. Another plus for the schools is that Channel One gives VCRs and televisions to schools that air its programming.

The partnership between corporate America and the nation's schools should be viewed cautiously but with an open mind. With educational resources shrinking to the point that some schools are using history books published 30 years ago, corporate funding of educational programs and materials has become more prevalent, more necessary, and more attractive. European countries have long been more open to corporate funding for education than the United States, believing the materials and programs the schools receive are well worth the price of exposing students to a corporate logo or an advertising message.

Modern Talking Pictures is one company that develops and executes corporate–educational partnerships. It has worked with a variety of brands, providing them with exposure to students and giving the schools worthwhile programs.

Other media companies also place advertising in schools. American Passage Marketing Corporation targets high school students with *GymBoards* in school locker rooms. Each board is customized with the names and colors of the school team as well as advertising. This program is particularly attractive because it allows advertisers to target teenage boys and girls separately. Another company, Market Source, places high-tech wall boards, called the High School Source, in schools. In addition to space for advertising, the boards include customized monthly calendars of school events and a moving LED message, which the school can customize for announcements.

Planet Report is the latest creation by Jeff Lederman, one of the founders of *Fast Times. Planet Report* consists of ad-supported poster and bookmark programs, distributed in elementary and high schools across the country. *Planet Report*'s giant 4' x 7' monthly newsposters are displayed in school libraries, cafeterias, hallways, and classrooms. Supported by advertising, the posters include a *Jeopardy*-type newsgame and reach about 8 million high school students. The company also distributes bookmarks, carrying logos and brief ads, to more than 85,000 schools.

The latest foray into school-based market is the 1999 launch of *BackStage Pass*, from RJE & Associates. Where *Channel One* focuses on the classroom and *GymBoards* focuses on the locker room, *BackStage Pass* wants to own the cafeterias. The president of the firm is Richard Ellis, a savvy record-industry marketing veteran. So, it's no surprise that at the heart of his vehicle is music. *BackStage Pass* exposes music artists to students in cafeterias through CD giveaways and posters, while the schools gain incentives for students to participate in their meal programs. Partnering with RJE & Associates in the distribution of the program is Snap Systems, a leader in automated food-service software. So, there's something in it for the record companies—that's why several labels are sponsoring the initial launch. And, there's something in it for the schools—that's why they're giving *BackStage Pass* such a valuable entree.

Chapter 4.

Teen Activities and Interests

What teenagers do with their leisure time segments them, profiles them, and offers opportunities to marketers. Much of what teenagers are is what they do. They tend to choose their friends based on shared interests. That's why teens who are into basketball hang out together, as do those who volunteer, work on cars, create music, go to the mall, or even do drugs. Teens look for and gravitate toward others who are like them. Their interests and activities can make for an instant bond.

In fact, we've found that teens are more accurately segmented by behavior than attitudes. Teens live a step or two ahead of themselves because so much of who they are is aspirational, and aspiration is different from behavior. This is why, in TRU's Teen/Types segmentation model, most of the variables we use to segment teens are behavior-based, rather than attitude-based. When presented with several types of activities and asked to choose the one they would most like to do, for example, many teens would choose a type that is different from the one they would select if they instead had to choose the activity that best describes what they actually do. Understanding what teens do and when they do it is key to creating relevant advertising for teenagers and reaching them when they're ready to receive your messages.

Teens still enjoy many of the activities they always have, from watching TV to dancing. They're also surfing the Web, going to religious functions, and cooking. In fact, many teen leisure-time activities are the same as those the rest of the population enjoys.

Often, the activities that the largest number of teens take part in are also the ones teens spend the most time doing. During the week, more teens watch TV than take part in any other leisure-time activity. They also spend more time watching TV (11.2 hours/week) than they spend with any other activity.

Some activities have high participation levels, yet teens spend little time doing them. Seventy-five percent of teens have read a newspaper during the past week, but they spent only 2.5 hours doing so.

Recognizing the difference between teen participation (the percentage of teens doing an activity) and involvement (the time spent doing it) is important if you want to promote your products by depicting an activity in advertising or sponsoring an event. So consider not only the size of the teen audience but also teens' level of involvement.

Today's teens are busier than ever, engaging in a greater variety of activities than teens did in the past. Teens also have more responsibilities than ever before. Still, we so often hear teens exclaim, "Life is boring." And they tell us that the age-old parent–teen dialogue can still be heard in households across the country:

"Where are you going?"

"Out."

"What are you going to do?"

"Nothing."

Teens also complain about being "stressed." What most seems to create this stress? It is their overly busy schedules. Finding time to study and socialize, to fulfill family obligations and take part in extracurricular activities is a stressful balancing act for most teens. Older teen with part-time jobs, boyfriends or girlfriends, find their free time is even more at a premium.

Although teen fashions, music, and lifestyles change, there are constants in teens' leisure activities. In many ways, the teen years are a time of learning about limits, of learning to make decisions, and of learning how to be responsible for one's time. Teen activities can be grouped according to whether the activities are self-directed or externally imposed.

We divide teen leisure-time activities into three groups based on their motivations. Group 1 activities are those teens choose to do and think are fun (e.g., dancing, hanging out, going to movies and concerts). Group 2 activities are those teens choose to do because they are good for them physically, intellectually, or morally (e.g., working out, going to the library, vol-

Leisure-Time Activities of Teens

Watching TV is the number-one teen leisure activity, as it is for adults as well.

(percent of teenagers participating in selected activities during the week prior to the survey, and number of hours teens spent participating in the activity, 1998)

	percent participating	number of hours
Watching TV	98%	11.2
Listening to FM radio	96	10.1
Listening to CDs, tapes, records	95	9.5
Hanging out with friends	88	8.6
Talking on phone (local calls)	87	6.2
Doing chores/running errands	82	4.3
Reading magazines for pleasure	76	2.8
Reading newspapers	75	2.5
Exercising/working out	75	5.1
Playing sports	72	6.3
Cooking/preparing meals	67	2.7
Using a computer at home	64	4.4
Reading books for pleasure	60	3.8
Shopping/hanging out at mall	60	3.1
Watching rented videos	56	4.1
Going to movie theaters	54	2.4
Cruising in car	52	3.7

Source: TRU *Teenage Marketing & Lifestyle Study*

(continued from previous page)

	percent participating	number of hours
Going to parties	52%	3.3
Studying	51	3.3
Going to religious functions	50	2.6
Playing home video games	49	3.1
Cooking/preparing dinner	48	1.9
Playing computer games	48	2.4
Grocery shopping for family	45	1.6
Dating/being with boyfriend/girlfriend	44	4.8
Using the Internet/World Wide Web	44	2.7
Using a computer at school/elsewhere	40	2.1
Talking on phone (long distance)	38	1.5
Going to sports events	38	2.0
Working at a regular paid job	38	5.9
Using an online computer service	37	2.6
Baby-sitting	36	2.6
Playing a musical instrument	34	2.3
Going to a library/museum/gallery	29	1.1
Going dancing	26	1.5
Going to amusement/theme park	25	1.5
Doing volunteer work	25	1.2
Playing online games	21	1.3
Reading magazines for school	19	0.7
Going to concerts	18	0.9
Playing arcade video games	15	0.7

Source: TRU *Teenage Marketing & Lifestyle Study*

unteering). Group 3 activities are those someone else says the teen must do (e.g., running errands, cleaning the house, taking care of a sibling, studying).

In part by design, most of the activities TRU measures come under the heading of "I choose/it's fun." These are leisure-time activities over which teens have significant control. If you incorporate "I choose/it's fun" activities into your advertising and promotional messages, your brand can benefit from the halo effect of a good time.

Teens also pursue activities of their own choosing for reasons of self-improvement or social benefit. Many teens need to feel they make a difference in the world. You can help teens raise their profile as contributors to the common good. By doing so, you send a message to teens that their spending and brand choices are important and have an impact beyond the sale in a way that is uniquely theirs. This is not to say, however, that teens are willing to spend more for a product just because a percentage of the sale is donated to a popular cause. But, if all else is equal, such a tie-in can be the tie-breaker.

The Importance of Socializing

There's probably no activity more important to teens from an emotional, psychological, and even marketing sense than socializing. Socializing includes hanging out with friends, participating in specific activities, dating, partying, even meeting in cyberspace. But teens socialize differently than in the recent past. When we first measured "cruising" in cars 15 years ago, for example, it was predominantly a male activity. Now girls are just as likely to cruise in cars, showing how much more independent and socially proactive girls have become in the last decade.

Dating especially has evolved, both in high school and on college campuses. Today, boys and girls often become friends before pairing off. Formal dating is rarer than it was 10 and 20 years ago, while group dating

High-Participation/ High-Involvement Activities

Watching TV and listening to music are the leisure-time activities that the largest share of teens spend the most time doing.

(activities in which a large percentage of teenagers participated during the week prior to the survey and in which teens spent a lot of time participating, 1998)

	percent participating	number of hours
Watching TV	98%	11.2
Listening to FM radio	96	10.1
Listening to CDs, tapes, records	95	9.5
Hanging out with friends	88	8.6
Playing sports	72	6.3

Source: TRU *Teenage Marketing & Lifestyle Study*

High-Participation/ Low-Involvement Activities

Although many teens read magazines, newspapers, and books, they spend little time doing so.

(activities in which a large percentage of teenagers participated during the week prior to the survey, but with which they spent little time, 1998)

	percent participating	number of hours
Doing chores/running errands	82%	4.3
Reading magazines for pleasure	76	2.8
Reading newspapers	75	2.5
Cooking/preparing meals	67	2.7
Reading books for pleasure	60	3.8

Source: TRU *Teenage Marketing & Lifestyle Study*

is more the norm. In focus groups about this topic, teen girls tell us that they seldom wait around for boys to ask them out on a date, and they might be put off if a boy did ask them out. When we asked a group of 16-year-old girls how they would react if a guy "they only kind of knew" called them up and asked them out, they exclaimed, "That would be just too weird!"

Instead, most couples are finding each other within a group of mixed-gender friends—certainly a positive sociological shift from years ago. But there's no question about it: teens still yearn to have a boyfriend or girlfriend. In fact, 85 percent of teens say that having a boyfriend or girlfriend is "in." Only the means to the end have changed, and teens become friends before they date. We're also seeing a return to the allure of more formal dating—coming particularly from girls, who seem to like the idea of traditionally romantic dating.

Of course, not all teens socialize to the same extent, and the frequency with which they socialize correlates not only to age but also to self-esteem and status within their social hierarchy. When you're accepted by and become part of a group that regularly congregates and communicates, you feel better about yourself.

We asked our national sample of teens the following question: "How many nights a week do you usually. . .stay at home (without friends). . . date/be with boyfriend/girlfriend. . .get together with friends?" The data show that nearly 9 out of 10 teens spend at least one evening by themselves at home during the week and at least one evening with friends. Only about half spend at least one evening a week with a boyfriend or girlfriend.

Girls go out on dates more often than boys. One reason for this is that teen girls often date older boys, and older teens spend more evenings out with friends or with boyfriends/girlfriends than do younger teens. Boys aren't as aspirational when it comes to dating.

Where Teens Spend Their Leisure Time

A few years ago we were conducting focus groups to expose teens to advertising ideas for a top youth-targeting brand. The storyboards depicted teens heading to a movie theater after school. This was an instant "disconnect" to respondents. Several said, "Hey, we don't go to movies after school. That just doesn't make sense." Once teens disconnect from an ad, it's almost impossible to get them back. So, something as seemingly innocuous as an afternoon movie can spell trouble for an otherwise strong message. Execution is key in advertising to teens. Even if strategies are sound and the advertising communicates on strategy, you can still lose teens if the execution doesn't feel or look real.

The after-school movie may be an obvious example of an activity that does not match the occasion. But it led us to develop a measure to determine which teen venues are appropriate for which occasions. Do teens do the same things after school that they do on weekends? Do they go to different places on a date than they would if they were hanging out with friends?

We presented our national teen sample with a list of activities and asked them to identify those in which they participated after school, on weekends, or on a date (or, more simply, with a girlfriend or boyfriend).

As expected, the findings show that teens frequent different places at different times—revealing the challenge of reaching a moving target. Nearly two-thirds spend their free time after school at home, while only about one-third spend their free time at home on weekends, and only 1 in 20 stays home during a date. The top three places teens go after school are home, to a friend's house, or someplace at or near school to take part in sports or other activities. On weekends, teens are most likely to go to a friend's house, a party, or a mall. On dates, teens are most likely to go to a movie, a restaurant, or a boyfriend's or girlfriend's house.

What Teens Do during the Week

While most teens get together with friends at least once a week, fewer than half of even the oldest teens date or spend time with a boyfriend/girlfriend weekly.

(percent of teens participating in activity at least one evening a week and average number of evenings spent participating in activity during a week, by gender and age, 1998)

			gender			
	total		boys		girls	
	%	#	%	#	%	#
Stay at home (without friends)	89%	3–4	87%	3–4	90%	3–4
Get together with friends	88	3–4	86	3–4	89	3–4
Date/be with boyfriend/girlfriend	43	2	40	2	46	3–4

			age			
	12–15		16–17		18–19	
	%	#	%	#	%	#
Stay at home (without friends)	90%	3–4	89%	3–4	84%	3–4
Get together with friends	85	3–4	92	3–4	90	3–4
Date/be with boyfriend/girlfriend	34	1	54	2	49	7

Source: TRU *Teenage Marketing & Lifestyle Study*

Teens frequent the widest variety of places on weekends, as shown by the double-digit percentages for all but one measured place—school. On dates, teens are surprisingly traditional; they go to movies, restaurants, their boyfriend's or girlfriend's house, or a party. Although dating practices have evolved, teens still go to the same places on dates.

One intriguing finding is that except for leisure time after school, teens prefer to spend their free time at someone else's home. On weekends, they get together with a friend, but not at their own home. When they date, they go to their boyfriend's or girlfriend's home, but again not to their own. This is another lifestage truth. Think back to your own teen years and, chances are, you'll remember who had the most popular house. Most teens have at least one friend who has what they often refer to as the party house. Usually, it's a friend whose parents aren't home, or, as teens tell us, whose parents "don't care." Although parents admonish their children when they're young not to behave differently in someone else's home from how they are expected to behave in their own home, when kids become teens they look for friends' homes where they can do just that.

Another interesting pattern in the data is that girls frequent a broader range of venues than boys. With the exception of sporting facilities, video arcades, and parties, significantly more girls than boys spend time at each of the listed venues, regardless of occasion.

In general, younger teens (aged 12 to 15) prefer to spend their free time at places requiring little planning or travel, such as the mall, movies, roller rinks, video arcades, or school (for school-sponsored activities). Older teens, particularly 16- and 17-year-olds, enjoy the widest variety of venues, including restaurants, friends' houses, the city, concerts, parties, and teen/dance clubs. These are the teens for whom a car (their own or a friend's) means newly found independence and empowerment.

Where Teens Prefer to Spend Their Leisure Time

Teens prefer to spend their after-school leisure time at home, and their weekend leisure time at a friend's house.

(percent of teens citing location as one where they prefer to spend their leisure time after school, on weekends, and on a date; respondents could pick up to three places, 1994)

	prefer to spend leisure time		
	after school	weekend	on a date[*]
Home	63%	30%	6%
Friend's house	55	52	6
School/around school	30	7	2
Sporting facility	28	25	4
Boyfriend's/girlfriend's house	26	34	36
School dances	18	20	17
Mall	17	44	11
Downtown/uptown/city	17	32	14
Video arcade	16	23	4
Restaurant	16	32	36
Park	15	28	17
Party	8	48	26
Bowling alley	8	22	9
Movie theater	8	43	55
Church/place of worship	8	36	2
Roller rink	7	24	9
Teen/dance clubs	7	23	15
Beach	7	39	13
Concerts	4	26	18

[*] Those who said they date/get together with their boyfriend or girlfriend at least once a week.
Source: TRU *Teenage Marketing & Lifestyle Study*

Where Teens Prefer to Spend Their Leisure Time, by Gender

A larger share of girls than boys would prefer to spend their leisure time at the mall.

(percent of teens citing location as one where they prefer to spend their leisure time after school, on weekends, and on a date, by gender; for locations preferred significantly more by one gender, 1994)

	boys	girls
AFTER SCHOOL		
Preferred by more girls		
School/around school	25%	35%
Boyfriend's/girlfriend's house	22	30
School dances	16	21
Mall	15	20
Preferred by more boys		
Sporting facility	31	25
Video arcade	19	12
ON WEEKENDS		
Preferred by more girls		
Party	45	52
Mall	40	49
Movie theater	40	46

Source: TRU *Teenage Marketing & Lifestyle Study*

(continued from previous page)

	boys	girls
Beach	36%	42%
Boyfriend's/girlfriend's house	31	38
Restaurant	29	35
Roller rink	21	26
Teen/dance clubs	18	28

Preferred by more boys

Video arcade	28	18

ON A DATE

Preferred by more girls

Movie theater	47	54
Restaurant	25	30
Concert	15	20

Source: TRU *Teenage Marketing & Lifestyle Study*

Favorite and Least-Favorite Weekend Evening Activities

Weekend nights hold a special allure for teens. It's the time when they can do what they want—be with friends, be with the opposite sex, and sometimes push the limits of age restrictions. On weekends, teens have a reprieve—albeit a temporary one—from the rigors of school, work and, often, family. But what do teens do on weekend nights? And what do they want to do? Knowing the answers to these questions gives marketers useful information for creating advertising that excites teens and for developing promotions that motivate them.

Most older teens spend weekend nights with friends. Younger teens are often saddled with family time (some do enjoy it—even on the weekend). Half as many teens say they spend time with a boyfriend or girlfriend on the weekend as say they spend time with family or friends. Just 17 percent go out on dates. One-third of teens go to someone's house (the same friend, no doubt, as discussed above). One-fourth spend time talking on the phone (even if they're restricted to their home, they can escape behind a closed door to talk with similarly restricted friends). More than one-third say they usually watch TV on a weekend night. As many teens rent movies as go to them.

As social as they are, teens want to spend even more time with their friends away from home. Their favorite venue for socializing is a party. In focus groups, when we ask teens, "What's going on this weekend?" a typical response is simply, "Don't know. . .but gonna check to see if there's a party." When asked what they most like to do on a weekend night, teens in our quantitative sample opted for going to a party. Parties are magnets for teens, providing an opportunity to be with friends, meet new ones, and do nothing but have fun. Parties pull together all of teens' favorite social activities in an unstructured and comfortable environment—friends, the opposite sex, music, dancing, food, games, and—for some—drinking and drugs. And, of course, teens' favorite parties are without parental supervi-

What Teens Like to Do on the Weekend

While teens prefer going to a party on weekends, they most often just hang out with friends.

(percent of teens citing activity as something they actually do, and would most like to do, on a weekend, 1996)

	actually do	would most like to do
Hang out with friends	48%	34%
Be with family	43	11
Watch TV	35	9
Go to someone's house	32	20
Go to a movie	25	28
Watch rented movies	25	13
Hang out with boyfriend/girlfriend	24	37
Talk on phone	24	10
Go to/have a party	22	42
Play sports	22	14
Go to a restaurant	21	13
Sleep	21	13
Go on a date	17	37
Work	17	10
Do homework	14	5
Go downtown	13	18
Play home video games	13	9
Read	13	8
Play PC games	12	10
Go skating/rollerblading	11	14
Stay home alone	11	7
Do something illegal	9	11
Go to a dance club	8	22
Go to a video arcade	7	11

Source: TRU *Teenage Marketing & Lifestyle Study*

sion—especially those for older teens. In fact, in our qualitative research we often use the party theme to get teens to think about and describe brand-user imagery. We might say, for example, "If Brand X were to have a party, what would it be like? Who would be there? What kind of music would be played? What would everybody be doing? What else? Would parents be there?" By asking the same series of questions about Brand Y, a distinct teen-relevant brand-user personality begins to emerge.

Teens also want to be active on the dating scene, and as many teens (37 percent) say they would most like to hang out with a boyfriend or girlfriend on a weekend night as say they would most want to go out on a date. Other activities teens would like to do include hanging out with friends, going to a movie, going to a dance club (mentioned by almost twice as many girls as boys), and going to someone's house.

Teens become more independent—both socially and financially—once they reach the age of 16. They earn their driver's license, and many of them find an outside source of income. Significantly more older than younger teens hang out with their boyfriend/girlfriend, go to or have a party, work, and date. Older teens participate in fewer activities than younger teens because they are so driven by a singular pursuit—socializing.

Television, sports, and video games are all more appealing to boys than girls. Significantly more boys play video games and would like to play them during a weekend night—on a home system, a computer, or at a video arcade. Also, more boys play sports and would like to play sports on a weekend night. More boys than girls watch television on weekend nights. Girls yearn more for social contact. More girls than boys talk on the phone, hang out with their boyfriends, and go to restaurants. Girls are also more interested in going to dance clubs. In fact, more girls go dancing than boys (which raises an interesting question—with whom are they dancing?).

Plotting what teens do on weekend nights against what they want to do yields four quadrants (see chart) showing the popularity—and aspirational qualities—of various weekend activities. Evaluating which

"Like to Do"
versus "Actually Do"

The quadrant map shows at a glance what teens do,
and what they want to do.

LIKE TO DO

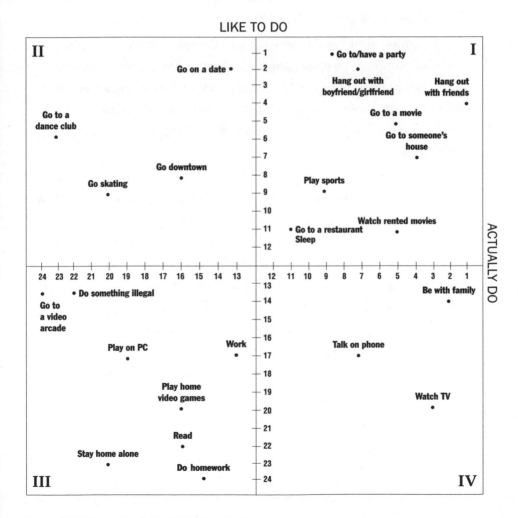

ACTUALLY DO

Source: TRU *Teenage Marketing & Lifestyle Study*

activities fall into which quadrant reveals those that present opportunities for marketers in developing and placing advertising, as well as those that marketers should avoid.

Quadrant I (do and want to): Quadrant I shows those activities which teens usually do and most want to do on a weekend night. Because teens both like and participate in them, these popular activities offer realistic scenarios for teen-targeted advertising. They also suggest venues at which to reach teens with place-based media.

Quadrant II (don't do but want to): We call this the "aspirational" quadrant. Although relatively few teens date, go downtown, skate, or go to dance clubs on weekend nights (perhaps because there are few opportunities to do so), more teens want to do these things. These are the weekend-night activities teens long for and that excite them when depicted in advertising.

Quadrant III (don't do and don't want to): These are the weekend activities that few teens do or want to do. Because these activities are less popular on weekend nights, they might be suitable for use in humorous advertising scenarios, such as showing a teen being freed from spending a weekend night alone doing homework.

Quadrant IV (do but don't want to): Although many teens watch TV, talk on the phone and spend time with their family on weekend nights, they would much rather be doing other, more sociable and exciting things. These activities are teens' "last resorts" when they have nothing better to do on a weekend night (or their plans have fallen apart). They are especially common activities for younger teens, who—as we say—are "parentally challenged."

Sports and Recreational Activities

Sports play a key role in many teens' lives, consuming their time, passion, and thoughts. Some thrive on competition and the thrill of excelling in and mastering new sports. Others are drawn to sports for the social aspect—sports facilitate group get-togethers, and team sports provide a sense of belonging and acceptance. Finally, some teens—mostly girls—appreciate sports for the exercise and resulting physical fitness they provide.

Playing sports is a mainstream teen activity. Most brand managers can feel comfortable in using sports or sports themes to reach most teens because most teens like sports, play sports, and follow sports. When going after a broad teen target, using a sports theme is natural. Teens are segmented by the sports they choose to play. If you're targeting a specific gender, age, or Teen/Type (i.e., Influencer, Conformer, Passive, or Edge—see Chapter 5 for more on these Teen/Types), it's important to understand which sports they favor. It's also important to understand that certain sports hold vicarious appeal to many teens even if relatively few participate in them.

Nearly three-fourths of teens participate in sports during an average week, and 62 percent participate in an organized league outside of school. Thirty-eight percent attend a sporting event during the week. Team sports, such as basketball, football, and baseball/softball, are top among boys both as sports in which they participate and as their favorites. Less-competitive sports, such as swimming, exercise/aerobics, and jogging/running, are top in participation among girls.

To repeat, it's not just a certain kind of individual who's into sports today—it's almost everyone. We see it every time we hold a focus group. Typically, about half the boys are wearing baseball caps and about equally as many boys as girls are wearing some type of athletic apparel—from college or professional team jerseys to sweats and jackets. And, of course, most teens wear athletic shoes (although lately more are wearing boots). We're seeing a unisex style in how teens dress, and sports apparel contributes greatly to this trend. Even many of the top youth apparel brands are adding a sport line, including Nolo, The Gap, and Tommy Hilfiger.

Teen Sports Affinity Index: Boys

Snowboarding is the sport with the highest affinity among teen boys.

(the Teen Sports Affinity Index is calculated by multiplying the percentage of boys who participate in a sport by the proportion of those who rank the sport as one of their three favorites, 1998)

Snowboarding	66	Swimming	35
Martial arts	61	Weight training	34
Surfing/windsurfing	58	Billiards/pool	34
Snowmobiling	58	Water skiing	32
Basketball	57	Track and field	29
Baseball	52	Camping/hiking	29
Hunting	48	Ice hockey	28
Football	46	Tennis	28
Wrestling	44	In-line skating	27
Motorcycling	44	Volleyball	26
Mountain biking	43	Bowling	26
Riding personal watercraft (e.g., Jet Ski)	43	Street hockey	25
		Bicycling	24
Skateboarding	42	Boxing	23
Soccer	40	Roller skating	22
Dirt biking	38	Sailing	22
Fishing	38	Mountain climbing/rappelling	20
Golf	37	Racquetball	20
Downhill skiing	35	Beach volleyball	17

Source: TRU *Teenage Marketing & Lifestyle Study*

Teen Sports Affinity Index: Girls

Swimming is the sport with the highest affinity among teen girls.

(the Teen Sports Affinity Index is calculated by multiplying the percentage of girls who participate in a sport by the proportion of those who rank the sport as one of their three favorites, 1998)

Swimming	64	Martial arts	36
Riding personal watercraft (e.g., Jet Ski)	56	Water skiing	35
		Mountain climbing	35
Horseback riding	54	Exercise/aerobics	33
Softball	54	Sailing/boating	31
White water rafting	54	Surfing/windsurfing	29
Basketball	51	Billiards/pool	28
Volleyball	50	Sailboarding	28*
Snowboarding	50	Bowling	27
Gymnastics	48	Weight training	27
Soccer	48	Jogging/running	27
Skateboarding	46	Cross-country skiing	26
Camping/hiking	42	Ice skating	25
In-line skating	41	Bicycling	24
Roller skating	41	Mountain biking	24
Beach volleyball	41	Wrestling	19
Tennis	40	Fishing	19
Downhill skiing	39	Snowmobiling	19
Track and Field	37	Handball	19

Source: TRU *Teenage Marketing & Lifestyle Study*

When we ask participants in the warm-ups before focus-group discussions to say what they would be doing if they weren't at the focus group, they often respond with "playing sports."

TRU measures teen participation in 51 sports, from swimming to snowboarding, in our syndicated study. Our clients use this information to decide which sports to tie into when advertising or promoting to teenagers. We ask teens to rank sports by their level of participation outside of school (in other words, sports of their choice rather than school-imposed sports) in the past year, and whether a sport is one of their three favorites. Although boys and girls are both highly involved in sports, the sports they participate in and favor differ.

Teens' favorite sports are not necessarily the ones in which they are most likely to participate. Teens face financial, geographic, and other obstacles to their participation in certain sports. Golfing and skiing are expensive, for example. Snowboarding requires mountains, while surfing requires an ocean. Additionally, teens may participate in a sport for reasons of health or because their friends pressure them into it, but they may not enjoy it.

Basketball is by far the most popular sport with boys. It's the sport with the highest participation rate and the one most often mentioned as a favorite. Basketball is the second-most popular sport among girls after swimming. Not surprisingly, the NBA has been the most successful of the major professional leagues at marketing its players and products, yielding the majority of teens' favorite professional athletes. (It will be interesting to see if the 1998–99 NBA lockout will have any lingering effects on teens' attitudes toward the league.)

Unlike basketball, which appeals to both boys and girls, many sports are preferred significantly more by one gender. Steer clear of these sports if you want to advertise or promote to a dual-gender audience.

Single-Gender Sports ·

Teen boys like football and fishing much more than teen girls do, while girls like swimming and exercising much more than teen boys do.

(percent of teens citing sport as one of three favorites by gender, for sports favored significantly more by one gender, 1998)

	boys	girls
Preferred by boys		
Basketball	33%	24%
Football	22	3
Fishing	12	5
Weight training	10	5
Golf	9	2
Hunting	7	1
Preferred by girls		
Swimming	18	43
Exercise/aerobics	4	18
Volleyball	5	18
Roller skating	4	14
In-line skating	6	13
Gymnastics	1	8
Horseback riding	1	7

Source: TRU *Teenage Marketing & Lifestyle Study*

The following responses from focus group participants reveal the differences in how boys and girls approach sports:

"More guys play sports for fun than girls. They're more spontaneous about playing. We'll play, like, in the summer, if we're all at someone's house and they happen to have a basketball net." —16-year-old girl

"Everybody plays sports now, so there really aren't jocks anymore. Except for the three-sport kind of guy." —17-year-old boy

"For girls, sports means more aerobics and exercise. We'll all go to a health club and work out." —16-year-old girl

"Sports are plain cool. Everybody likes them and wants to be at them." —14-year-old male

When deciding which sport to tie into promotionally or to use thematically or executionally in advertising, consider both behavior (participation) and attitude (favoring). To gain a better understanding of teen attitudes toward sports, TRU developed the Sports Affinity Index. This index reveals the sports that enjoy an extraordinary level of enthusiasm among participants. The Teen Sports Affinity Index is based on the percentage of teens participating in a sport who also name the sport as one of their three favorites. A perfect score would be 100, meaning that all participants name the sport as one of their favorites.

By using the percentage of participation in the sport as the base for the calculation, the index picks up emerging sports: those with low levels of participation but which are hugely popular among participants. By tying into these popular alternative sports, you can separate your company from the many others that portray traditional mass-participation sports in their teen marketing. Teens can be attracted vicariously to certain sports in which they may not have the opportunity to participate (again, because of the expense, geography, etc.). Sports with a high Affinity Index score transcend participation numbers. They excite teens, grab their attention, and offer them something special.

Teen Boys: Sports Participation and Favorite Sports

Basketball is not only the sport in which the largest share of teen boys have participated, it is also their favorite.

(rank order of sports in which teen boys participated in the past year and sports that are one of teen boys' three favorites, 1998)

Participated in past 12 months	One of three favorites
1. Basketball	1. Basketball
2. Swimming	2. Baseball
3. Football	3. Football
4. Bicycling	4. Swimming
5. Baseball	5. Billiards/pool
6. Billiards/pool	6. Fishing

Source: TRU *Teenage Marketing & Lifestyle Study*

Teen Girls: Sports Participation and Favorite Sports

Swimming is the sport in which the largest number of teen girls have participated in the past year, and it is their favorite sport.

(rank order of sports in which teen girls participated in the past year and sports that are one of teen girls' three favorites, 1998)

Participated in past 12 months	One of three favorites
1. Swimming	1. Swimming
2. Exercise/aerobics	2. Basketball
3. Running/jogging	3. Softball
4. Basketball	4. Exercise/aerobics
5. Bicycling	5. Volleyball
6. Bowling	6. Running/jogging

Source: TRU *Teenage Marketing & Lifestyle Study*

The rank order of the index differs from the previous sport list. Three of girls' top sports are water sports. In contrast, boys' top water sport, water skiing, comes in at number 13. With the exception of weight training among boys, exercise-oriented sports have low indices, indicating that although many teens participate in them, few consider them favorites. Sports such as skiing, mountain biking, dirt biking, white-water rafting, and horseback riding have low participation levels, but the teens who participate in them do so enthusiastically. Consequently, these adrenaline-producing, heart-thumping sports emerge with high scores on the Affinity Index. They offer you an opportunity to associate your brand with a sport that's new and exciting. If you watch ESPN2 and MTV Sports, you'll see a variety of sport hybrids—what teens and marketers alike refer to as "extreme" or "radical" sports—to which you can link your brand. Mountain Dew, for one, has effectively connected its brand image to rugged, high-energy outdoor sports.

Despite the appeal of extreme sports, traditional sports still hold a powerful draw. Baseball/softball and basketball, two of the most heavily played sports, have high indices among both girls and boys. Based on the Teen Sports Affinity Index, basketball, baseball/softball, and downhill skiing are the sports with the strongest appeal for boys and girls combined. For boys only, you should consider football and a few of the individual sports like dirt biking and martial arts. For girls only, swimming, horseback riding, gymnastics, and volleyball are the best candidates.

Chapter 5.

Teen Trends and Social Hierarchy

Probably no other segment of the population is as involved in or motivated by lifestyle trends as teenagers. From the latest in language and music to fashion and "what to do," teens are searching for and are influenced by what's new and now.

When adults—and marketers specifically—think about teens, they often focus on teenagers' fascination with fads and trends. Teen trends are also a hot media topic. In fact, one of the most common questions reporters ask us at TRU is, "What's the latest teen trend?" Staying attuned to teen trends is a challenge for marketers. Teen trends are one of the most interesting aspects of teen lives. They are also highly important to teen marketers who want to associate their brand with what's current and relevant. Being an integral part of a trend is an enviable and rare situation; tying into a trend is smart and doable.

We help marketers identify what's current in teen lifestyles by probing what's in and what's out in our semiannual syndicated study. Even twice a year is not enough to keep up with teens' "in" and "out" lists, because teen fads can change overnight. That's why we supplement our semiannual trend analysis with a variety of Teen Topic sheets, distributed more frequently. It's key for marketers to understand that teens never stop looking and grasping for what's new. Therefore, you need a constant, timely, and reliable source of teen trend information.

Puzzled about where to begin? Certainly, syndicated studies that you can subscribe to, such as TRU's, provide ongoing information on trends. Digesting teen media information and conducting your own primary research are two other key methods for keeping attuned. We also recommend that you look where teens themselves look. This way, your trend-immersion process runs concurrently with that of teens, rather than a step or two behind. To pinpoint where teens learn about the latest and greatest, we asked teen respondents in our national quantitative study to name the one or two sources they most rely on for the latest trends.

Where Teens Find Out about Trends

Teens rate friends as the most important source for new trends.

(percent of teens citing source, 1994)

Friends	47%
Magazine	32
TV shows	29
Myself	21
Music videos	19
Advertising	14
Coolest people in school	13
DJ (radio)	9
Older brothers/sisters	8
Movies	8
Celebrities	6
Weirdest people in school	4
VJ (video)	4
Younger brothers/sisters	3

Source: TRU *Teenage Marketing & Lifestyle Study*

Teens struggle with and are highly influenced by peer pressure. They are consumed by friends—what friends think, what friends do, what friends say, wear, and buy. So, it should come as no surprise, then, that teens rate friends (47 percent) as their most important source of new trends. Another 13 percent say they learn about trends from the coolest people at school, while 8 percent learn about trends from older kids in the neighborhood and school.

The message is clear: some of the best teen research costs nothing. Observe! Go where teens go. Watch them, listen to them, see what they do and how they do it. We furnish our clients with a list of exactly that—what they should do to actively immerse themselves in teen culture. (Incidentally, we title this continually updated paper, "Wise Up To Teens: A Primer on Teen Trends.")

Once you realize just how influential friends are, the logical next question is, where do their friends learn about trends? The answer is, they learn about trends from a combination of sources, most of them entertainment or media. In fact, the second-most important trend source is magazines. Magazines rate highly as a trend source because of the devotion of girls: more than twice as many girls as boys name magazines as one of the two best places for finding out about trends. It's not surprising that magazines rate so highly on this measure with girls. Not only do teen girls devour magazines that are written especially for them, but much of the editorial content in these magazines is devoted to fashion. So, when asked to think about trends, respondents naturally associate trends with fashions, and girls think of magazines—from teen magazines like *Seventeen, YM,* and *Teen,* to more adult-oriented fashion magazines, such as *Vogue* and *Cosmopolitan.* Teen boys, on the other hand, don't have any regularly published magazines directed exclusively at them. They are also less fashion-conscious than girls and spend less time reading magazines. In turn, they rate magazines significantly lower than do girls as a trend source.

Teen Trends:
Safe for Marketing Use

Advertisers won't turn off teens by depicting these products, styles, or activities in advertising.

(trends that are consistently in among all teens, 1996–98)

Alternative music

Baggy clothes

Baseball caps

Boxer shorts

Caring about the environment

Cell phones

College clothing

College sports (football, basketball)

Coloring your hair

Computers

Dating

Designer jeans

Eating healthy

Electronic beepers

Fast cars

Going to the beach

Going to the movies

Having a girlfriend/boyfriend

High school sports

Homecomings

In-line skating

Internet

Long hair on girls

Music videos

Online computer services

Partying

Playing sports

Pro sports (football, basketball)

Pro-sports clothing

Proms

R&B music

Rap music

Shopping

Short hair on girls
(especially among girls!)

Short hair on guys

Straight hair

Taking photos

The word "cool"

The word "sucks"

Working out

Source: TRU *Teenage Marketing & Lifestyle Study*

TV is the third-most frequently named source of trend information for both genders. If you're a TV fan, you've noticed the proliferation of new TV programs with a noticeable teen slant, from "Dawson's Creek" and "Party of Five" to "Buffy the Vampire Slayer," "Sabrina the Teenage Witch" and, of course, almost anything on MTV. Adding to TV's importance in fueling trends is the fact that television is such a big part of everyday life. The frequency of television viewing by itself makes TV an influential source of trend information.

Speaking of MTV, 19 percent of all teens and 24 percent of African-American teens name music videos (which TRU measures separately from TV) as one of the two most influential sources for finding out about new trends. To African Americans, music videos rank second only to friends as a trend source. The music genres of African-American origin—rap, R&B, hip hop, and dance—dominate airplay on many of teens' favorite radio and music-video stations. Teens, both black and white, look to music videos not only for the latest in music but also for the latest in fashion and language. Many of today's (and yesterday's) teen fashions originated with rappers.

A study of the hip-hop generation by a Philadelphia-based social sciences group reported that urban minority teens respect rappers more than any other type of celebrity, including athletes. These teens believe rappers are more honest than other celebrities and that rappers portray teens' lives more accurately and relevantly than do athletes with multimillion dollar contracts. Given these perceptions, perhaps it's not surprising that significantly more African-American than white teens say they look to music videos for lifestyle cues.

Twenty-one percent of teens on this measure (and 64 percent on a similar measure that focuses exclusively on fashion) say they are the trendsetters (or, at least, they don't follow trends). We have found that fewer than 10 percent of teens are true trendsetters, however. This is the group

Teen Fads:
Unsafe for Marketing Use

**While fads can be used successfully in advertising,
they may turn off many teens.**

(items that have been consistently out among all teens, 1996–98)

Being a vegetarian	Liquor
Being patriotic	Long hair on guys
Bell-bottoms	Lots of jewelry
Caring about politics	Lots of makeup
Cigarettes	Pierced noses
Classic Rock	Snowboarding clothes
Comic books	Techno music
Dieting	The military
Drugs	The phrase "Tha Bomb"
Funky hair	The word phat
Going to coffee houses	Tight clothes
Heavy metal	Top-40 music
High-top athletic shoes	Vinyl records/albums

Source: TRU *Teenage Marketing & Lifestyle Study*

we've dubbed Influencers. The implication of this finding to marketers is to carefully craft messages so as to avoid communicating to teens a straightforward trend-following message. No teen really wants to think of himself or herself as blindly following the latest fad. Rather, they respond positively to being portrayed as individuals with a diversity of styles and preferences.

Do teens take cues from advertising, or do advertisers take cues from teens? This is a question marketers frequently ask. In fact, it works both ways. We know advertisers take cues from teens or there would be no need for teen research. Our clients are getting more sophisticated than ever in using research—they're using it more often and more creatively. Just as important, teens take cues from advertising. Fourteen percent name advertising as a prime source of trends. Because teens typically deny the influence of advertising, this figure is undoubtedly understated. Nevertheless, teens admit that advertising is a more important trend source than DJs, VJs, movies, celebrities, and the coolest or weirdest people at school.

Again, if you want to know what's in with teens—or, even more of a challenge, what's going to be in with teens *next*—pay attention to the things teens do. Read what they read, watch what they watch, and go where they go. Nothing is more important than keeping your eyes and ears open!

What's In, What's Out

May adults view teens as extremely fickle, quickly adopting the latest fad or trend only to discard it just as fast. This perception is true to a point, but to be successful, you must separate soon-to-die fads from die-hard trends.

TRU's syndicated study asks teens what's "in" and what's "out." The results paint a timely, rich picture of teens today. The list includes a lot of "out" items, and every now and then a client challenges us by asking, "If you really knew what's 'in,' why are so many things you measure 'out'?" There are several answers to that question.

Unstable Items: Use at Your Own Risk

Some of the items on this list may be safe to use if you're targeting a single gender or narrow age targets.

(items that were in as of the fall 1998 study but have been unstable over the years, items that have been measured for too short a period of time to predict their stability, and items that are just too close to call)

Backpacks

Bath/body shops

Birthday parties

Candles

Cargo pants

Cargo shorts

Chunky heeled shoes

Class rings

Corduroys

Cussing

Daily organizers/planners

"Dawson's Creek"

Hemp necklaces

Home video games

"Jerry Springer"

Khaki shorts

NBA clothes

NFL clothes

"Party of Five"

Platform shoes

Reading the paper

Sharing costs on dates

Skateboarding

Soccer

"South Park"

Tattoos

Temporary tattoos

Volkswagen Beetle

Watching the news

Wide-legged jeans

Source: TRU *Teenage Marketing & Lifestyle Study*

First, we measure some items that are "out" because many advertisers believe they are "in," such as used jeans, preppy fashions, heavy metal, classic rock, and so on. Second, we try diligently to identify emerging trends. We want to identify opportunities that our clients can tie into *before* they become accepted by the mainstream. Finally, we're not perfect! Although we regularly conduct formal focus groups to help us compile the list to be tested and immerse ourselves in teen culture through observational research and digesting a huge realm of teen and young-adult media, qualitative research cannot substitute for quantitative. While we may hear from any number of teens in a few markets that something is "in," our national sample may disagree.

To compile our list of items to be tested, we use three main sources: 1) TRU's most recent syndicated study, to learn what's rising and should be included on the list or what's falling and should be dropped; 2) teens and young adults (remember, teens are aspirational) themselves, both in focus groups designed for this purpose and through regular and planned observation (in other words, we go where teens go—from malls to clubs to social events where we observe and talk with teens); 3) media sources, from MTV, The Box, and "Dawson's Creek" to a long list of magazines and catalogs.

When I first ordered a subscription to *Seventeen* years ago back in 1982, I was one of only two TRU employees. Predictably, I received a form letter from the editor, congratulating me on becoming "an American girl in the know." Now, each of our staff members is assigned a variety of magazines to browse through, clip, and route each month. (I still receive *Seventeen*.) Last year, we began formalizing the procedure by writing blurbs on each item, adding TRU's perspective and e-mailing it to TRU subscribers. Our clients' response to this service, which we call *teen.bits*, has been overwhelming, reflecting corporate America's recognition of just how crucial it is to stay closely attuned to the teen market.

If you've ever guessed wrong in advertising to teens, you know that teens can be unforgiving. If they feel misrepresented or patronized, they often reject the advertised service or product. Knowing what's "in" and what's "out" can help you avoid some of the pitfalls in advertising and marketing to teens. Successfully differentiating between fads and trends can save you heartache and money. Trends are safe—and recommended—in teen marketing. Fads are inherently unstable and dangerous. Designer jeans are a trend, but Girbaud was a fad. Rap is a trend, but Vanilla Ice was a fad.

The data on what teens view as "in" and "out" provide insights into executional elements in advertising and promotion, revealing hot product categories. To help marketers distinguish between fads and trends, we've classified more than 100 items TRU has been tracking over the past few years into three categories: "safe for marketing use," "unsafe for marketing use," and "use at your own risk." Keep in mind that some of the items appearing on the "unsafe" list may be safe and highly appropriate if you're targeting a single gender or a narrow age group. Although we classify home video games as "unstable" among the total teen population, for example, they are highly stable among boys. Similarly, although going to coffee houses is "out" among total teens, it's "in" among older girls. And although miniskirts are "out" among girls, they're "in" among boys. (It's hard to believe we spent time and money figuring that one out, isn't it?) And, as stated earlier, some trends that are classified as "out" are, in fact, emerging; they're "in" among Influencers and will soon be adopted by the mainstream majority.

Teenagers' Social and Trend Hierarchy

Everyone knows there's a social pecking order among teens, particularly in high school. Teens cluster in groups that carry certain labels, such as jocks, nerds, stoners, ropers, granolas, preppies, geeks, headbangers, skaters, gangbangers, and wanna-be's of all kinds. Each market, even each school, has its own names for teen groups or cliques. While the names might be different, the hierarchy is the same both across town and across the country.

Status and image drive teen hierarchy. The teens at the top are considered the "coolest"—the ones other teens emulate or try to emulate. Below the top teens are the majority that form the mainstream, less-secure teens who strive to fit in by adopting the fashions and behaviors they think their peers will find "cool."

Then there are the teens who want to fit in but can't and accept this fact. Finally, there are teens who don't care about the teen social hierarchy, marching to the beat of a different drummer. These are the teens who, in many cases, start the trends.

This hierarchy not only defines the lives of teenagers, it also can be applied to marketing objectives. Sixteen years ago, TRU became the first company to segment teenagers by statistically grouping them into lifestyle or psychographic segments. (This analysis was initiated by the late motivation researcher and TRU co-founder Dr. Burleigh Gardner.) Two years ago, we concluded that our system was no longer as useful as it had been because the segments had begun to vary significantly by age and were not ringing as true to us as in the past. Because teens are already so highly segmented by age, a teen lifestyle segmentation system that contains an age bias would be virtually useless. Also, as soon as the system doesn't feel "real" to us, based on our talking to teens every day, we would tend to disregard it. So we revamped our Teen/Types system.

To create the new model, we first identified the variables that most segment teens by lifestyle and attitudes. These variables include basic values, self-perceptions, the meaning of "cool," revealing "in" and "out" items, leisure-time priorities, taste in music (teens who are into alternative music are different from teens who are into rap), shoes, and jeans brands of choice (again, a teen who wears Wrangler jeans is different from one who wears

Polo jeans). We then statistically segmented teens using a hierarchical cluster analysis. The concept of the system remains the same: to successfully match marketing goals with teens' natural hierarchy. We wanted to statistically determine how teens are grouped on a trend-adoption curve. We wanted to update the system, as new trends in activities, sports, fashions, music, media, and products emerge. We particularly wanted the model to reflect how teens are changing in the real world. Unlike other qualitative or intuitive segmentation models of teenagers that we've come across, Teen/Types is qualitatively based but is determined by a statistical analysis of key quantitative variables. Importantly, the resulting segments are neither arbitrary nor self-determined. Instead, they are based on statistically identified commonalties in lifestyle and attitude among segments of teens.

The new system has again resulted in four segments, with a hierarchy similar to TRU's past segmentation system. What has changed is that there are now two cool groups rather than one. Each of these cool groups is distinctive, reflecting that today there is more than one way to be cool. While pigeonholing people into one of four groups is less than perfect, this segmentation system has proven to be a highly accurate and useful marketing tool for our clients.

There is a definite hierarchy in the teen social world, and it is reflected in Teen/Types. New products, fashions, and activities often start with The Edge teens—the new segment we've identified—and sometimes with The Influencers, whose visibility and prominence broadcasts these trends to others. They are then adopted by The Conformers, and finally by The Passives. A few examples of trends that started with Edge teens and have become mainstream include alternative music, hair coloring, tattoos, funky nail-polish colors, rave parties, and body piercing. Airwalk and JNCO are two brands which began with Edge teens and have now—quite profitably—gone mainstream. Noted examples of trends that originated with Influencers include rap music, baggy jeans, and pro-sports clothes. Two Influencer

TRU's Four Teen/Types

TRU has uncovered four major teenage typologies:
The Conformers, The Passives, The Edge, and The Influencers.

(teen types as a percent of teens and average age; 1998)

	percent	average age
The Conformers	49%	15.4
The Passives	21	15.6
The Edge	17	15.8
The Influencers	13	15.2

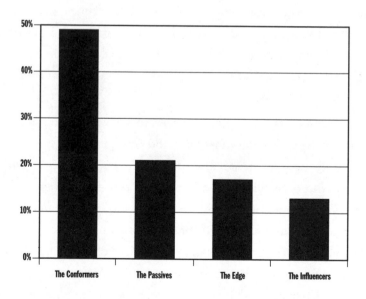

Source: TRU *Teenage Marketing & Lifestyle Study*

brands, which have since been adopted by the majority, are Tommy Hilfiger and Polo.

While the four Teen/Types vary in size, the average age of each group is about 15. The variables that most strongly discriminate the Teen/Types are values, attitudes, lifestyle preferences, and activities, rather than age. This segmentation system reveals the attitudinal and lifestyle differences that set teens apart from one another, even within the same age group.

The Edge

Teens of this type are often at the cutting edge of teenage lifestyle and fashion. What's ironic, though, is that they like to think of themselves as outside of the typical teenage social spectrum. These are the rebellious, independent, alternative, cool teens with whom many trends begin. But these are also the teens who would most object to being labeled as trendsetters. These teens like to think of themselves as being apart from the social mainstream, but in fact they're often ahead of it. Contradictions, such as these, define these teens. For example, they're anti-style and anti-fashion, yet they also have their own brands, which are ever-changing and which personify their anti-fashion attitude.

These are social teens, though some adults might view them as antisocial. They want out of the house as often as possible, to be with their friends. They're the least traditional, the least family-oriented of the four types. They're experimental and adventurous. They like to push the edge—at school, at home, and in what they do for fun. They're the most into extreme sports and the least into traditional sports. These are the teens who break the rules. For social marketers, these are the teens we would most characterize as being at risk.

Edge teens aren't the best students, although they are bright. Consequently, they're not optimistic about their future success, but they're not bothered by that prospect as they live for the moment. They want to have fun. . .now. It's not surprising, then, that they're not involved in the community, nor particularly concerned with any social issues.

These teens are heavily into music—but not mainstream music. They're by far the biggest fans of ska and punk, which are the truly upcoming alternative genres. They also favor alternative and metal, but are not fans of rap, hip hop, and R&B. Their musical preferences reflect that this is essentially a Caucasian segment; still, they are at the cutting edge of white music.

They like to think of themselves as different, rejecting the stereotypical portrayal of teens. They are not friends with those who would be characterized as jocks or preps, yet they accept differences.

Edge teens stand out from their peers in what they can get away with from parents. More Edge teens than others say they either successfully sneak—or their parents let slide—riskier behaviors and more extreme fashions and styles. This point is important, because those teens who are often the first to try something new need this kind of parental license. The Edge seems to have the requisite freedom more so than the other segments. In fact, when asked to describe peer trendsetters in qualitative research, teens will exclaim, "They're those kids whose parents don't care!"

The Influencers

This most popular social group is also the smallest, comprising just 13 percent of the teen population. Despite its size, this Teen/Type is the most influential among its peers. It is a highly select group, to which membership is greatly sought after and valued. These are the teens most other teens "wanna be." For marketers, these are the popular teens—those you want to reach first because their actions are often adopted by the majority.

Because we have already identified a second influential group, it's important to understand how Influencers differ from Edge teens. Influencers are more mainstream cool and popular. They also care greatly about being popular, and they revel in their status. These are good-looking teens who care about how they look and what they wear. They are fairly easy to identify on personal appearance alone. We often ask a subsample of our respondents to participate in a photo project and send them disposable cameras with which to take photos of various aspects of their lives. We make sure they have someone else take several shots of them so we can see what these teens look like. When the photos come back to us, someone labels the back with respondent code and Teen/Type. The rest of us play a guessing game, trying to identify Teen/Type. Influencers are simply the best-looking teens. It never fails to impress us how far good looks go at this age.

Though Edge teens believe others think they're cool, they are not as invested as Influencers in achieving or maintaining this status. Edge teens are more independent and don't consider themselves normal. Similarly, while Influencers admit the importance of fashion and brands in their lives, Edge teens profess to be anti-fashion.

Ethnicity drives some of the differences between these two Teen/Types—especially when it comes to music and fashion. Influencers are a racially diverse group, disproportionately African American (36 percent) and Latino (18 percent). Still, 43 percent of Influencers are white. In sharp contrast, the Edge segment is disproportionately white (85 percent). Conformers look to either Influencers or Edge teens for cues, although more strive to adopt the mainstream cool of Influencers. Interestingly, some Influencers (usually white Influencers) take fashion and lifestyle cues from Edge teens. But it's not until the Influencers are seen sporting a new trend that most Conformers (and eventually Passives) will follow.

The two key traits that set Influencers apart are (1) their outgoing nature and energetic social lifestyle, and (2) the confidence they hold in themselves and in their status among peers. In fact, these teens derive much of their confidence from the social status they already hold. They know they've arrived: they admit "things are going extremely well" for them and that most people who know them think they're "cool." Additionally, Influencers simply enjoy being teen.

Although Influencers are self-confident, they still feel a need for affirmation, a need to constantly stand out among peers. They are particularly conscientious about maintaining their appearance and are concerned about wearing the latest and greatest. Influencers are active, relatively free-spending consumers. It is part of their psychological makeup to own and be seen wearing what's current and cool. Not surprisingly, then, Influencers shop a wider variety of stores than other teens.

Along with Edge teens, this is the group which most strongly states, "I'm often the first one to try something new." Influencers have a more direct impact on the trends adopted by Conformers than Edge teens, and it is this quality that most attracts marketers to Influencers.

The Conformers

Conformers represent the massive mainstream of teen life. They comprise the largest Teen/Type—nearly 49 percent of the teen population. They might best be characterized as typical teenagers and—as their name indicates—as conforming to the latest teen behaviors, styles, and trends.

Conformers lack the confidence and social status of Influencers. It is probably their insecurity that contributes to their compliance with already-developed fads and their reliance on external trappings. What stands out most about this group is that nothing stands out! They tend to be average participants in most activities. They tend not to take extreme views or have deep-seated concerns; they are not the ones most likely to buy particular products. Yet—and this in itself is noteworthy—they are effective in emulating Influencers, although some Conformers—depending upon their school's social makeup and (to some degree) their ethnicity—opt to emulate Edge teens rather than Influencers. But whichever of the top-two trend groups they emulate, what's key is that Conformers look to other peers for adoptable fashions, styles, attitudes, and behaviors.

Conformers seem to have low self-esteem: fewer Conformers than Influencers or Edge teens think they're "cool." Therefore, they aggressively seek out lifestyle cues already adopted by others to help them feel more confident in how they see themselves and in how they wish to be perceived by peers.

Conformers socialize, but to a lesser degree than Influencers. For instance, they are not as actively involved in social or athletic events as Influencers, yet they participate in almost all the same things—parties, sports, shopping.

Conformers tend not to try new things first. They are the followers of trends, not the leaders. Conformers essentially are "shadows" of the Influencers.

What is most important about Conformers for marketers is that they actively emulate the top teen social groups, have the financial means to do so, and represent the largest share of the teen population. This is the group from which marketers profit. Advertising and promotions that show what the "cool" teens are wearing, doing, and owning can be especially effective with Conformers, giving them cues about what to strive for and to adopt. Additionally, marketing communications that offer solutions for typical teen problems, and thus promise to promote self-confidence, would probably be especially compelling to Conformers.

The Passives

Like Conformers, Passives yearn to be more popular and more like other teens. They differ in that they are passive in their attempts to emulate those teens. They are the last of all groups to pick up on fashion trends; they spend less time listening to music; and they tend to be the least active in general. Passives exist on the outskirts of the mainstream of teen life, lacking the confidence and other personal attributes needed to elevate their status.

This Teen/Type is disproportionately male. In one way, this perhaps explains the general characteristic of not being stylistically "in," as males are generally less fashion-involved than females.

Passives lag behind other Teen/Types in social activities, including going dancing, going to the movies, going to sports events, going to parties, talking on the phone, and going to the mall. Passives do have friends, however—usually other Passives with whom they get together a couple nights a week. But even when they do get together as a group, they are less active than others.

Although Passives would not choose their particular rung on the teenage social ladder, they appear to accept it. More than half the Passives agree "things are really going well" for them. They are content to maintain their status quo. While they inwardly may yearn to be like their cool peers, relatively few consider themselves cool. They are not motivated enough (or unable) to be proactive in improving their situation. While acknowledging that they're not the "in" group, more than half the Passives believe they're part of a relatively normal teen group—that most of their friends are pretty much like them. This perhaps contributes to their passive nature, since they feel securely surrounded by others like themselves.

Not surprisingly, Passives don't like hip hop, rave, punk, or ska. They're not socially active enough to be dance fans or experimental enough to favor emerging music.

Although Passives spend less money than other teens, they are still a worthwhile target, representing 21 percent of the teen population. They are at the second level of adoption, behind the plurality of Conformers. Because they are adopters, they should respond favorably to the same type of messages that appeal to Conformers. Furthermore, advertising and new products that offer social solutions and optimism for their life stage will be especially effective with Passives.

What Teens Think about Labels and Groups

Most teens don't like being labeled, but they admit it is part of teen life.

(percent of teens who agree with selected statements, 1996)

Once you're labeled as part of a group, it's hard to lose the label.   64%

Being labeled in a group that you don't want to be in can cause a lot of stress.   61

These groups just happen, they're a part of school.   60

These groups are stupid.   58

Not being in a group that you want to be in can cause a lot of stress.   45

These groups make being at school hard.   38

These groups are important.   13

People in my school aren't labeled.   13

Source: TRU *Teenage Marketing & Lifestyle Study*

What Teens Themselves Say about Cliques

What makes our Teen/Types segmentation system so powerful a tool for marketers is that it mirrors teenage America. It is rooted in teens' own reality. In fact, we have formally presented Teen/Types to high school students, and they remarked about how real it is. In the next sentence, however, they'll tell us "how stupid labeling each other is." So, we decided to quantify what teens think about this type of segmentation—about cliques and labels. We found that although teens nationally disdain labeling, they admit it's part of their world and can cause a lot of stress.

To teens, the most stressful aspect of labeling is being classified as a member of an undesirable group. Yearning to be considered a member of a desirable group, but not making it, is also stressful. But teens accept that these groups are part of school life, that they just happen and can't be avoided—although more than one-third of teens say these groups make going to school more difficult. Only 13 percent of teens say these groups don't exist.

The findings underscore the fact that teens exist in a harsh world at school, populated by a variety of socially distinct groups—some of which are thought of highly and others not. Although most teens agree these classifications are "stupid," they accept them as a part of their everyday reality and deal with the consequences of being included or excluded. It's important for marketers to recognize that many products (e.g., cars, music, clothes, shoes, and other fashion items) play a role in these groups. Products and brands can be a badge of acceptance, a vehicle for admittance, or even part of a uniform for group members. In turn, products are associated—either positively or negatively—with the teen groups who use them.

These comments from four high school students bring this reality a little closer:

"People can make or break your reputation just because they don't like you."

"If people think you're in a certain group, they tend to treat you a certain way."

"Everyone is going to get labeled—it just happens that way."

"Guys don't really pay attention to these things. Guys don't really care."

Chapter 6.

Teens and Music

Music is probably the most influential and pervasive medium in teenage lives. It can reflect a teen's own personal experience, and it unites teens into a collective whole. But music not only reflects the teen experience, it also defines it. And it always has. To no other age group is music as culturally significant as to teens.

Because of music's power to attract and speak to teens, it is an effective marketing tool when used appropriately. From creating original jingles to signing on the biggest stars as endorsers, advertisers have used music to reach teens for more than 40 years. In the past 15 years or so, the number of companies and brands using music to communicate with teens has exploded, however.

In the early 1980s, Pepsi's use of Michael Jackson helped to define its image as distinct from Coke's. By effectively using the star who at the time was the hottest musical act among teens, Pepsi boosted its brand image. Teens perceived it as youthful, "cool," and relevant. Teens developed an ownership of Pepsi that remains to this day.

All teen marketers want to do the same for their brands, to make them relevant and compelling to teens. Music can help you do so. There are two ways to associate a brand with music or to use music in marketing or advertising to teens. One, tie into a specific act, like Pepsi did with Michael Jackson. Two, tie into a musical genre but not a specific artist. Each of these options has certain advantages.

Bringing aboard a current musical act can bring immediate attention to your brand, helping to create awareness. Unless your company is blessed with a huge budget and can move quickly into production, however, you probably will be better off using music without a celebrity. The greatest disadvantage of tying into a musical act is that its popularity is usually short-lived. More often than not, musical stars live or die on their latest product. Typically, it's only superbrands like Pepsi or Coke that can afford

Most Popular Musical Genres among Teens

Rap and Alternative are the most popular musical genres among teens.

(percent of teens saying genre is in, 1998)

	percent
Rap	71%
Alternative	71
R&B	64
Hip Hop	58
Dance	56
Top 40	42
Classic rock	42
Heavy metal	38
Reggae	32
Ska	29
Country	28
Punk	27

Source: TRU *Teenage Marketing & Lifestyle Study*

Highest All-Time TRU*Scores among Musicians

The key to using a musical celebrity is to select one who is on the way up, but hasn't yet peaked.

(16 all-time highest TRU*Scores for musical acts; TRU*Scores are the percentage of teens familiar with an act who like the act "very much")

TRU* Score	Performer	Wave
60	Michael Jackson	Spring 1984
57	Madonna	Fall 1985
54	Bon Jovi	Spring 1987
54	M.C. Hammer	Fall 1990
53	Men at Work	Fall 1983
53	Journey	Spring 1984
53	Whitney Houston	Fall 1986
53	M.C. Hammer	Spring 1991
53	Boyz II Men	Spring 1993
52	Van Halen	Fall 1984
52	Subway	Fall 1995
51	Journey	Spring 1989
51	Boyz II Men	Fall 1993
50	Green Day	Spring 1995
50	Boyz II Men	Spring 1992
50	Bruce Springsteen	Fall 1985

Source: TRU *Teenage Marketing & Lifestyle Study*

to pay huge sums for short-term endorsement deals and quickly produce elaborate commercials that air during an act's short-lived ride at the top.

The key to using a musical celebrity is to select one who is on the way up but hasn't yet peaked. Because teens' musical taste is much more diversified than it once was, it's equally important to consider the genre in which the artist performs.

We use a measure called TRU*Scores to determine the relative popularity of celebrities. TRU*Scores show the percentage of teens familiar with an act who like the act "very much." Michael Jackson still holds the all-time highest TRU*Score for a musical act, a 60 he achieved in the winter of 1983 when *Thriller* was riding high on the charts. The score means that 60 percent of teens who were aware of Michael Jackson at the time liked him "very much."

The advantage of TRU*Scores is that they compare acts based on their popularity among those who are familiar with them, not on the size of their audience. The measure also uncovers the lesser-known acts that score well. Given greater exposure, these acts may become widely popular. Acts with a high TRU*Score—from the mid-30s and up—but a low awareness quotient have special potential as endorsers. Of course, this quantitative assessment is only your first step in choosing a celebrity. Matching an act's image to your corporate or brand image is the other determinant in deciding whether to pursue a deal.

Because of our experience in developing and working with TRU*Scores, we have become fairly skilled at predicting musical trends among teens, particularly the rise and fall of certain acts. What follows are some rules we've developed about teen musical preferences. These rules can guide you in deciding which type of music or celebrity would work for your brand.

Teens show an overwhelming preference for new music. To a teen, new music doesn't mean recent or within the last couple years. It means the newest music of all. Teens are attracted to new music not only because of its intrinsic quality of being current, but also because of a basic teen tenet: teens prefer things that are uniquely for them. This is true not only of music but of other lifestyle choices as well.

New musical acts can achieve fame with lightning speed. Because MTV connects teens globally, performers whose videos are in heavy rotation can gain a mass audience and teen fame almost overnight. Musical acts can lose their popularity just as rapidly. Just as MTV can propel an act to fame, it can also burn out an artist through overexposure (typically, showing the same video over and over). Because of teens' accelerated physiological and emotional growth, their preferences and tastes constantly change. One-fourth of the teen audience of a musical act that was "in" just two years ago will have aged out of the segment. The remaining three-fourths may associate the act with a time when they were just kids.

Nothing can match the excitement of a debut. This is another reason why new acts can lose their appeal rapidly—they cannot debut twice. Goo Goo Dolls, Silverchair, Ace of Base, Presidents of the USA, Hootie & the Blowfish, Tiffany, and New Kids on the Block are just a few examples of artists who debuted strongly with teens but lost their appeal as quickly as they gained fame. Because a debut is a singular occasion, artists (and their labels) must find other ways to match the excitement of newness after a debut.

One obvious way to do this is to create quality music. Certainly, this separates genuine talent from one-hit wonders. But even quality music may not be enough to maintain popularity among teens. Artists who innovate continuously are popular longer than those who do not innovate. Madonna has been one of the few artists who could reinvent herself enough to recapture a teen audience. Still, she has never come close to matching the popularity she enjoyed among teens when she debuted, and now that she is a mother and the star of "Evita," teens certainly view her as being more "adult contemporary" than relevant to their world.

Commercial endorsements accelerate the erosion of an artist's popularity among teens. As much as teens enjoy seeing one of their favorite music stars in a TV commercial, they often view commercial endorsements as selling out. The exposure also means that an artist has gained acceptance by the mainstream, and performers who are also embraced by mom and dad or by younger brothers and sisters are often resoundingly rejected by teens. Teens prefer artists whom they can call their own.

Such was the case with M.C. Hammer. He debuted to tremendous teen popularity and sustained it for a full year. Then he went commercial. Mattel introduced him in doll form as "Barbie's celebrity friend." He was featured in a Saturday-morning cartoon. He also sold Pepsi and British Knights sneakers in commercials. What happened was predictable: little kids, and some parents, started to love Hammer, but big kids wanted to pretend they never had.

Assuming that an artist's music and image are appealing, the common denominator in the popularity of musical acts among teens is newness. "Some music is only popular because it *is* new," one teen told me bluntly during a focus group.

An artist's popularity also can spiral downward from overexposure, triggered by endorsements, merchandise licensing, advertising, and publicity. This creates a Catch-22 situation when signing on a musical star. The star's effectiveness in communicating to teens will last only a short period of time, and the endorsement itself is likely to wear out the artist's popularity.

Because of these problems, record labels are monitoring their artists' commercial activities carefully. They understand that the short-term riches gained from endorsement deals are often outweighed by the premature death of an artist's career. Of course, acts that are intrinsically faddish and destined to fade rapidly, such as Vanilla Ice, Milli Vanilli, and even the hugely successful Spice Girls, will want to grab commercial endorsements while the going is good.

Hammered: The Fast Rise and Fall of a Mainstream Rapper

While teens enjoy seeing one of their favorite music stars in a TV commercial, they often view commercial endorsements as selling out.

(M.C. Hammer's TRU*Scores by study wave, fall 1990 to spring 1993; TRU*Scores are the percentage of teens familiar with an act who like the act very much)

Wave	TRU*Score
Fall 1990	54
Spring 1991	53
Fall 1991	40
Spring 1992	31
Fall 1992	25
Spring 1993	20

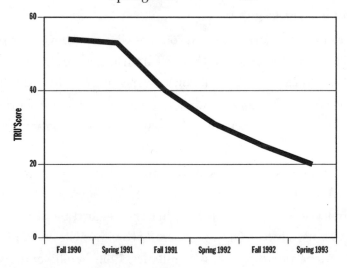

Source: TRU *Teenage Marketing & Lifestyle Study*

Musical acts have a one-year window of opportunity for gaining popularity among teens. In the 16-year history of TRU's syndicated study, with the single exception of Boyz II Men, no act achieving a strong TRU*Score of at least 35 (meaning 35 percent of teens aware of the act like it "very much") has been able to top that score in more than three waves (one-and-one-half years). This statistic alone shows how fickle teens are when it comes to musical performers.

Before Boyz II Men, Janet Jackson and Mariah Carey came close to breaking the three-wave rule. But the popularity of both fell after two consecutive waves of TRU*Score increases. Both artists shied away from commercial endorsements and, like Boyz II Men, both are genuinely talented. Mariah Carey, although not topping her highest debut score, has found greater longevity among teens than any other artist over the past few years. She has all the ingredients—a great voice, pop songs that especially hook girls, looks that especially hook boys, and dance music that crosses over to all ethnic segments. Two other acts which have maintained high popularity over the past few waves of our study are No Doubt and Puff Daddy. Still although they scored well for three consecutive waves, they were unable to top their initial success.

Acts with little talent can also rise to fame quickly, but they fall just as fast. Teens can't be fooled for long, although long enough for manufactured acts—propelled by gimmicks—to gain fame and fortune. To sustain any respectable level of popularity, an artist needs to be legitimate. Teens are discerning enough to reject acts that lack real talent. Let us hope the Spice Girls, Vanilla Ice, New Kids on the Block, and Milli Vanilli put their money into long-term investments.

Certain genres breed greater teen loyalty. While top-scoring artists (with TRU*Scores over 35) begin to decline in popularity after a maximum of one year, even an act with a lower score can develop loyal fans among teens. Teen loyalty depends somewhat on the musical genre, with some genres developing more loyal fans than others.

Acts with Fleeting Popularity

Most musical acts enjoy short-lived popularity among teens.

(highest and lowest TRU*Scores for selected artists through fall 1998; TRU*Scores are the percentage of teens familiar with an act who like the act very much)

	highest	lowest
Michael Jackson	60	6
Madonna	57	18
Green Day	50	16
Bruce Springsteen	50	8
Vanilla Ice	45	8
New Kids on the Block	45	5
Ace of Base	36	19

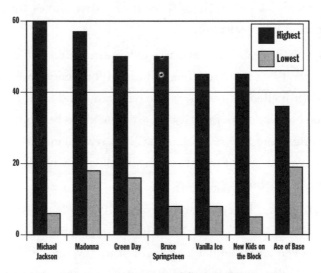

Source: TRU *Teenage Marketing & Lifestyle Study*

Acts with
Loyal Fans

Although musical acts may not achieve the highest TRU*Scores,
they can develop a loyal following.

(highest and lowest TRU*Scores for selected artists through fall 1998; TRU*Scores are the percentage of teens familiar with an act who like the act very much)

	highest	lowest
Boyz II Men	53	45
Mariah Carey	41	31
Pearl Jam	37	31
Smashing Pumpkins	37	31
Metallica	31	23
Guns 'N Roses	30	29

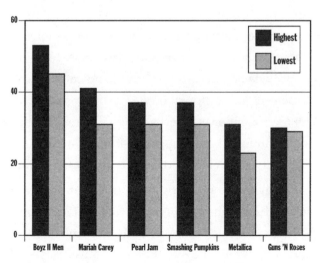

Source: TRU *Teenage Marketing & Lifestyle Study*

The success of Boyz II Men, like that of Mariah Carey, is explained by their appeal to all teen segments. As teens' musical tastes have become more fragmented, Boyz II Men's and Mariah Carey's vocal talents and non-alienating image helped them win unprecedented popularity among the entire teen population.

Hard-rock and metal groups generate greater loyalty among teens, especially compared with rap and alternative acts, which come and go so quickly these days. Metallica, for one, may never be as popular among teens as some of the top rap and alternative acts. But their fans are more loyal, and, therefore, their TRU*Scores are more stable year after year. When Guns 'N Roses were together, their popularity among teens was predictable; they achieved the same 29 or 30 TRU*Score in five consecutive waves. (Of course, what the members of this band did offstage was less predictable, and few companies dared to associate their brands with Axyl, Slash, and the gang.) R&B acts, which often rely on the song writing talents of others and whose dominant ingredient is great vocals, are also more stable in teen popularity than alternative or rap acts.

TRU*Scores are an important measurement for marketers because they reveal the popularity of performers among all teens, not just record-buying teens. It's important to recognize that while most teens buy music, a significant minority do not. According to our syndicated study, more than one in five (38 percent) teens did not buy a CD or pre-recorded tape in the past year. With few exceptions, advertisers want to reach the masses; they don't want to discriminate based on music-buying status. One exception would be a record club, which would want to target music-buying teens.

Teens who buy music regularly have different musical tastes than those who don't. Heavy music buyers are more adventurous and enjoy non-mainstream genres much more than do non–music buyers. For example, far more heavy music buyers than non–music buyers like techno, punk, reggae, and ska. They also like rap, alternative, and R&B more than nonbuyers. Those who don't buy much music enjoy country more than heavily buying teens do, and they like Top 40 and classic rock about as much as heavy buyers do. The following tables compare the musical preferences of heavy buyers (those who have shopped at a record store more than five times in the past 30 days) with teens who haven't shopped at a record store in the past 30 days.

African-American genres are the most popular among teens. Whatever is popular among African-American teens influences the white majority. This is true not only in music, but also in fashion and language. Not long ago, the musical preferences of white teens determined an artist's overall popularity among the general teen market. Today, African-American teens determine the musical preferences of the teen majority, with essentially black genres—rap, hip hop, dance, and R&B—being favored by most teens. For example, it's estimated that 80 per cent of rap records are purchased by white teens. While white teens cross over to these rhythm-based genres, black teens do not cross over to the essentially white genres of alternative and metal. Latino teens, notably, are the most musically adventurous, with diverse tastes. They like all teen genres, from rap to alternative.

The popularity of black genres is particularly noteworthy since African-American performers were, to some degree, barred from mainstream commercial exposure as late as the 1980s. The unprecedented success of Michael Jackson's *Thriller* and the acceptance of his videos on MTV broke through this racial barrier. Today it is not uncommon for white artists to achieve popularity by working in a black genre.

The table on the next page 165 shows the continuing influence of African-American performers. It lists the top-scoring artist in each of TRU's past 28 waves, with black performers denoted in boldfaced type. Beginning in the fall of 1990, African-American artists led the scoring for an unprecedented nine straight times. It was not until the spring of 1995 that a white act, Green Day, managed to claim top popularity.

Heavy Buyers vs. Non-buyers: Musical Genre Preferences

Teens who buy a lot of music have different musical tastes from those who don't.

(percent saying musical genre is in by music buying behavior, 1998; heavy buyers are those who have shopped at a record store more than five times in the past 30 days; nonbuyers have not shopped in a record store in the past 30 days)

	heavy buyers	nonbuyers
Preferred significantly more by heavy buyers		
Rap	74%	65%
Alternative	71	61
R&B	69	56
Hip hop	64	52
Dance/rave	60	47
Techno	43	25
Top 40	42	37
Reggae	35	27
Punk	34	24
Ska	33	22
Preferred significantly more by non-buyers		
Country	27	37
Classic Rock	39	42
Preferred equally by both heavy buyers and non-buyers		
Heavy Metal	37	37

Source: TRU *Teenage Marketing & Lifestyle Study*

Heavy Buyers vs. Nonbuyers: Musical Performer Preferences

Heavy music buyers prefer different musical acts than those who are not heavy buyers.

*(TRU*Scores for musical acts by music buying behavior, fall 1998; heavy buyers
are those who have shopped at a record store more than five times in the past 30 days;
nonbuyers have not shopped in a record store in the past 30 days; TRU*Scores
are the percentage of teens familiar with an act who like the act very much)*

	TRU*Scores	
	heavy buyers	non-buyers
Preferred significantly more by heavy buyers		
Puff Daddy	54	41
Mase	54	38
Usher	47	38
Wyclef Jean	36	25
Third Eye Blind	35	29
Preferred significantly more by non-buyers		
Toni Braxton	22	26
LeAnn Rimes	18	24
Preferred by both heavy buyers and non-buyers		
Sugar Ray	33	30
No Doubt	30	29
Backstreet Boys	23	22

Source: TRU *Teenage Marketing & Lifestyle Study*

Rap is here to stay because it speaks more powerfully to teens than any other genre. It has been said that rap is the first recent major cultural phenomenon that did not come from baby boomers. This is one reason for its popularity among teens. They own rap; it speaks directly to them. Rap also appeals to teens because, like dance and R&B, it's a rhythmic genre.

Over the past few years, rap has evolved considerably, as evidenced by the differing styles of Puff Daddy and Snoop Doggy Dogg. Today, there are "mainstream" rappers, gangsta rappers, female rappers, jazz rappers, and other hybrid rap performers.

Hip-hop artists have been successful in prolifically recycling older songs through sampling—digitally copying a track of a record—and through cover versions. These artists have been criticized in some circles for this practice; however, perhaps only through such treatments would teens be exposed to these songs. Probably the best known example is Puff Daddy's "I'll Be Missing You," a tribute to Biggie Smalls, which was based on a substantial sample of Sting's "Every Breath You Take." Puff Daddy has also crafted hits that are based on samples from Led Zeppelin, as Janet Jackson has from Joni Mitchell, and Public Enemy from Stephen Stills. Even the Jose Marti classic "Guantanamera" has turned hip hop, thanks to Wyclef Jean, formerly of the Fugees. (Incidentally, "Guantanamera" has also been transformed into a children's song, "One Ton Tomato," by the talented musician and creator of music for kids, Sherban Cira.)

It looks like alternative bands are also getting into the act of sampling. The group Garbage, for example, repeats the famous hook from the Beach Boys' "Don't Worry Baby" in their single "Push It."

Although teens favor rap, they still love great singers. The most consistently popular performers among teens are those who combine good vocals with a strong R&B rhythm. In what may be a backlash against the proliferation of nonmelodic rap, there are a growing number of great vocal R&B groups, such as Boyz II Men, 112, and En Vogue. Teens are also enthu-

Top Musical Acts: 1984 to 1998

African-American performers are frequently the most popular musical acts among teens.

*(most popular musical acts in past 20 waves of
Teenage Marketing & Lifestyle Study)*

TRU Wave		TRU Wave	
Spring 1998	**Puff Daddy**	Spring 1991	**M.C. Hammer**
Fall 1997	No Doubt	Fall 1990	**M.C. Hammer**
Spring 1997	No Doubt	Spring 1990	Paula Abdul
Fall 1996	**Fugees**	Fall 1989	New Kids on the Block
Spring 1996	Mariah Carey	Spring 1989	George Michael
Fall 1995	**Subway**	Fall 1988	George Michael
Spring 1995	Green Day	Spring 1988	**Whitney Houston**
Fall 1994	**R. Kelly**	Fall 1987	Lisa/Cult Jam
Spring 1994	**Snoop Doggy Dogg**	Spring 1987	Bon Jovi
Fall 1993	**Boyz II Men**	Fall 1986	Bon Jovi
Spring 1993	**Boyz II Men**	Spring 1986	Bruce Springsteen
Fall 1992	**Kris Kross**	Fall 1985	Madonna
Spring 1992	**Boyz II Men**	Spring 1985	Van Halen
Fall 1991	**Bell Biv DeVoe**	Fall 1984	Journey

Note: Boldfaced type indicates black performers.
Source: TRU *Teenage Marketing & Lifestyle Study*

siastic about solo artists whom they judge to be talented vocalists, such as Mariah Carey, Aaliyah, Usher, Brandy, and Erykah Badu.

Classic rock and country are less relevant to teens. Some teens tell us they respect the great rock-and-roll artists, such as the Beatles, the Stones, Led Zeppelin, or the Grateful Dead, but they recognize that this music belongs to another generation (namely, their parents'). In each wave of our syndicated study, we measure the popularity of one or two classic rockers. Predictably, their scores are low—in many cases, embarrassingly low. The Beatles fared poorly among teens even at the time their catalog was released on CD and received a great deal of media attention. Eric Clapton received a low score even when his album *Unplugged* was riding high on the charts and his performance on MTV was shown repeatedly. The only exception to the poor performance of classic rockers is Queen's TRU*Score of 32, received when the movie *Wayne's World* was showing in theaters. Wayne, Garth, and their buddies lip-synching to the Queen classic "Bohemian Rhapsody" (which became a heavily rotated MTV video) was perhaps teens' favorite scene in this blockbuster movie. Clearly, it takes a lot before a classic rock act scores well among teens.

Country music has been one of the fastest-growing genres among adults and teens over the past few years. Still, country music is limited to a sort of cult following among teens, and particularly teens in the Northeast reject it. Teens do not feel that they "own" country, nor is it particularly relevant to their lives. Country has produced only a few artists (Garth Brooks, LeAnn Rimes, Shania Twain, Tim McGraw, and the Dixie Chicks) whom teens respect. And unlike dance or rock, country does not offer the rhythm that so engages teens.

Teens' musical taste is highly fragmented. Where baby boomers had rock and Motown, today's "echo boomers" can literally spout off a dozen or so styles of music they favor, from metal, hip hop, and alternative to rave, house, techno, rap, and ska. The latest TRU*Score data strongly underscore this finding: the top-five music acts in our current wave represent four distinct genres: rap, R&B, alternative, and dance. From a marketing perspective, this fragmentation phenomenon is a two-sided sword. It facilitates targeting; for example, if you want to reach African-American teens, stick to rap or R&B. On the other hand, it's more difficult than ever to reach teens en masse using a single style of music. But, don't let this deter you from tapping into the power of music to reach teens.

There are two ways to deal with teens' fragmented musical tastes: 1) be inclusive (take a look at Gap ads, which rotate between rap, swing, and techno); and 2) err on the side of using whatever music is most appropriate for your specific marketing effort, because teens will embrace a truly creative effort (consider the example of the popular Mountain Dew ad which features the song "Tonight" from *West Side Story*).

Chapter 7.

The Power of Celebrity

Celebrities are an integral part of youth culture. To teens, they are more than musicians, athletes, actors, or fashion models. They are role models, heroes, and even icons. They do more than entertain teens. They nationalize the teen experience, speaking for a cohort and inspiring trends in lifestyles, fashions, attitudes, and behavior. Celebrities can bring attention, authority, and added appeal to your teen-directed advertising and promotions. As much as adult America is attracted to celebrities, teens are lured in a unique way. Their enthrallment with celebrities can be leveraged in a big way.

Celebrities are human beings, however, and associating your brand with a celebrity can be risky. Although not an endorser of a teen brand, O. J. Simpson is the most dramatic example of the risk you take when you tie into a celebrity. Michael Jackson and Tonya Harding (both of whom endorsed major teen brands) are other examples of celebrities who, because of allegations of wrongdoing, became damaged goods to companies looking for endorsers. Juwan Howard, Allen Iverson, Latrell Sprewell, and Dennis Rodman are more recent additions to the list of "Marketer Beware."

Though teens have become more cynical about celebrities because so many have disappointed them, the right celebrity can still bring instant attention and credibility to your product or brand. This is particularly true of younger (aged 12 to 15) teen boys, who get especially caught up with celebrities—athletes in particular. These younger boys are the easiest teen segment to market to. I was reminded of this when we were testing a Nintendo TV spot for the company's "Ken Griffey, Jr. Presents Major League Baseball." (Ken Griffey, Jr. is teen boys' favorite baseball player, according to our current TRU*Score ranking.) The primary objective of the Nintendo research was to learn whether the execution clearly communicated its intended messages. But we heard something else of great importance during the research. As soon as the boys discovered that Ken Griffey, Jr. had lent his name to the game, their expectations of the game increased greatly. In

Teens' Favorite Celebrities

One in five girls names Leonardo DiCaprio as her favorite celebrity, while boys say Jim Carrey is number one.

(percent of teens citing non-music, non-sport celebrity as their favorite, 1998; for celebrities mentioned by at least 3 percent of teens)

Boys		Girls	
Jim Carrey	13%	Leonardo DiCaprio	20%
Will Smith	11	Will Smith	9
Pamela Anderson Lee	6	Sandra Bullock	7
Tyra Banks	5	Matt Damon	5
Tim Allen	5	Tyra Banks	4
Bruce Willis	5	Julia Roberts	4
Harrison Ford	4	Brad Pitt	4
Jerry Seinfeld	3	Tom Cruise	3
Adam Sandler	3	Jim Carrey	3
Nicholas Cage	3	Meg Ryan	3
		Claire Danes	3
		Sarah Michelle Gellar	3

Source: TRU *Teenage Marketing & Lifestyle Study*

this case, just the use of a celebrity's name heightened the image of the product. Griffey, Jr. did not even appear in the commercial, although his father did. The right athlete can be a powerful marketing tool.

There are many other examples of the successful use of celebrities in marketing, none bigger than Michael Jordan. Jordan is teens' all-time favorite celebrity. He is vitally important to Nike's bottom line; the "Air Jordan" shoe line alone represents a substantial portion of Nike's basketball shoe sales. Being associated with Michael Jordan has also benefited Gatorade, McDonald's, Coca-Cola (before Gatorade), Wheaties, Wilson, Hanes, and other brands and licensees.

Maybe there will never be another Michael Jordan, but there are plenty of other exciting celebrities with whom you can associate. Grant Hill, Penny Hardaway, and Kobe Bryant appear to be Michael's heirs-apparent in basketball marketing, but an athlete from another sport or a celebrity from another field may emerge as the next teen superhero.

If you want to tie into celebrities, music and sports are the first two places to look. After music, sports is the area of interest shared by the largest number of teens. When we asked teens in our quantitative study which types of celebrities they most like to see in advertising, the winners by far were music and sports stars. Significantly more boys than girls chose sports stars, while significantly more girls than boys chose music stars.

After athletes and musicians come supermodels, a category that is relatively new. When we ask girls what they think about these glamorous models they frequently tell us, "I just can't relate to *that*!" Supermodels are beyond a typical teen girl's aspirational set. Consequently, twice as many boys as girls named supermodels as the celebrities they want to see in advertising.

During qualitative research we conducted, however, high school boys were not enthusiastic when shown a brochure featuring a supermodel on its cover. One boy finally explained that he would prefer to see someone

Celebrity Types Teens Prefer in Advertising

Boys prefer to see sports stars in advertising, while girls prefer music stars.

(percent of teens preferring celebrity type in advertising, by gender, 1993)

	boys	girls
Sports stars	42%	16%
Music stars	12	33
Supermodels	22	12
Animated characters	11	11
Movie stars	8	16
TV stars	4	12

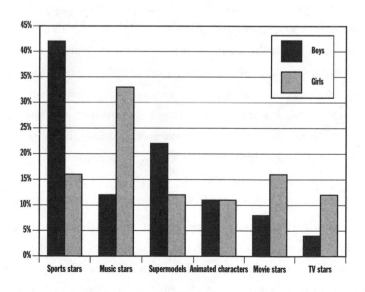

Source: TRU *Teenage Marketing & Lifestyle Study*

on the cover whom he would "actually have a shot at, like one of the best-looking girls at school" over the glamorous, older model. It appears that supermodels are also outside boys' aspirational set!

After supermodels, teens name movie stars, animated characters, and TV stars as the type of celebrity they most like to see in advertising. Note that teens' top three choices—sports stars, music stars, and models—are real people, rather than actors or characters in roles. Teens want honesty and clarity in advertising (above almost all else), so it follows that they want real-life endorsers rather than actors.

In addition to musical performers, we also track the popularity of sports and other stars with our TRU*Score system. By comparing the TRU*Score trends of celebrities in different fields, we have developed the following guidelines to help you determine which type of celebrity to sign up.

Sports stars and certain actors and models are more popular than music stars. Over the past three waves of our syndicated study, sports stars have averaged a TRU*Score of 32. Actors / models have a TRU*Score of 36 (one wave only), while the score is only 27 for music stars. It is important to remember that a larger share of teens are familiar with actors / models and musical artists than with sports stars. On average, 68 percent of teens are familiar with music stars, and 68 percent are familiar with actors / models. But only 55 percent of teens, on average, are familiar with athletes. Fewer teens are familiar with sports stars simply because many girls don't know who these athletes are, especially once they get past the "marquee" names of Michael Jordan, Grant Hill, Shaquille O'Neal, and Mark McGwire.

The popularity of sports stars is more stable than that of musical acts. Musical acts typically enjoy an extremely short span of popularity because teens like music that is new. The popularity of athletes lasts longer than that of musicians because each sport season brings them renewed attention. Eventually, however, age or injuries end athletic careers and the popularity of an individual sports star among teens. Unlike athletes or musicians, actors can rejuvenate a waning career by starring in a new, successful TV show or movie. This can make the popularity of actors / models more stable than that of musicians or athletes.

The appeal of sports stars, actors, and models is broader than that of musical performers. Some of the sports starts, actors, and models teens admire are also admired by their parents. Teens and parents are equally likely to be fans of Michael Jordan or Bill Cosby, for example. But in general, teen celebrity preferences are distinct from those of adults, as revealed in a comparison of celebrity preferences reported in our teen studies with a 1993 survey by Video Storyboard Tests. Candice Bergen was the most popular celebrity among adults at the time but ranked 32 out of 39 among teens. Cher was third-most popular among adults but next to last among teens. Though the study didn't measure Leonardo DiCaprio, Puff Daddy (or, for that matter, any of teens' current favorites), it is safe to assume that there is an equal difference between adult and teen ratings for these stars.

Certain musical acts appeal specifically to teens. From thrash metal to gangsta rap, complete genres of music alienate adults. Teens love this. It gives them an important sense of ownership. The fact that adults don't like certain types of music is attractive to teens, since they want things that are uniquely their own. Though adults might wear many of the same fashions as teens or get involved in the same activities, it's the rare parent who cranks up Metallica or dances to Mase.

Commercial endorsements increase the popularity of sports stars but erode the popularity of musical celebrities. Teens want music performers to remain pure. They see them as artists and may reject them for selling out if they endorse a commercial product. On the other hand, commercial endorsements can actually increase the popularity of athletes. Teens like Anfernee Hardaway as much for his "Li'l Penny" commercials for Nike as for being an all-NBA guard. The same was true for Larry Johnson and

Celebrities with Endorsement Potential

Celebrities who are not yet well known, but extremely popular among their fans, have the greatest endorsement potential.

(familiarity ranking is based on the percentage of teens who say they are familiar with a celebrity; popularity ranking is based on the percentage of teens familiar with a celebrity who really like the celebrity; 1998; 1 is highest rank)

	familiarity ranking	popularity ranking
Sports stars		
Jerry Rice	4	15
Kobe Bryant	10	24
Kordell Stewart	11	23
Terrell Davis	15	27
Warrick Dunn	18	35
Kevin Garnet	23	34
Music stars		
Usher	25	3
Mase	29	2
Dru Hill	30	9
Missy Elliot	33	13
Wyclef Jean	37	15

Source: TRU *Teenage Marketing & Lifestyle Study*

his popular "Grandmama" commercials for Converse a few years ago. Tiger Woods, Grant Hill, Kevin Garnett, and Kobe Bryant, to name just a few, are athletes whose starring roles in athletic-shoe commercials have broadened and heightened their teen appeal.

How can you narrow the field of celebrities who could successfully endorse your brands? Select a celebrity who is on the way up, rather than someone who is at the peak of popularity. This is because teens are most attracted to what or who is new and because the budgets for many teen brands are relatively small. To find rising stars, we look for celebrities with a low familiarity ranking (meaning few teens are familiar with him or her) and a high popularity ranking (among the few teens who are familiar with the celebrity, he or she is highly popular). For example, Jerry Rice (despite all his years in the NFL) ranks 15th in familiarity among teens, but among those familiar with him, he ranks fourth in popularity.

During the time this study was fielded (1998), the celebrities in the accompanying chart showed special potential as endorsers. All enjoyed a high degree of popularity among the relatively few teens who were familiar with them. If a celebrity is highly popular among the small audience familiar with him or her, then greater exposure should mean broader popularity.

The gap between a celebrity's familiarity and popularity is only the first screening step in deciding whom to sign on as an endorser. The next step is to examine the image and personality of the celebrity to assess whether there is a fit with your product, brand, and company. A gangsta rapper, for example, would be a bad bet, regardless of how popular he is.

Using Sports Celebrities as Endorsers

While rap and alternative are teens' top musical preferences, basketball is king in sports. In the past several waves of our study, most of the highest TRU*Score for athletes have belonged to basketball players, and to Michael Jordan in particular. In fact, in the 15 years of doing the study, there has been no other celebrity from any field who has approached MJ's popularity. But it's important to recognize that Jordan is unique and, in this case, is the exception to the rule that teens prefer younger, newer-on-the scene celebrities. When Shaquille O'Neal first came out of college, for example, his TRU*Score rivaled Jordan's. After several years in the league, Shaq's scores have plummeted to the point where WNBA player Lisa Leslie has matched his numbers. O'Neal's decline did not go unnoticed by Reebok, for which Shaq was the marquee endorser. In fact, last year Reebok dropped Shaq as an endorser and discontinued his line of shoes. How do you explain the decline of an athlete who is not only at the height of his career but who is also a true personality? In qualitative research we've done, teen boys have complained that Shaq is too commercial. They object not to his advertising appearances (for Reebok as well as Pepsi), but to his fledgling film and recording careers. Simply put, these guys think Shaq should spend more time learning how to shoot a free throw than making "bad movies and rap records." Additionally, teens seem to be attracted to the more athletic, versatile players who can do it all on the court, like Jordan, Scottie Pippen, Grant Hill, and Penny Hardaway. Shaq's too one-dimensional a player for these basketball fans.

Still, it's no coincidence that basketball players are the pro athletes used most often in advertising, not only for athletic shoes but also for fast food and soft drinks. Teens like to see sports stars in commercials. This does not mean that teens don't discriminate, even among basketball players. They favor players who are the most exciting and physically gifted. Behind the popularity of basketball players is the tremendous job the NBA has done in marketing itself and the sport. It will be interesting to see if the recent lockout has marred this special relationship with teens. The NFL, the NHL, and Major League Baseball, in particular, lag behind. In all fairness, the NBA probably has an inherent advantage in creating stars. Its sport can better feature the individual than football or hockey. The NFL is further challenged in developing stars by the fact that its players wear hel-

TRU*Scores for Athletes

Basketball players, particularly Michael Jordan, are the most popular athletes.

(all-time highest TRU*Scores for athletes, fall 1992 through spring 1998; TRU*Scores are the percentage of teens familiar with an athlete who like the athlete very much)

TRU* Score	Athlete	Wave	TRU* Score	Athlete	Wave
66	Michael Jordan	Fall 1992	54	Tiger Woods	Fall 1997
64	Michael Jordan	Spring 1992	54	Magic Johnson	Spring 1993
63	Michael Jordan	Fall 1993	54	Grant Hill	Fall 1995
62	Michael Jordan	Spring 1993	54	Jerry Rice	Fall 1995
62	Shaquille O'Neal	Fall 1993	54	Anfernee Hardaway	Fall 1995
61	Michael Jordan	Spring 1994	54	Shaquille O'Neal	Fall 1992
60	Shaquille O'Neal	Spring 1994	54	Anfernee Hardaway	Spring 1996
60	David Robinson	Fall 1992	54	Shaquille O'Neal	Spring 1993
59	Scottie Pippen	Fall 1992	54	Scottie Pippen	Spring 1992
58	Emmitt Smith	Spring 1994	54	Scottie Pippen	Spring 1993
57	Michael Jordan	Fall 1994	54	Grant Hill	Fall 1996
57	Magic Johnson	Spring 1992	53	Bo Jackson	Spring 1992
56	Michael Jordan	Spring 1995	53	Grant Hill	Spring 1996
56	Michael Jordan	Fall 1995	53	Michael Jordan	Spring 1996
56	Anfernee Hardaway	Fall 1996	53	Jerry Rice	Spring 1995
56	Magic Johnson	Fall 1992	53	Anfernee Hardaway	Spring 1997
56	Shaquille O'Neal	Fall 1994	52	Michael Jordan	Spring 1998
56	Scottie Pippen	Spring 1994	52	David Robinson	Fall 1993
55	Michael Jordan	Fall 1996	52	Shawn Kemp	Fall 1993
55	Michael Jordan	Spring 1997	52	Magic Johnson	Fall 1993
55	Michael Jordan	Fall 1997	52	Jerry Rice	Spring 1994

Source: TRU *Teenage Marketing & Lifestyle Study*

mets which cover their faces. Exacerbating this issue, the NFL has clamped down on players who remove their helmets after scoring a touchdown. Some football stars are starting to move up, however, especially among boys. (Football stars historically receive higher scores in our spring studies, which are fielded during football season.) All-star running back Barry Sanders along with legendary receiver Jerry Rice have current scores that match those of Jordan and baseball great Ken Griffey, Jr. As the table shows, 9 of the top 10 and 27 of the 30 highest scores to date belong to basketball players. Not a single female athlete makes this list.

Individual sports, such as tennis, track and field, boxing, ice skating, and auto racing, have been unable to produce the types of stars teens can relate to. The most prominent exception is golf, which has produced an extremely relatable star in Tiger Woods. After his Masters win in 1997, Woods received the second-highest TRU*Score, behind only Michael Jordan. Until Woods came along, I had thought it was impossible for any golfer to score that highly among teens. But Woods is an exception: he's young, multiracial, extremely talented, and full of personality. What's more, to teens, he doesn't fit the traditional image of a pro golfer, which has added to his great appeal. And, importantly, he was featured in some popular Nike ads. Still, teens' attention span is short, so Woods must start winning the big tournaments again to resuscitate his already declining popularity among teens. Already the next generation of athletes is beginning to make its mark—in addition to Tiger Woods, Kobe Bryant in basketball and Venus Williams in tennis are currently among teens' top 10 sports stars.

Using Actors and Models as Endorsers

We have measured non-music, non-sport celebrities in only a few waves of our syndicated study to date. But even in this early analysis, we've detected patterns that may help you assess the popularity of actors and models.

Teens' Favorite Movies

Titanic is by far the favorite movie of teen girls, mentioned by more than 1 in 10.

(percent of teens citing movie as their favorite, by gender, 1998; for movies cited by at least 2 percent of teens)

Boys

Star Wars	3%
Men in Black	3
Titanic	2
Jurassic Park	2
Braveheart	2
Friday	2
Happy Gilmore	2
Money Talks	2
Dumb and Dumber	2
Liar, Liar	2
Scream	2
The Rock	2
Austin Powers: Int'l Man of Mystery	2

Girls

Titanic	11
Grease	6
Scream	3
Soul Food	3
Romeo and Juliet	2
Dirty Dancing	2
My Best Friend's Wedding	2
Friday	2

Source: TRU *Teenage Marketing & Lifestyle Study*

Many of the most popular actors have roots in comedy, emphasizing the importance of using humor to attract teens. Teens' favorite TV shows are situation comedies, and their favorite commercials are those that use humor.

Also, several of the top-rated celebrities star in current TV shows, reflecting the impact of network TV in the lives of teens. Will Smith, who at that time was starring in "The Fresh Prince of Bel-Air," received the highest TRU*Score of any celebrity. Only living legend Michael Jordan has topped Smith's score of 63 in earlier waves.

Movie-going is one activity that teens universally enjoy. It is also an activity that spawns celebrity. Movies provide a large measure of escapism and entertainment for teens; additionally, theaters are easily accessible for most teens. Not only are theaters popping up in virtually every mall, but second-run movies are available everywhere—on videocassette, cable, and on demand via pay-per-view. Many teens have amassed videocassette collections of their all-time favorites—the films they watch repeatedly without becoming bored.

In a recent TRU study, we asked teens to write in (no list provided) the one movie they like so much that they can watch it over and over again. We also asked them to write-in their favorite celebrity who's not from the worlds of music or sports. For favorite movie, not surprisingly, the tragic love story *Titanic* sailed into first place as teens' most consistently watchable movie. And despite the epic's nearly three-and-a-half hour running time, girls flocked to see the box-office titan starring their favorite heartthrob, Leonardo DiCaprio, again and again. Leo's high-seas heroics likely helped him win the most votes as teens' favorite celebrity. But Leo has only the girls to thank—out of his 106 votes, only four were cast by boys!

Teen faves don't have to be brand new. Twenty-year-old *Grease* became a teen hit all over again after its re-release allowed teens to see the musical classic on the big-screen for the first time. Like *Titanic*, the popularity of number-two rated *Grease* was largely fueled by girls.

Horror films are back in a big way with teens, thanks to teen girls' number-three favorite, *Scream*. The stylishly satirical slasher film paved the way for a revival of the genre, which has done surprisingly well with girls. Many of teens' favorite TV actresses—including Neve Campbell, Jennifer Love Hewitt, Courtney Cox, Sarah Michelle Gellar, and Katie Holmes—have broken into films by playing tough-as-nails scream-queens.

A final note: actors and comedians have an inherent advantage over musicians and athletes in advertising. They can truly act.

Chapter 8.

Teen Values

To communicate with teens effectively, you need to understand their complexity. That means you need to develop a deep understanding of their often conflicting behaviors, lifestyles, attitudes, and values. And you can't stop there. You need to understand what teens look like, how they act, what they think, how they feel, and what they believe others feel about them. You need to know what they prefer and how they prioritize. You need to know how teens see themselves and those close to them. You need to know the fundamental motivations that drive teen behavior: teen attitudes and values. You need information and insights that come from digging deep, that transcend typical behavioral data or qualitative insights. When you accurately link a relevant product benefit to a core teen value, you can hit a deep emotional chord, while identifying your brand more closely with teens.

For more than 10 years, TRU has been tracking key teen values in our syndicated study through a battery of attitudinal statements, known as the Teen Value Monitor. More than 20 statements comprise this measurement. For each one, teens are asked to express their degree of agreement or disagreement. The results show trends in key teen values over time. Attitudes change more slowly than behavior, even among teens. When attitudes do change, teen behavior is also likely to change, as attitudes are often a precursor to behavior. TRU's Teen Value Monitor reveals the teen mindset and "heartset." It provides a unique portrait of how teens are feeling about themselves and the world in which they live, and how these feelings and values shift over time. The results provide rich direction for guiding marketers in communicating effectively with teens—in going for that often-elusive but ever-compelling emotional chord.

Teens are complex individuals. How they see themselves doesn't always match up with either their own behavior or how their peers see them. But marketers need to realize that teen self-perceptions are real—they reveal critical insights into the individual.

Teen Value Monitor

Today's teens like to do things with their family more than the teens of five years ago; they are also more likely to say religion is an important part of their life.

(percent of teens who strongly or somewhat agree with statement, 1993 and 1998)

	1998	1993	percentage point change
Things are really going well for me. I've worked hard to get where I am and feel I'll always be successful.	75%	69%	6
I really like to do things with my family.	71	63	8
I think I'm pretty normal—most kids I know are pretty much like me.	67	61	6
I always try to have as much fun as I can—I don't know what the future holds and I don't care what others think.	65	69	–4
It's very important for me to get involved in things that help others and to help make the world better—even if it's not that important to others my age.	63	63	0
My religion/faith is one of the most important parts of my life.	63	53	10
I care a lot about whether my clothes are in style.	61	61	0
Most people who know me or just see me think I'm cool.	53	46	7
It's important to me to fit in with my friends and other kids I like, and—to be real honest—sometimes their opinions can really influence me.	51	48	3
I'm often the first one to try something new.	49	46	3
Success means making a lot of money.	45	36	9
I wish I were more popular—I watch the kids who are popular and wish I were more like them.	28	27	1

Source: TRU *Teenage Marketing & Lifestyle Study*

Teen Values by Gender

Girls are more likely to feel normal than boys, while boys are more likely to equate success with money than girls.

(percent of teens who strongly or somewhat agree with statement, by gender, 1998)

	boys	girls
Things are really going well for me. I've worked hard to get where I am and feel I'll always be successful.	75%	76%
I really like to do things with my family.	71	71
I think I'm pretty normal—most kids I know are pretty much like me.	64	71
I always try to have as much fun as I can—I don't know what the future holds and I don't care what others think.	63	67
It's very important for me to get involved in things that help others and to help make the world better—even if it's not that important to others my age.	58	69
My religion/faith is one of the most important parts of my life.	61	67
I care a lot about whether my clothes are in style.	58	64
Most people who know me or just see me think I'm cool.	55	52
It's important to me to fit in with my friends and other kids I like, and—to be real honest—sometimes their opinions can really influence me.	54	48
I'm often the first one to try something new.	45	52
Success means making a lot of money.	51	38
I wish I were more popular—I watch the kids who are popular and wish I were more like them.	29	27

Source: TRU *Teenage Marketing & Lifestyle Study*

Teens are characterized by contradiction. They want to carve out their own identity, yet they want to belong to a group. They thrive on all-out fun, yet they approach many parts of their life with seriousness and even reverence. Most maintain an inherently rebellious edge, yet they embrace traditional institutions.

These Teen Value Monitor measures provide more than a snapshot of teens' value perceptions at a point in time—they characterize this particular cohort, showing how it differs on fundamental values from its predecessors. It's key to put these layers of teen data and insights together—to view them holistically. It's important for your brand to connect in some relevant way to at least one of these key teen values.

A Sense of Belonging and Acceptance

Many adults view teens as rebellious and non-conforming. If you hold this simple opinion without understanding the nuances surrounding it, you may be at a loss for how to appeal to this group. TRU's research destroys this teen stereotype, revealing how much teens want to be accepted by others. For example, more than twice as many teens say they like being with their family than say they yearn to be more popular.

I recently conducted a series of focus groups for a leading snack-food brand, which has never specifically targeted teens. Brand managers recognized, however, the importance of the teen market and requested research to understand how teens use their product, and what they think and feel about the brand. The research uncovered not only that the product is typically consumed alone at home, but also that teens have warm feelings for the brand based on a positive connection to home and family. I suggested that a potential advertising theme be home—specifically, that this brand can be totally indulged in at home, almost as an escape from the pressures associated with being a teen. One of the senior account people at the brand's advertising agency immediately began to reject this concept, explaining that it goes strongly against her "personal understanding" of what being a teen means. Fortunately, her client persuaded her to keep her mind open to the fact that teens are only stereotypically anti-family. We showed her that teens, in fact, greatly value family and appreciate home as an anchor in their lives. Therefore, connecting to this key value would be not only relevant to teens, it would be distinctively honest in marketing to them. (This concept was recently tested independently as one of several new positionings for the brand; it was found to be overall the strongest of the tested ideas.)

As important as family is to teens, a paramount motivation of teens is their desire to fit in with their peer group. The need to fit in and be accepted is a constant of this lifestage and can be effectively leveraged in advertising. About two out of three teens consider themselves "like most other kids," and a slightly smaller percentage care a lot about whether their clothes are "in style." Nearly half find it so important to fit in that they admit to being influenced by peer pressure.

Today's teens come across as confident and secure: they say things are going well for them and that they will always be successful. They consider themselves normal. More than half even believe others think they're cool. Fewer than one in three express a desire to be more popular.

We believe, however, that this popularity figure is understated. Teens don't often confess to feeling pressured by a quest for popularity. In fact, for most teens, it's more a quest to be accepted. Regardless, this quest leads to stress. So, in part because they're feeling so much stress, the idea of being carefree—of having fun at any cost—is particularly compelling. Yet it's important to recognize that teens are not without inner conflict. They want to fit in, but they don't want to be like everyone else. Of course they also feel tremendously pressured by peer dynamics. In fact, peer influence (whether direct or, as is more common, indirect) is a ceaseless motivator of teen behavior.

It's also risky to view teens as a homogenous group. Not only their lifestyles are markedly different based on demographics, so are some of their attitudes. For example, more girls than boys agree with the statements, "I think I'm pretty normal—most kids I know are pretty much like me" and "I care a lot about whether my clothes are in style." More younger (12-to-15-year-old) than older (16-to-19-year-old) teens think they're normal, care about their clothes being in style, wish they were more popular, and strive to fit in with others. More white than African-American teens admit to feeling peer pressure. More African-American than white teens care about their clothes being in style, say others think they're cool, and that things are going well for them. The oldest teens are the most optimistic. More 18- and 19-year-olds than younger teens agree that things are going well for them and that they will always be successful.

Based on these measures, teens today appear self-assured, confident, and optimistic about their future success. Yet, at the same time, teens continue to struggle with peer issues. As part of this natural identification with the peer group, teens—to a certain extent—want to separate themselves from adults and younger kids. Again, this desire to fit in with peers cannot be underestimated, as it drives so much teen behavior.

Despite being so peer-influenced, teens are fairly well-grounded. More than 70 percent say they like to do things with their family, and more than 60 percent say religion is one of the most important aspects of their life. In fact, these two traditional attitudes are on the rise among teens.

Again, there are demographic differences. More African-American than white teens say religion is one of the most important aspects of their life and that it is important to get involved and help others. More Hispanic than white teens agree with the statement, "I really like to do things with my family," reflecting their greater family orientation. In fact, in some anti-smoking campaigns in which we were involved, the basic messaging strategy for reaching Hispanic teens was that of impact on the family. We tested several advertising positionings for convincing kids not to smoke, from addiction and decreased athletic performance to short-term health consequences and role-modeling. What we learned—in Massachusetts and Arizona—was that the fear of letting parents down in any way was an espe-cially powerful motivator for Latino teens.

It is important to segment teens not only by demographics, but also by lifestyle. TRU's Teen/Types system delineates four groups based on teen social hierarchy (see Chapter 5). These groups are characterized not only by their lifestyles—that is, how and with whom they spend their time—but by attitudes and values. The top teen social group, Influencers, for ex-ample, are the ones most interested in helping others. Yet they are also the most materialistic. They want to be known—to be seen—as being involved. They also care greatly about maintaining their status and, to them, one way of doing so is to buy and wear whatever's currently in teen vogue. Edge teens, on the other hand, are significantly less religious and family-oriented than the general teen population. These are the teens who are most rebellious. Although they represent a relatively small percentage of the total teen audience (less than 20 percent), in many ways it is their ac-tions that adults and advertisers often mistake as being representative of most teens.

It's critical to recognize that teens have a serious side, placing impor-tance on religion, family, and even the greater good of society. Combine that with their desire for fun, and you find that teens of the late 1990s are unusually well balanced. Yet they also have a materialistic side. Nearly half equate success with making a lot of money. And their penchant for materialism has been growing over the last five years, although it still does not approach the level it achieved during the end of the greed-is-good 1980s.

There are significant differences in belonging/acceptance measures by age. The need to belong to a close-knit group is more important to older teens. Younger teens, in contrast, yearn for widespread acceptance. As ado-lescents age, their confidence and sense of self grow. With this growth comes a diminished need to be accepted by everyone and a greater desire to de-velop stronger bonds with fewer people.

One of the attitudes we track quantifies the importance of peer pressure. We ask teens whether they agree or disagree with the statement, "It's important to me to fit in with my friends and other kids I like, and, to be real honest, sometimes their opinions can really influence me." As expected, the youngest teens are most willing to admit they are peer-influenced. Teens aged 12 to 15 give more credence than older teens to the opinions of others. Consequently, their self-image is largely dependent upon how they perceive others seeing them. As teens age, they become less concerned about being popular, fitting in, and wearing what everybody else wears. They begin to develop a stronger sense of confidence in their unique attributes, feelings, and opinions. Nevertheless, a substantial minority of 18- and 19-year-olds also admit to being influenced by peer pressure, showing how powerful and long-lasting peer pressure can be. And, controversial new social theories assert it is these perceptions of peer dynamics that not only color a teen's self-esteem, but also shape how individuals feel about themselves well into adulthood.

We also track a less direct peer pressure statement: "I care a lot about whether my clothes are in style." Not only does this statement indicate how fashion conscious teens are, it is also a measure of independent thinking vs. group pressure. The operative phrase in the statement is "in style," meaning accepted by peers. As with the more direct statement about peer pressure, the youngest teens are most likely to agree with the statement, while the oldest are least likely.

The statement, "I think I'm pretty normal—most kids I know are pretty much like me," is designed to reveal how comfortable teens are with their view of themselves. Typically, if a young person does not feel normal (recognizing that the boundaries of normalcy have expanded in the past few years), they probably feel insecure and lonely.

One of TRU's favorite techniques to use in qualitative concept testing is what we call a Teen/Type match. We ask teens to list the names of the social groups in their school. With great ease, they identify many. We hear the old standards: nerds, jocks, and preps. We also hear labels that are indigenous to certain regions: "ropers" in Texas, "surfers" in California, "granolas" in the Northwest, "white hats" in the Midwest (preppy teen boys who wear white baseball caps). Of course, there are also gang and ethnic-related labels, such as "taggers," "gangbangers," "wacks," "wiggers" (white kids who wish they were black), and "R.I.C.s" (racial identity crisis). We put the list aside and move on to exposure and rational evaluation of the tested concepts. Finally, we return to our list of Teen/Type labels and ask, "OK, which of these groups would like (buy, wear, try, etc.) this new idea?" If the answer is "nerds" or "geeks," there is a big problem with the concept. On the other hand, if the more popular types are the ones perceived to buy into the idea, then the concept has withstood the all-important test of the teen social hierarchy.

Sometimes, for our own curiosity, we ask, "Which of these groups do *you* fit into?" More often than not, teens will tell us, "I don't fit into any of these. I'm just normal!" Teens who feel normal are close enough to the teen mainstream to feel they belong and are accepted. Being normal is a safe and desirable place to be for most teens. Those who don't feel normal fit into one of two camps: 1) those who are uncomfortably (often awkwardly) outside the teenage social mainstream; or 2) the more fortunate ones who think they're too cool, independent, or individualistic to be classified as normal.

Striving for Identity

One of the challenges in marketing to teens is that the age group is marked by contradictory attitudes. Perhaps the most obvious contradiction is that as important as it is for teens to belong to a group and be accepted by others, it's equally important for them to carve out their own identity. Respondents will tell us in one breath, "Hey, I want to fit in, but I don't want to be like everybody else!" These opposing psychological needs drive many teen behaviors.

Although teen responses to our belonging/acceptance measures seem mature and perhaps uncharacteristic of teens, their responses to the stereotypically teen statement, "I always try to have as much fun as I possibly can—I don't know what the future holds and I don't care what others think," are very teenlike. Nearly 70 percent strongly or somewhat agree with this statement. This is a timeless, engaging teen perspective. This attitude uniquely appeals to and is characteristic of this lifestage: embracing the moment with a disregard for consequences. It is perhaps the quintessential teen statement. In fact, this message has been at the heart of several teen-directed campaigns, such as Pepsi's compelling "Be Young. Have Fun. Drink Pepsi" of a few years ago.

Just fewer than one-half of teens consider themselves innovative. The same proportion believe others see them as cool. Those who agree with these statements are boldly confident in their peers' judgment of them.

The oldest teens are most comfortable with who they are. They are no longer trying to prove how "cool" or trendsetting they are. They believe in the Sprite credo of "Image is Nothing." More of the younger teens (aged 12 to 17) have a "play now, pay later" attitude. Nearly half of those under age 18 say they are often the first to try something new and are perceived by others as cool. Girls under age 18 are more likely than boys of the same age to think of themselves as carefree seekers of fun at any cost.

Minority teens are more likely than white teens to say others think they're cool. Sixty-three percent of African-Americans, 54 percent of Hispanics, and 41 percent of whites say others think they're cool. Minority teens' perception that others think they are cool is supported by the fact that many white teens emulate their behavior and fashion.

The Serious Side

As much as teens just want to have fun, there's also a serious side to them. Nearly two out of three say that "it is very important to get involved in things that help others and to help make the world better, even if it's not important to others" their age. This serious attitude, while in contrast to the carefree mindset described above, adds another dimension to today's teens.

Teens in the late 1960s and early 1970s were more consumed with the politics and issues of the times than are teens today. In the 1980s, teens were more driven by material concerns. Today's teens appear to be more balanced, more diverse in their thinking.

Most teens enjoy being with their families, for example. Their traditional values also include religion. More than 60 percent of teens say "religion/faith is one of the most important parts" of their lives. In fact, over the past five years the two values that have experienced the greatest shift are family and religion—both showing an upward trend. So, today's teens are surprisingly traditional, embracing these two key adult institutions. It's easy to get caught up in the data and lose perspective of how teens prioritize these issues. As much as they appear globally concerned, what most excites them is fun. This shows why Pepsi's "have fun now" strategy was so timely and explains why it engaged so many teens. Teens are adventurous, precocious, and naturally rebellious. Although they can envision their future as adults, they feel that future is a far-off place and now is the time to have fun. Although many teens live for their social lives, "having as much fun as I can" is not quite as high a priority in their lives as it was in prior years—dropping four points in five years from the number two to the number four teen value. Aware of the seriousness of AIDS, for example, which is the number-one teen social concern, many of today's teens may have slightly tempered their fun-at-all-costs attitude in favor of more responsible fun.

Great Expectations

At the end of the 1990s, teens appear cautiously confident. Three out of four say "things are really going well" for them and that they will always be successful.

Past TRU surveys have shown that only one in three teens hopes to live the same lifestyle that his or her parents live now. These data can be interpreted in a number of different ways. First, most teens want to live better (i.e., be more affluent) than their parents. Underscoring this interpretation is the fact that teens from lower-income homes are much less likely to say they hope to live a similar lifestyle as their parents. Second, some teens will not agree with this statement because of their own rebelliousness. As one commented, "When I'm my parents' age, I'm gonna make different choices. Even though you'll be an adult, you don't have to act like one."

Based on how teens see their current situation and their future, marketers who portray teen confidence and strength should find their message well received. Understand that teens today are a diverse, well-balanced group. They reveal a serious side—placing importance on traditional values such as religion, family, and helping others—and they want to have a great time! When creating teen-targeted messages, marketers need not fear portraying the divergent sides of this multifaceted group. Teens often reveal many personalities—from staid to self-conscious to silly—and are generally comfortable admitting to this diversity. The best strategy is to portray teens as honestly and realistically as possible, even if it means exposing their more serious side when appropriate.

Chapter 9.

The Essence of Being Teen

Subscribers to TRU's syndicated studies receive not only printed reports and supplemental information throughout the year, they also receive what we call a "Key Findings" presentation. I've come to believe that, to many of our clients, this is the most important part of their subscription. As much as we'd like to think our clients read every word of our reports, we believe—as competition for our clients' reading time increases—a personal presentation of our research is more important than ever.

How does the idea of a 90-minute research presentation sound to you? It's probably not a big turn-on if you're a busy marketer. That's why, after completing one of the more than 100 presentations we deliver each year, we're gratified to hear attendees remark, "I never knew research could be so interesting or useful," or "That was the most fun I've ever had during a presentation!"

We work hard to make our presentations lively, interactive, and anecdotally rich to keep our clients focused during the 90 minutes—and, of course, to keep them coming back for more. But the secret of our success is really quite simple. It's the content! I strongly believe there is no other demographic segment as interesting to adults as teens. In fact, our "Key Findings" presentation generally follows the table of contents of this book, presenting the latest findings and insights on teen demographics, buying, media, activities, trends, and attitudes. But it is the final section that is the most fun to present—and the most well received by our clients. We call it "The Essence of Being Teen," because it includes an ever-evolving battery of questions that measure attitudes that are uniquely teen. Understanding teens at an intimate level—being able to recognize the nuances that hit the strongest chords—can spell the difference between developing products, promotions, and advertising that teens can identify with and coming up with campaigns they ignore.

The Meaning of Cool

As much as teens discount the importance of being cool, it remains the most deeply entrenched teen motivation. But realistically, it is not cool for teens to say, "Hey, I buy that product because it's cool."

What Makes a Person Your Age Cool?

A sense of humor and good looks are the main attributes of cool, according to teens.

(percent of teens citing attribute as one that makes a person cool, 1997)

Funny	49%
Good looking	49
Outgoing personality	45
Has lots of friends	38
Popular with opposite sex	34
Smart	28
Good athlete	26
How they dress	25
Independent	20
Big partier	17
Owns cool stuff	13
Rebellious	8

Source: TRU *Teenage Marketing & Lifestyle Study*

The teenage needs of belonging and acceptance are the psychological underpinnings for their striving to be cool. Since being cool is rooted in these deep needs, it can be teens' overriding motivation, driving many of their behaviors—from socializing to purchasing. And it is a timeless need. Although the trappings of cool often change, the teen desire to be cool is timeless.

How teens determine who is cool reveals their innermost motivations, insecurities, and peer values. By recognizing the importance of cool as a working concept and knowing how teens define cool, you can choose talent and portray teens and young adults more effectively in advertising. By showing cool teens using your brand (or by showing cool activities, places, brands, attitudes, etc.), you can benefit from a halo effect.

Several years ago, we set out to define cool from a teenage perspective. We started qualitatively, talking to teens one-on-one and in focus groups. We found that cool means different things to different teens, but that it was universally regarded as being incredibly important. From our qualitative research, we compiled a list of attributes that some teens equate with cool. Then we asked respondents in our quantitative study this question: "Think about somebody your age who's considered very cool. What makes that person so cool?"

If you remember your teenage years, then you probably know the answer to this question. Although teen preferences and lifestyles change over time, the importance to teens of being good looking has not changed. This finding is good news for the marketers of health and beauty aids. The motivation to look good is as strong as ever, and it's not only central to the way teens feel about themselves, it's also a key factor driving teen consumer behavior.

In high school, you can get by almost on looks alone, according to our data. I've talked to many adults who reminisce about the best-looking girl or boy in high school (also usually the most popular) who hasn't achieved much since then (typically to their delight!).

Personality also plays a large role in coolness ratings. In fact, the quality of "being funny" now ranks as high as being good looking. Humor is key in teen life. Teens' favorite TV shows typically are sitcoms, and their favorite commercials are usually characterized by humor. Teens who are able to make their peers laugh are thought of as being not only entertaining, but also cool. Teens also place weight on gregariousness—being outgoing is the third-most important personality trait to teens.

The attributes teens most use to describe their cool peers are interrelated. The fourth-most popular response, for example, is "has lots of friends." Teens who have lots of friends are typically outgoing and often good looking. So, if a teen possesses one or two of the top cool attributes, chances are he or she will also embody several other attributes.

Good looks has always been one of the most important attributes of coolness, but other attributes have waxed and waned over the years. Being independent, a partier, and rebellious probably would have ranked much higher 20 years ago. Today, only 8 percent of teens cite being rebellious as an attribute of coolness, probably because there is less for teens to rebel against these days. Teens feel the generation gap with their parents less than previous teen cohorts did, and they do not feel alienated from society. In fact, "system" and "society" are words we seldom hear teens use these days. Finally, it's more challenging to be rebellious in our almost-anything-goes society. Teens tell us it is tough to push the limits these days because there are none.

In contrast, teens 20 years ago probably would have considered the attribute of "being a good dresser" superficial. It certainly would have ranked below being independent and being rebellious. But today, personal style is important to teens.

Boys and girls place different priorities on some attributes of coolness. Boys are more likely to think a cool person is defined by traditional macho attributes such as being popular with girls and being a good athlete. Girls are more likely to define coolness by outward appearance and personality traits: being good looking, outgoing, and fashionable. As teens age, their definition of cool matures. Eighteen- and 19-year-olds place greater importance on being smart, outgoing, and funny than younger teens. Younger teens, struggling to fit in, define coolness more by outward appearance: being good looking, having lots of friends, being popular with the opposite sex, being a good athlete, and being fashionable.

Teens' top-five coolness attributes have remained constant over the past few years (although the rank order has changed slightly). This stability affords marketers some comfort in knowing how teens define cool and how best to portray a cool teenager in advertising. But be careful: talents' physical appearance is of great importance. Actors should be good looking, but realistically so. Teens often complain about talent in advertising being too perfect, too different from kids they know. Additionally, actors should exude personality—humor and gregariousness—because teens' definition of cool is multifaceted.

Teens and Age Aspiration

The more you talk to teens and analyze their behaviors and attitudes, the more you begin to understand that they live a step or two ahead of where they really are. They are constantly thinking about their immediate future— usually from a social perspective. Because they are surrounded by older teens, they see the benefits of being older.

A few years ago I attended a youth-marketing conference at which a speaker discussed the issue of teen age aspiration. The speaker explained that young teens want to be 16, while 16-year-olds want to be 18, and 18-year-olds want to be 21. At the time, I believed this to be an accurate representation of what most adults (i.e., most marketers) thought about the issue. After the speaker's presentation, I asked her where she got her data, since it was an issue we were exploring at TRU. Her findings, she said, were based on her observations and on talking informally with kids—the same qualitative sources we had been relying on.

Age Aspiration

The youngest teens wish they could skip most of their teen years, aspiring to be age 17.

(actual age of teens and age teens wish to be, 1996)

Actual age	aspired age
12	17
13	17
14	18
15	18
16	18
17	19
18	19
19	20

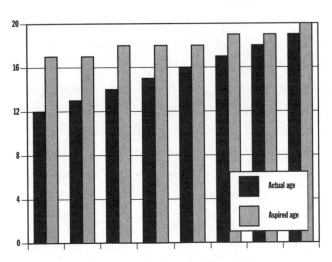

Source: TRU *Teenage Marketing & Lifestyle Study*

By happenstance, we were preparing to send the questionnaire for our semiannual syndicated study to the printer the next day. We were able to squeeze in one final question, which I penned while at the conference, "If you could be any age right now, what age would you be?"

The results show the question was well worth asking. On average, 12-year-olds want to be much older—16 or 17. They literally want to skip most of their teen years! Although perhaps startling, this finding makes sense. The youngest teens watch their older brothers and sisters, the kids ahead of them in school, the older kids in the neighborhood, and older teens in TV and movies (typically portrayed by twentysomethings!). As they watch, they think, "Wow, they're having more fun than me. They're driving, dating, and their faces are even clearing up!"

By the time teens reach age 18 or 19, they're thinking, "Hey, I have it pretty good right now. Not a lot of responsibility, but a lot of independence. I think I'd like to be just a year or two older." Older teens are in no particular hurry to enter the adult world of serious responsibilities. They're pleased with the balance they have achieved between adult freedoms and teen fun.

The gap in teens' actual age and the age they aspire to be shrinks as they get older. The youngest teens (12-to-15-year-olds) aspire to be three to five years older than they are. They are less content with their current life stage and love to imagine themselves as being older, actually longing for the aging process to accelerate. Younger teens look forward to the independence and greater variety of activities that come with maturity, such as driving, dating, working, going to college, and moving out. Older teens are more content with their current age, enjoying all the things younger teens yearn to do.

The message to marketers is one of strategic convenience: Err older. In positioning a product or brand, aim high in the tone of your message and the talent you choose to portray it. Talk to older teens, since younger ones aspire to their level. By doing so, you can narrow what is an overly broad audience. Just make sure the kids at the young end of the target get your message.

These findings can also guide you in deciding upon the age of the actors to use in teen-directed advertising. If your target is 12-to-15-year-olds, consider using 17-year-old actors. You'll grab the youngest teens because they aspire to be as old as the actor. At the same time, the ads will still appeal to 16- and 17-year-olds because they will identify with people their own age, allowing you to appeal to a broader age target.

What Teens Like about Being Teen

Despite all the pressures, obstacles, and stresses teens face today, out studies show that most teens enjoy their lifestage. We asked our teen sample this question: "Do you like being a teenager?" Nine out of 10 said "yes."

Despite such a high rating, teens, of course, are not trouble-free. Not surprisingly, the oldest teens are somewhat less satisfied with being a teenager than their younger counterparts. The older teens are ready to move on; they've been teens long enough. Some are troubled with and tired of adult stereotypes of teenagers. They await the greater independence associated with being adult.

We also asked our respondents what they like about being teens. Reflecting the importance of social relationships in their lives, teens cite close friends and having a boyfriend/girlfriend as what they most like about being teens. Other findings from TRU research confirm the paramount importance of friends to teens.

"Friends are the best part [about being a teen]. We always have a great time together and they're there when you can't talk to your parents," said one 14-year-old girl.

"Freedom" and "partying" rank second and third among the best facets of being a teen. Both involve social interaction. Teens enjoy the free-

What Teens Like
about Being Teens

Friendships are what teens like most about being teens.

(percent of teens citing factor as what they like about being teen, 1993)

Close friends	32%
Boyfriend/girlfriend	25
Freedom	24
Partying	24
Not getting caught	19
Able to drive	17
No adult responsibility	14
Dating	14
School events	13
Going to school	9
Few worries	8
Few expectations	6

Source: TRU *Teenage Marketing & Lifestyle Study*

What Teens Like about Being Teens, by Gender

Both boys and girls say friends are what they like most about being teens, but boys rank freedom second while boyfriends rank second for girls.

(percent of teens citing factor as what they like most about being a teen, by gender, 1993)

Boys

Close friends	28%
Freedom	26
Partying	25
Having girlfriend	22
Able to drive	19

Girls

Close friends	36
Having boyfriend	29
Partying	23
Freedom	22
Not getting caught	21

Source: TRU *Teenage Marketing & Lifestyle Study*

dom to be with friends, away from their family. They especially like to party with friends. (Of course, partying means different things to different teens.)

"The greatest thing is that we're old enough to do a lot of things while not having adult responsibilities to worry about," said a 16-year-old boy.

"Being able to do what you want is great; adults can't act stupid like teens can," commented a 15-year-old girl.

"Being a teen is great because you're able to have fun, be with friends, party without having to worry about much," said a 16-year-old girl.

Nearly 20 percent of teens say their favorite part of being a teen is "doing things you're not supposed to and not getting caught." Younger teens are slightly more rebellious in this way than their older counterparts: 22 percent of 12-to-15-year-olds agree with the statement versus 18 percent of 16-to-19-year-olds. Perhaps because older teens have been getting away with things for a few years, the thought of breaking the rules is no longer as exciting as it once was. Younger teens, on the other hand, are still in the early stages of pushing the limits. Most are thriving on it.

To some teens, partying is synonymous with "doing things you're not supposed to do." Thirty-seven percent of teens cite one of these responses, revealing how appealing it is to teens to do things their parents may frown upon.

"Being a teen is great because you can do whatever you want and not get caught," said a 15-year-old boy.

"I like being able to fool around, being lazy and free, and doing things behind my parents' backs and not getting caught," said a 16-year-old girl.

There are significant gender differences on this measure. Girls are more likely than boys to cite "close friends" and "not getting caught" as the best aspect of being a teen. Boys are more likely to cite "being able to drive."

These likes also vary by age. More younger (12-to-15-year-olds) than older (16-to-19-year-olds) teens cite "dating" and "not getting caught." Teens aged 16 and 17 are most likely to name "driving" or "not having adult responsibilities." These teens have just gotten their driver's licenses and are enjoying greater freedom and independence. They are also beginning to recognize the responsibilities that come with adulthood and have a greater appreciation of their relatively carefree lifestyle. Significantly more 18- and 19-year-olds than 12-to-17-year-olds mention "freedom" as what they most like about being a teen. Many of these young adults are on their own for the first time, either at college or in the work force.

What Teens Dislike about Being Teens

TRU also asks respondents what they dislike about being teen. By understanding what teens (and teen segments) dislike most about their current life stage, marketers can offer solutions and empathy for the problems teens face.

When asked, "What do you most dislike about being a teenager?" more teens name "peer pressure" than anything else.

"Peer pressure. . .because you don't act yourself. You try to be someone you're not just to try to please someone else," said a 17-year-old girl in a focus group.

"Peer pressure. Almost every teenager is pressured into alcohol, drugs, sex, etcetera. Many people want to try to fit in, and they will ruin their life to fit in," said a 14-year-old girl.

"Trying to resist peer pressure. If there wasn't so much pressure, many teens would make it through life a lot easier," commented an 18-year-old girl.

"Peer pressure makes you go against your beliefs sometimes. It's really hard to say 'no' when you want to fit in so bad," said a 15-year-old boy.

What Teens Dislike
about Being Teens

Peer pressure is the number-one factor teens hate about being teen.

(percent of teens citing factor as what they dislike about being a teen, 1993)

Peer pressure	33%
Not taken seriously	23
Not enough money	21
Age restrictions	19
Parent pressures	19
Lack of respect	17
Grades	15
Curfew	14
Going to school	13
Parent hassles	12
Physical changes	11
Worrying about fitting in	11
Standardized tests	9
Too much responsibility	7
Trends changing fast	6
Treated badly at stores	5

Source: TRU *Teenage Marketing & Lifestyle Study*

"There's a lot of peer pressure; there are always people trying to change you and make you fit in with them, especially about joining a gang," said a 16-year-old boy.

"It's really hard sometimes being a teen because you're constantly being judged by what you do, wear, or what type of music you listen to," complained a 14-year-old girl.

Peer pressure is omnipresent, motivating, and punishing. It affects teen decisions far beyond the brand of jeans they wear or what friends they choose. It influences teen involvement in sex, drinking, drugs, and gangs. Younger teens are most affected by peer pressure. Older teens, who have more experience with peer pressure, cope with it more easily. Yet even the oldest teens admit to being affected by it.

The second most common complaint about being a teen is not being taken seriously. Significantly more older teens (18- and 19-year-olds) cite this than do younger teens. Twenty-seven percent of 18- and 19-year-olds say the worst part of being a teen is age restrictions. Our qualitative research has found that older teens often feel frustrated with their in-between status. They believe themselves to be mature and responsible—sometimes more mature than the adults around them.

"I can tell you when I drink with my friends, I'm a lot more responsible than some of my parents' friends," said an 18-year-old boy.

"The worst part about being teen is not being old enough to do some things, but being old enough to do others. It's difficult to figure out what we can and can't do," said a 15-year-old boy.

"It's tough dealing with the transition from child to adult. You're not really accepted by the adult community because you're not old enough, but you're too old to act like a child. Sometimes it's really frustrating," complained a 15-year-old girl.

The third-ranking teen dislike is a universal problem: not having enough money. To many teens, money can spell the difference between being a participant and being left out. Many teens, especially younger ones, rely almost exclusively on allowances and parental handouts for spending money. Although most of teens' income is discretionary, many feel pressure to keep up with the latest fashion and entertainment trends, which can be expensive. Money is an important part of teens' social lives. As teens have told us, "not having the funds" can seriously hamper their romantic aspirations.

Teens feel pressure not only from peers but also from parents. Nineteen percent name "pressure from parents" as one of the things they most dislike about being a teenager.

"Having your parents always telling you what to do," is how one 13-year-old boy put it.

A 19-year-old girl explained that she disliked "the pressure from parents to act older and mature. But at the same time, they treat you like a little kid."

"Parents are always trying to get you to be what they want you to be rather than what you want to be," said a 17-year-old boy.

Separately, another 12 percent complain about "parent hassles." Overall, 26 percent of teens name either parent pressure or parent hassles. Although the generation gap is narrower today than a generation ago, teens and parents still struggle to get along.

"Parents expect you to read their minds! They want you to do something, but they don't tell you to do it. Then, they yell at you for not doing it!" said a 15-year-old girl.

"Parents are a hassle. They're too pushy, overprotective, bossy, nosy, and they don't let you do anything," said a 16-year-old girl.

"It's really hard trying to get parents to understand why you do things. They always say, 'We never did that when we were your age.' It's like, who cares?" said a 13-year-old girl.

"Parents—you can't live with them, you can't live without them!" exclaimed a 15-year-old boy.

"The toughest thing about being teen is what you look like because no guy wants to go out with an ugly girl and no girl wants to be around an unpopular girl," said a 12-year-old girl.

"It's hard going through all of these physical changes, like acne and reaching 'maturity,'" complained another 12-year-old girl.

"School is tough. There's so much to worry about, like grades, home-work, and tests. And, you have to get past [school] in order to do anything else," said a 14-year-old boy.

Are Teens Happy?

Teens have a positive outlook on life. They are happy, having fun, and not afraid to admit it. Teen life does not come without a price, however—two-thirds admit to being bored some or most of the time, and more than 40 percent say they have been depressed.

Teens are evenly split about whether they are having fun "most" or just "some" of the time. Only 5 percent say they rarely or never have fun. The teens who answered "most of the time" are evidently finding pleasure in all three facets of their lives: home, school, and free time (see Chapter 10 on the three parts of a teen's world).

Teen life is fast-paced and multifaceted enough to keep them inter-ested most of the time. Although more than half say they are bored some of the time and another 14 percent are bored most of the time, nearly one-third say they are rarely or never bored.

Just over 40 percent of teens admit to feeling depressed most or some of the time. While these teens are not relying on a clinical definition of depression, they evidently distinguish being depressed from being bored. Because teen life is marked by constant change—physiological, emotional,

Are Teens Happy?

The majority of teens, 55 percent, say they are happy most of the time.

(percent of teens saying they experience feeling most or some of the time, 1996)

	most of the time	some of the time
Having fun	48%	45%
Happy	55	37
Bored	14	52
Depressed	7	34

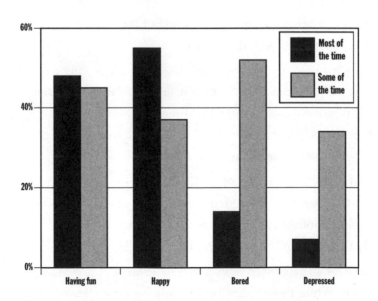

Source: TRU *Teenage Marketing & Lifestyle Study*

and intellectual—it is no surprise that teens react to this change by feeling depressed at times. In fact, only 12 percent say they are never depressed.

According to these data, the older teens are, the harder it is to have fun. Significantly more of the youngest teens (12-to-15-year-olds) than either the middle (16- and 17-year-olds) or oldest teens (aged 18- and 19-year-olds) say they have fun most of the time. That fact that more pre-driving, pre-dating teens say they are having fun indicates, perhaps, their simpler definition of fun. More attainable, everyday pleasures add up to fun for the youngest teens, while older ones are more difficult to please. What's particularly revealing is that significantly more of the youngest teens admit to being bored. The increased independence of age, while not necessarily making life more fun, does make it less boring.

Girls' greater emotional peaks and valleys are evident in our data. Significantly more females than males say they are happy most or some of the time, and more say they are depressed most or some of the time.

It is important to recognize that teens are extremely emotional. They are in a constant state of change which leaves them feeling unsettled and, at times, powerless. Advertising that depicts or appeals to a variety of teenagers' emotions is likely to be seen as accurate and relevant. Few teens are always happy or always depressed, but most are bored at least some of the time. Boredom—or complaining about being bored—seems to be a natural part of this life stage. Products, services, and messages that combat boredom may be especially welcomed by teens.

Teen Expectations and Hopes

TRU regularly asks teens about their hopes and expectations to gain insight into what teens feel about the future. The results give marketers the opportunity to talk to teens about their dreams, communicating with them in a relevant and compelling way. Our studies show that teens *expect* to have a traditional adult life (own a home, marry, have a successful career,

Teen Hopes and Expectations

While teens hope for fame and fortune, they expect more mundane things like homeownership, marriage, and children.

(percent of teens citing whether they hope or expect event will occur in their adult life, 1997)

	expect	hope
Owning a home	85%	35%
Going to college	82	32
Having a successful career	72	48
Getting married	72	41
Having children	65	41
Earning a lot of money	52	61
Owning a nice car	51	54
Travel the world	25	70
Become famous	15	65

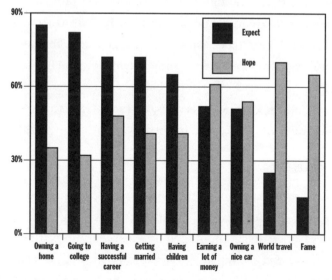

Source: TRU *Teenage Marketing & Lifestyle Study*

have children), but they *hope* for a more glamorous lifestyle, marked by wealth, travel, and fame.

What teens are most likely to expect in their adult lives they least hope for, and what they most hope for is what they least expect. Teens envision leading the same adult lifestyle as their parents. They expect to marry, have children, and buy a home. Not only do teens think owning a home is the norm (without fully understanding what buying a home entails), they are also optimistic (perhaps, naively so) about their financial ability to buy a home in the future.

A majority of teens *expect* to marry and have children, but few *hope* to marry and have children. At this stage in their lives, as they struggle with their parents, they can't relate to the idea of having their own family someday. Yet, they expect to follow society's norm of marrying and having children.

Teens are not the disenchanted, pessimistic youths so often portrayed in the media. Our data, in fact, paint an altogether different picture. Young people believe they will someday live the American Dream, and they hope for an enchanted future. Although teens don't necessarily expect to attain many of the materialistic trappings of success, they hope to attain them. Frequently seeing extravagant lifestyles portrayed in television, movies, and—for some—their own communities, makes attaining such a lifestyle that much more alluring.

Teens' confidence in their future ability to purchase a home is strong—nearly 9 out of 10 expect to own a home someday. A sizable number don't feel they will ever become parents, however. Seventy-two percent of teens expect to marry, yet only 65 percent expect to have children. Fewer than half hope to marry or have children. Similarly, more teens expect they will marry than actually hope to do so. Evidently, some perceive marriage to be more of "what I'm supposed to do" rather than one "what I want to do."

Nearly two-thirds of teens hope to become famous, yet only 15 percent expect to achieve fame.

In marketing to teens, it is critically important to avoid portraying their future as offering no more than typical adult fare, such as jobs, marriage and children. Marriage, parenthood, and homeownership are too mundane and too distant to appeal to teens who dream of excitement and glamour. Teens will respond favorably to advertising that offers them the opportunity to realize their hopes, rather than simply meet their expectations.

Since teens want advertising to be real, it's important for marketers to strike a balance when using hopes and expectations as themes. Clearly, hopes are more alluring, exciting, and aspirational. Yet, if teens find a situation portrayed in advertising to be completely unbelievable or unattainable, they may reject it. Teens respond to ads and products that reach for some of their hopes, that are both aspirational *and* believable.

A few years ago I conducted some one-on-one interviews with male high school athletes to see their reaction to a new advertising campaign for a major athletic footwear company. Two of the boys not only told me that someday they would appear in these commercials as NBA stars, they genuinely believed it! You would think teens could recognize that the odds against achieving sports celebrity are astronomical. But they want to believe in it. Creating advertising that balances what teens long for with what they find believable is an ongoing challenge in marketing to teens.

What Teens Look Forward To

While it is important to understand what teens think about their future as adults, it's also important to know what they're looking forward to in the near future.

In focus groups, we asked teens to list events, occasions, or situations that they were looking forward to experiencing. We then asked our na-

What Teens Most Look Forward To

Teens most anticipate events that will occur in their immediate future.

(percent of teens citing event as something they look forward to, 1993)

Graduating	29%
Summer	24
Driver's license	23
College	21
Job	18
College acceptance	16
Vacation/travel	16
Starting career	15
More freedom	14
Moving out	13
Prom	9
Athletic event	8
Weekends	8
Adult responsibility	6
Fraternity/sorority	2

Source: TRU *Teenage Marketing & Lifestyle Study*

What Teens Most Look Forward To, by Age

The youngest teens are most looking forward to getting a driver's license, while the oldest teens eagerly anticipate starting a career and going to college.

(percent of teens citing event as something they look forward to, by age, 1993)

	age		
	12 to 15	16 and 17	18 and 19
Graduating	30%	40%	17%
Summer	27	25	18
Driver's license	35	16	3
Going to college	16	25	26
Getting a job	20	17	16
College acceptance	19	21	4
Vacation/travel	18	11	16
Starting career	11	11	27
More freedom	16	15	9
Moving out	9	12	20

Source: TRU *Teenage Marketing & Lifestyle Study*

tional sample of teenagers to select the one or two things from the list of 15 that they most eagerly anticipated doing.

Graduation is the most frequently cited event, followed by summer, getting a driver's license, going to college, and getting a job. Teens are most excited about milestones in their immediate future because it is easier for them to visualize them. Therefore, it is essential to examine these data by age group. Fourteen-year-olds look forward to different events than 19-year-olds.

Unlike the age-aspiration measure, which varies little by age, the results of this measure are not as convenient for marketing applications. Clearly, teens are short-term thinkers. The closer in age a teenager is to a specific event or milestone, the more eagerly he or she awaits the event. The results of this measure, shown in the table on page 222, reveal the relevant events and lifestage experiences that can be incorporated into advertising or promotions to appeal to each teenage segment. The event most imminent in the target segment's life is likely to prove the most motivating.

Adults' Biggest Misconceptions about Teens

Teens commonly complain that parents "just don't understand us." Adults think they are all alike, teens say, relying on stereotypes to describe them. Although parents can survive a guilty verdict on this measure, advertisers cannot.

Through a series of focus groups with TRU's panel of Influencers, we crafted a list of 14 adult misconceptions about teens, according to teens. Then we quantified the list in our large national study.

According to teens, the biggest misconception adults have about people their age is that they are not mature enough to handle responsibility. Interestingly, 19-year-olds are just as likely as 12-year-olds to feel this way. This finding underscores how important it is for teens to believe ad-

Biggest Adult
Misconceptions about Teens

Most teens say the biggest adult misconception about them is that they are not mature enough to handle responsibility.

(percent of teens citing factor as a big adult misconception about teens, 1994)

Not mature enough	52%
Cause trouble	47
Lazy	35
No problems/worries	29
Take drugs	25
Not intelligent	24
Lack commitment	23
Watch too much TV	22
Don't strive	22
Sexually active	21
Bad drivers	21
Unconcerned about world	20
In gangs	19
Drink alcohol	16

Source: TRU *Teenage Marketing & Lifestyle Study*

Biggest Adult Misconceptions about Teens, by Gender

Teen boys cite drug-taking as one of the top-five adult misconceptions about them, while teen girls cite being sexually active.

(percent of teens citing factor as a big adult misconception about teens, by gender, 1994)

Boys

Cause trouble	52%
Not mature enough to handle responsibility	49
Lazy	37
Take drugs	28
No problems/worries	27

Girls

Not mature enough to handle responsibility	56
Cause trouble	43
Lazy	34
No problems/worries	32
Sexually active	24

Source: TRU *Teenage Marketing & Lifestyle Study*

vertisers respect their intelligence, or, to put it in teen vernacular, that companies do not "dis" them.

"One of the worst parts about being teen is having people think you're not mature or responsible enough to do things when you know you can," said a 14-year-old girl.

Many teens resent the fact that adults view teens as troublemakers. In focus groups, teens complain about the small but vocal minority of people their age who cause adults to write off the entire age group.

"There's a few troublemakers in school who give all of us a bad name," said a 15-year-old girl.

"You are always getting compared to the negative statistics of teens, and it puts a limit on your privileges," commented a 14-year-old girl.

"The toughest thing about being teen is making adults understand that all teens are not alike. We're not all under a bad influence," said a 19-year-old.

"Since most adults think all teens are on drugs and in gangs, they don't give credit to those teens who are doing their best to stay away from that stuff," said a 17-year-old boy.

Being perceived as immature and causing trouble are not the only stereotypes that teens find troubling. Teens rank being lazy as the third-biggest misconception, followed by not having problems or worries. None of the top four misconceptions focus on a specific behavior (such as taking drugs or drinking alcohol). Perhaps these general stereotypes are most bothersome to teens because they are the hardest to disprove. Someone either does or does not do drugs, but it's much more difficult to combat the image of immaturity, irresponsibility, or laziness.

"I hate it when adults stereotype all teens as being lazy and troublemakers," complained a 16-year-old girl.

"Adults think teens don't have problems and worries but we do.

There's a lot of pressure to fit in and we worry about getting into a good school and our futures," said a 17-year-old boy.

Not surprisingly, there are some gender differences worth noting on the misconception measure. Four of the top five misconceptions are cited by both boys and girls. But more boys than girls think adults assume teens take drugs, while more girls than boys believe adults assume teens are sexually active. Significantly more younger than older teens feel that adults assume teens cause trouble, are lazy, and watch too much TV. Conversely, more older teens say adults assume teens don't have problems and that they lack commitment.

Significantly more minority teens than white teens say taking drugs, causing trouble, and being in gangs are adult misconceptions. Significantly more white teens, on the other hand, say adults believe teens watch too much TV and are not mature enough to handle responsibility.

Biggest Everyday Worries

According to teens, one of the biggest adult misconceptions about them is that they don't have problems or worries. But teens worry a lot. They worry about everything from grades and planning their future to performing well in sports and wearing the right clothes. These worries can be leveraged in advertising to teens. Although teens will tell you that they care about issues like AIDS or saving the earth, they are motivated more by how they look and whether they have cash in their pocket. When we quantified teens' everyday worries, here's what we found.

Girls are bigger worriers than boys—they are more concerned about five of the top-six worries than are boys. While girls worry about everything from how they look to what people think about them, boys worry more than girls only about having enough money.

Everyday worries differ significantly by age. Eighteen- and 19-year-olds are primarily concerned with "having enough money" and "planning

Biggest Everyday Worries of Teens

Teens biggest worry is grades, but money and looks are close behind.

(percent of teens citing factor as a big worry, 1993)

Grades	52%
Having enough money	48
How you look	47
Planning your future	38
Getting along with parents	30
Being talked about behind your back	27
Having a boyfriend/girlfriend	25
Getting into college	25
Doing well at sports	22
Wearing the right clothes	14
Having a couple of really close friends	13
Having lots of friends	12
Being sexually active	11
Unplanned pregnancy	10
Being able to drive	10
Getting a date	10
Gangs	9
Being considered cool	9
Getting into trouble with authorities	8

Source: TRU *Teenage Marketing & Lifestyle Study*

your future." All other worries seem relatively unimportant to the oldest teens. "Grades" is the number-one concern among younger teens, especially 12-to-17-year-olds, a finding consistent with the fact that 55 percent of teens say studying is "in." (Eighteen- and 19-year-olds are less concerned with grades because 20 percent of them are not in school.)

"If you don't get good grades now, it will affect the rest of your life," explained a 17-year-old boy.

Don't be misled by this finding. Just because grades are the biggest teen worry doesn't mean most teens are constantly striving for academic excellence. There are other reasons why grades are such a big concern, from being grounded by parents to being ruled ineligible to play on sports teams because of low grades. Not making good grades can really cramp a teen's style.

Grades are also key because they are the single quantification of a student's progress—a measure with emotional, social, intellectual, and achievement ramifications. If you have ever awakened in the middle of the night in a cold sweat over a nightmare in which you failed to study for your high school history final, it shouldn't be difficult to understand this pressure on teens. It can totally consume them.

"Man, if it weren't for grades, I'd like to stay a student forever," said a 15-year-old boy.

"Grades are like a constant gun pointed at your head," said a 14-year-old girl.

After grades, the youngest teens are most concerned with how they look (53 percent), particularly 12-to-15-year-old girls (63 percent). Girls in this age group are 17 percentage points more likely than 16-to-17-year-old girls and 26 percentage points more likely than 18-to-19-year-old girls to say "how you look" is one of their biggest everyday worries. This finding is consistent with our Teen Value Monitor measure showing that girls aged 12 to 15 are the most insecure about how others perceive them.

Biggest Everyday Worries
of Teens, by Gender

Boys' biggest worries are grades and money,
while girls worry most about looks and grades.

(percent of teens citing factor as a big worry, by gender, 1993)

	boys	girls
Grades	50%	54%
Having enough money	50	45
How you look	37	58
Planning your future	36	40
Getting along with parents	25	36
Being talked about behind your back	24	30

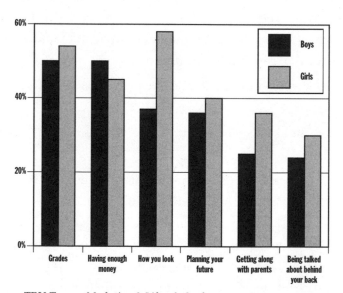

Source: TRU *Teenage Marketing & Lifestyle Study*

Biggest Everyday Worries of Teens, by Age

Teens aged 12 to 17 are most worried about grades, while older teens worry most about money.

(percent of teens citing factor as a big worry, by age, 1993)

12 to 15

Grades	57%
How you look	53
Having enough money	39
Being talked about behind your back	34
Getting along with parents	32

16 and 17

Grades	55
Having enough money	48
Planning your future	47
How you look	43
Getting into college	39

18 and 19

Having enough money	66
Planning your future	63
How you look	39
Grades	37
Getting along with parents	26

Source: TRU *Teenage Marketing & Lifestyle Study*

Another big worry for the youngest teens is "people talking about you behind your back." In fact, this is the third-biggest worry for 12-to-15-year-old girls, and it is anything but new to teens. Generations of teenagers have shared the same concern, and it's connected to a certain stage of maturation. Teens who are going through puberty, or who recently went though puberty, are most concerned about being talked about.

This concern offers some potent leverage for advertisers, particularly those with products that can aid teens during this physiological transition. Teens buy the acne treatment they think will most effectively prevent or eliminate acne. They buy the brands of clothing that are most accepted by their peer group. Once teens find products they trust, they are hesitant to abandon them for others. Since teens are consumed with concern about their physical appearance, if you can offer teens improved or no-risk looks, you're sure to strike a responsive chord.

"One big worry for teens is what other people think of you. If someone who is popular says something bad about you, everyone starts talking about you," said a 12-year-old girl.

"There's a lot of pressure about who your friends are because if they're not really your friends, they'll talk about you behind your back," said a 15-year-old boy.

A few years ago Clearasil ran a highly successful campaign, leveraging the teen fear of being talked about behind one's back with the even bigger worry of how one looks. One TV spot showed a girl holding up a white sheet with red polka dots asking her friends, "Whose face does this remind you of?" She and her friends replied in unison by yelling out the unfortunate boy's name. Naturally, in the course of 30 seconds the boy's face cleared up and he even got the girl! When we asked teens about this spot, many said it was mean. In the same breath, however, they said it was real. The campaign evolved with less harsh executions, which kept the advertising fresh and effective.

When marketers think about teens, they often think about the fads and trends that so permeate teen lives. It's easy to get caught up in this, because teens do so as well. Teens probably are more invested in trends—especially those involving fashion, music, and language—than any other population segment. Most of TRU's competitors, in fact, concentrate specifically on this area. It is an important one, and difficult to track (let alone predict). While we gather quantitative data every six months on what's in and what's out and are doing ongoing qualitative research on this topic, our focus has always been on the greater, psychological motivations and behaviors that characterize teen lives and offer the greatest opportunities to marketers. Still, we make a concerted effort to keep our clients attuned to the latest and greatest in teen life. But we view this as a joint responsibility. We advise our clients what to read, listen to, watch, and observe to immerse themselves in teen culture. We also maintain an ongoing list of the teen media clients should pay attention to, including not only teens' favorite TV shows, magazines, and music, but also Web sites, catalogs, events, retailers, and venues. The fact is, if you are committed to keeping up with teens, you must not only read about them, but also read what *they* read, watch what *they* watch, and go where *they* go.

To get a teen perspective on keeping up with trends, we asked our teen sample to identify the trend sources that are important to them. Not surprisingly, the data show teens—especially girls—readily take cues about fashion and style from the people and media around them. Although most teens claim they rely on themselves for fashion ideas, it's really only Influencers and Edge teens for whom this is true. While Influencers are quick to adopt whatever's new, typically they are not quite experimental enough to start trends. They are more the broadcasters of trends. Once the mainstream teens (Conformers, followed by Passives) see that Influencers wear or do something new, it becomes safe to adopt that style or behavior.

Most teens—including Influencers, Conformers, and Passives, who collectively make up more than 83 percent of the teen population—are trend-involved. Most teens actively seek out cues for what's the latest and greatest. Few are self-confident enough to truly rely on themselves. The data show, however, that teens *want* to think this is true of themselves.

After themselves, teens of both genders name friends as the biggest source of fashion ideas. In fact, 72 percent get fashion cues from other people—friends, older siblings, cool kids, older kids, or people on the street. Additionally, 38 percent get cues from celebrities—music videos, movie stars, music stars, pro athletes, models, TV stars, and TV commercials. Finally, 55 percent get cues from media or merchandising sources—magazines, catalogs, and stores.

Although more fashion retailers are developing Web sites to showcase their merchandise in an interactive format, fewer than 2 percent of teens currently say they get fashion ideas from the Internet.

The number of teens who claim they set fashion trends is striking, especially in the face of data showing just the opposite. Teens want to feel they are in control when it comes to fashion and style. Marketing messages that appeal to this desire, stressing (to the masses) the importance of individual style, will resonate with teens. This is one of the reasons why Old Navy has been so successful in marketing to teens. Where else can you choose among tens of colors of the same stylish T-shirt. The idea is customization—allowing teens to customize themselves within the norm of what's acceptable and popular.

The list of the most important sources teens go to for trends suggests that fashion marketers should consider increasing their presence in magazines and catalogs. They should also recognize the strength of stores themselves, from layout to point-of-purchase information and knowledgeable sales people to whom teens can relate. Finally, understanding that many youth fashion trends originate with (or, at least, are broadcast by) urban

Where Teens Get Ideas about What to Wear

Most teens say they, themselves, are the number-one source for ideas about what to wear.

(percent of teens citing source for ideas about what to wear and how to wear it, 1998; up to four sources could be cited)

Myself	64%
Friends	56
Magazines	30
Catalogs	28
Stores	27
Older brother/sister	15
Coolest kids in neighborhood/school	14
People on the streets	13
Music videos	11
Older kids in neighborhood/school	9
Movie stars	9
Music stars	9
Pro athletes	9
Models	8
TV stars	8
Parents	8
TV commercials	8
Younger brother/sister	2
Internet	2

Source: TRU *Teenage Marketing & Lifestyle Study*

Where Teens Get Ideas
about What to Wear, by Gender

Girls are much more likely than boys to get ideas about what to wear from friends, magazines, catalogs, and stores, while boys are more likely than girls to get ideas from pro athletes.

(percent of teens citing source for ideas about what to wear and how to wear it, by gender, 1998; up to four sources could be cited)

	boys	girls
Myself	65%	63%
Friends	50	61
Magazines	16	45
Catalogs	17	40
Stores	22	33
Older brother/sister	16	14
Coolest kids in neighborhood/school	15	14
People on the streets	13	13
Music videos	12	10
Older kids in neighborhood/school	9	9
Movie stars	8	11
Music stars	8	10
Pro athletes	14	3
Models	4	12
TV stars	6	10
Parents	8	8
TV commercials	9	7
Younger brother/sister	1	3
Internet	2	1

Source: TRU *Teenage Marketing & Lifestyle Study*

African Americans, it's clear that there is a tremendous benefit to having black celebrities—particularly music stars—don your labels.

Teens and Social Issues

Teenagers are more societally conscious today than at any time in the recent past, that is, they are aware of a greater variety of social issues than ever before. When we ask teens to name the causes they care most about, they cite a wide variety ranging from AIDS and teenage pregnancy to ozone damage, guns, gangs, education, and child abuse. To a great extent, the media—from network television to in-school news programming, from music videos to benefit concerts—fuel this increased awareness.

Companies may find it beneficial to link their images and brands with social causes when marketing to teenagers. Cause-related marketing creates good will. It lets teens know you care about them. Your brand may benefit if consumers know that purchasing it contributes to a cause that is important to them.

To do this successfully, it's important to select the most compelling causes for the teen segment you're targeting. Because of teens' fickle nature and their attraction to whatever is newest, you must stay attuned to whatever teens consider to be the current hot issues, being careful to avoid controversial causes, such as abortion or partisan politics. You should also steer clear of issues that are used by too many other marketers. Based on these guidelines, we believe the issues with the most potential for cause-related teen marketing right now are education, drinking and driving, violence, child abuse, and race relations.

It is in vogue for teenagers to affiliate themselves with one or more causes. This is yet another way teens seek belonging and acceptance. As sincere as some teens are in their cause-related concerns and activities, you should keep in mind that many teens use causes to help them carve out an identity.

Affiliation with causes appears to start at a younger age than ever before. My son, who is now 15, won first prize when he was a first-grader with his antidrug poster carrying the message, "I don't think I'd be your friend if you took drugs." Early and positive association with a cause not only increases a teen's awareness of issues but also enhances his or her self-esteem. Still, for issues like drugs, tobacco, and alcohol, it's important to target individuals in the transitional stage—between parroting what parents and other adults say about these issues and being open to experimentation. There are many wasted messages out there, targeting kids who are either too young or too old to be persuaded by advertising about these issues. It is also important to examine data on these subjects carefully. Most national data, for example, show the average age of tobacco initiation to be about 11 years. Our extensive qualitative research shows, however, that most teens experiment once or twice around age 11, but don't become regular users until around age 13 or 14.

There is often a gap between teen attitudes and behavior. Seventy-one percent of teens say that eating healthy is "in," for example, but we found that those 71 percent of teens ate the same amount of junk food as the 29 percent who did not regard eating healthy as "in."

Twice a year we formally sit down with teens to discuss social issues. We want to know which issues they are aware of, which they care about, and which they are actively involved in. We do this to understand why teens in our quantitative study find some issues more relevant than others. We ask respondents in our study to choose the three issues that are most important to them from a list of more than 20.

Contrary to the common belief that today's teenagers are apathetic, they care about quite a lot. In general terms, teens are moved by issues they are personally confronted with, issues they fear, and issues that undermine their personal well-being. They are moved less by intangible notions that may not directly affect them. As part of the first generation to grow up under the cloud of AIDS, today's teens are aware of the magni-

Teen Social Concerns

AIDS is the number-one teen social concern, followed by education and child abuse.

(percent of teens citing social concern as one of the three concerns they care most strongly about, 1998)

AIDS	29%
Education	25
Child abuse	25
Drinking and driving	24
Racism	23
Abortion	21
Drug abuse	18
Violence	15
Sexual assault	13
Environment	12
Cigarette smoking	12
Nuclear war	11
Animal rights	11
Unplanned pregnancy	10
War	8
Suicide	8
Alcoholism	6
Homelessness	6
Women's rights	6
Eating disorders	6
Divorce	5
Unemployment	5
Health care	5

Source: TRU *Teenage Marketing & Lifestyle Study*

tude of its threat. In contrast, because protecting the environment is viewed as a few steps removed from their everyday lives, this issue carries less immediacy.

Not surprisingly, some social concerns are racially polarizing. Significantly more African-American than white teens consider AIDS (44 versus 25 percent) and education (38 versus 23 percent) as top concerns. Racism ranks higher among African-American (34 percent) and Hispanic (31 percent) teens than among white teens (18 percent). Significantly more white than minority teens are concerned with drinking and driving (more suburban white teens drive) and cigarette smoking (white teens have a higher incidence of tobacco use).

Differences also exist across gender lines. Significantly more girls than boys cite personal issues such as child abuse, abortion, sexual assault, unplanned pregnancy, and eating disorders, while boys list drug abuse, violence, smoking, war, and unemployment as top concerns.

The hottest teen issue, according to our latest data, is drinking and driving. Among white teens this issue jumped from fifth to first place in just six months. But an examination of the leading teen issues over the past few years shows AIDS and education to be at the top. Teens recognize that they are personally at risk of contracting AIDS, although their behavior lags far behind their awareness. In our qualitative research, we find that teens intellectually understand the importance of using condoms, but in practice they often engage in unsafe sex. Teens have a variety of reasons and rationalizations for not practicing safe sex. As much as teens understand the risk of AIDS, they simply don't believe it will happen to them. "We teens think we're invincible," explained a 16-year-old girl.

The second-most common explanation for not using condoms is "heat of the moment." As one 17-year-old boy said, "When you're in the right situation, you're feeling things, not thinking things."

Compounding this problem is alcohol and drug use. When teens (or adults) are under the influence of alcohol or drugs, they do not think as

Teen Social Concerns, by Ethnicity

AIDS is the number-one social concern of African-American and Hispanic teens, while drinking and driving is the number-one concern of white teens.

(top five social concerns of teens, by ethnicity, 1998)

White	African American	Hispanic
Drinking and driving	AIDS	AIDS
AIDS	Education	Racism
Child abuse	Racism	Child abuse
Education	Child abuse	Abortion
Abortion	Violence	Education

Source: TRU *Teenage Marketing & Lifestyle Study*

clearly as they normally would. Many teens have told us that when they are drunk or stoned, they're more willing to have sex (especially girls) and less likely to use (or demand) a condom.

Additionally, sexually active teen girls have told us they are embarrassed to buy condoms. Teens of both genders find going to the store, choosing (or asking) for condoms, and paying for them awkward, to say the least. Some retailers will not sell condoms to teens, claiming they are underage (although the same clerks will sell them cigarettes). One thing most teens agree on is that condoms should be easily accessible. Even socially conservative teens do not think abstinence is a realistic goal for all teens. For marketers to fully understand teenagers, they must recognize—and never discount—the pervasive power of teen sexuality.

Our research indicates that teens are not satisfied with the quality of their education. They think the nation's educational system faces profound problems. With so many schools experiencing budget cuts affecting teachers, textbooks, equipment, facilities, and classroom sizes, it's little wonder that today's teens consider education a primary problem. This issue is especially important to minority teens.

One indication of teens' declining confidence in the educational system is how they talk about teachers. Our focus-group research has shown that teens' anecdotes about their teachers have become increasingly negative over the past few years. Additionally, on two separate quantitative measures, the data show that teens think less of teachers today than in the past. Twelve years ago, teens rated educators as top role models—after only parents. Today, educators barely make it onto the list of role models. Teens also say they rarely turn to teachers, guidance counselors, or coaches with problems when they need advice. They would rather go to friends, parents, or siblings.

An important teen issue is race relations. Diversity and multiculturalism are not only media buzzwords, they are also the words teens use to define their cohort. Even today, many teens complain that their parents have racist views and sometimes prohibit them from socializing with peers of different ethnic backgrounds. We were struck by this finding after conducting qualitative research at Amundson High School, located in the heart of Chicago's north side. Amundson is probably unique, at least in Chicago, because of its ethnic diversity. Amundson students speak 39 languages and represent 49 nationalities. They are proud of their diversity and of how well students of various ethnic backgrounds get along. The students are united by their individual interests more than by their ethnicity or nationality. Those involved in sports cluster together, as do those interested in theater or student government, regardless of race or ethnicity.

Many teens at the school told us their parents forbade them to date someone of a different ethnic background. Whether it's African-American parents not wanting their child to associate with a Vietnamese student, or Caucasian parents not wanting their child to date a Filipino, the students we spoke to were exasperated by this problem. One 16-year-old Puerto Rican girl admitted that her father said he would—literally—kill her if she ever dated an African American. The students were frustrated by these restrictions, particularly since the punishment for disobeying their parents could be severe—from being grounded to being ostracized by the family. These teens believe their generation is much more enlightened about race relations than their parents' generation. Puzzlingly, most of these teenagers are the children of baby boomers, who once lodged similar complaints against their own parents.

The fact that today's teens are so concerned about race relations should encourage companies to be inclusive in marketing to teens. When choosing talent, consider showing a diversity of ethnicities, or develop multiple executions for reaching the diversity of teens.

Another close-to-the-heart issue, especially for urban minority teens, is violence. For teens living in inner cities, which can be literal war zones, gangs and violence are a part of daily life. Gangs and wanna-be gangbangers are not confined to the cities, however. Even upper-middle-class suburbs and small towns suffer increasing gang violence. As with the issue of race relations, significantly more minority teens than white teens name violence as one of their top three concerns.

A couple of years ago, we were conducting focus groups with high school boys about relationships. In the warm-up to the discussion, we asked the boys to introduce themselves and tell us about the weirdest way they had ever met a friend-to-be. One of the boys told about how he was shot by another boy. Although the backroom observers found the answer unexpected and provocative, to say the least, the focus group seemed to take it almost matter-of-factly. The respondent didn't give us many details about the incident, except to say that the experience brought him and the other guy together and now they are close friends. His comments speak to the reality of the world in which many teens grow up, one of pervasive violence that threatens their personal safety. Today, many teens need friends not only for companionship but also for protection in the volatile environment in which they live. That this young man befriended the person who shot him also speaks to the tolerance and open-mindedness of many of today's teens.

Abortion and child abuse are issues of special importance for girls. Like their parents, teens are on both sides of the abortion issue, and often passionately so. It may surprise some adults to know that many teens are against abortion, mirroring the attitudes of their parents. A significant number of teens believe abortion is an act against God, as do many adults, showing how deep-seated this attitude is. Remember, nearly two-thirds of teens say religion is one of the most important parts of their lives.

Unlike the abortion issue, there is only one side to the issue of child abuse. This issue became one of teens' top concerns after a handful of celebrities revealed their own history of childhood abuse, and as other celebrities have had child-abuse claims leveled against them. Of course, many teens have been victims of abuse themselves or know a friend who has.

We're pleased about the resurgence of interest among teens in the issue of drinking and driving. About eight years ago, drunk driving approached the top of the list, but then it slipped—until this year.

An issue that is continuing to lose favor among teens is the environment. There's a fine line in social marketing between talking relevantly to teens about an issue and bombarding them with too many messages. In focus groups, teens have told us they are tired of being lectured to about the environment by educators, other adults, and peers. Teens tell us that they and their friends make fun of "the kids who push the environment down our throats." For an issue as personally relevant to teens as the environment to decline so much in popular concern is alarming. It shows that the pedantic handling of an issue can greatly diminish its attractiveness to teenagers.

Concern about drug abuse has also declined among teens in the past few years. Part of the blame for this erosion lies with the advertising community. Although teens have been hit hard with antidrug and antidrinking-and-driving messages, the execution has often been laughable. Words like "no" and "don't" might work when you're talking to five- and six-year-olds, but teens find these reprimands and warnings preposterous. The best way to turn teens off is to preach to them. The best way to reach them is to find messages that resonate with them personally.

It's notable, then, that Philip Morris' recent youth anti-smoking ads feature the slogan, "Think. Don't smoke." We've clearly found that the most effective, gripping anti-tobacco ads are those that—through what they say and how they show it—compel teens to think.

Associating your brand with a teen issue may be one way of making it more relevant to teens, but there are risks associated with cause-related marketing. Teens are savvy, they expect honesty, and they must believe the association is sincere. Teens also expect companies to be socially responsible. Choosing which cause to tie into is a function not only of teens' current attitudes but also the fit between your brand and the cause. The causes that seem to be ripest for a corporate tie-in based on their relevancy to teens, their stability, and their relative lack of controversy are AIDS (ranking among the top two issues in every demographic segment), race relations (a top-three concern for minority teens and the number-six issue for white teens), education (the number-two issue overall), and drinking and driving (now the number-one issue among white teens).

Chapter 10.

Teen Life: Home, Play, School

It wasn't too long ago that marketers believed teens were too difficult to reach. Teens, it was thought, were too volatile, too unpredictable, and too risky to target—unless, of course, you sold acne medication or records. Today, a growing number of marketers know better as marketing vehicles that allow advertisers to reach teens throughout the day proliferate.

Teens' lives can be sectionalized in a way that is strategically important for marketers. There are three parts to teen life: 1) their own time, which they spend with friends and social activities; 2) family time, when parents often control what teens do; and 3) school, where teachers primarily control their time.

There are many ways to reach teens at play, at home, and at school—thanks to new media vehicles and more creative thinking regarding advertising, promotions, and sampling. Think of the many opportunities to reach teens at malls, for example, or at sporting events, concerts, and amusement parks. These are venues teens frequent with friends, often in a mood that makes them receptive to your messages. At home, marketers can reach teens through the mass media, including online services. And, from Channel One to GymBoards, from Scholastic to product sampling, there are more in-school media and sponsorship opportunities than ever before.

As you follow teens through the day, your strategy should be one of pervasiveness. The key to successful teen marketing is to be wherever teens are. Actually, one of the best examples of a pervasive media strategy is the one tobacco companies seem to use. From early morning radio advertising to outdoor ads, T-shirt logos, and product placement in movies, tobacco companies have successfully pervaded teens' lives. When the state of California decided to wage an anti-tobacco campaign, the advertising agency executive in charge, Bruce Silverman (currently executive vice president of Western Media), used the same weapon—an antitobacco pervasiveness strategy. How can an anti-tobacco campaign be successful, asked Silverman, unless it is fought by the same media strategy of pervasiveness?

Ways to Reach Teens

Just some of the ways to reach teens where they play, live, and learn.

At Play

Stores

Sports events

Concerts

Movie theaters

Video arcades

Theme parks

Teen clubs

Promotions linked to activities and interests

At Home

TV

Magazines, catalogs

Radio

Teen newspaper sections

Online/Internet

Direct marketing

At School

Channel One

Scholastic

react

GymBoards

Sampling

Sponsorships

Cause-related efforts

School newspapers

Backstage Pass

Planet Report

Source: TRU *Teenage Marketing & Lifestyle Study*

All marketers can learn from such a strategy and begin to appropriately pervade teens' lives with their products, messages, and images. One product that has done so successfully is the video game. Teens play and see ads for video games at home. They play video games at friends' homes and at arcades; they talk about them before, during, and after school.

Pervading teen life requires attention to detail. Understanding how teens view the three parts of their lives allows you not only to reach them where they are but also to deliver accurate and relevant messages. This chapter takes you through each part of teen life, offering insights and strategies for reaching teens in their own world.

The first step in pervading teen life is understanding how teens view and prioritize the three parts of their lives. To gain this understanding, we asked our respondents the following question: "Which part of your own life right now is most important to you—family, friends, or school?" When forced to choose only one of the three, teens in dramatic fashion name family. This choice—undoubtedly surprising to marketers and parents—is another indication of teens' underestimated maturity and larger perspective on life. They recognize the permanency of family and seem to value it above all else.

More than twice as many teens chose family (60 percent) than friends (24 percent) as the most important part of their lives. Only 16 percent chose school as most important. Half the sample named school as the least important part of their lives, while 37 percent named friends and just 12 percent said family was least important.

Our qualitative research uncovered the reasoning behind these answers. School, teens explained, is an essential and fundamental part of their lives. It's only when school is directly compared to family and friends that its importance diminishes. Significantly more girls than boys (64 versus 56 percent) chose family as the most important part of their lives. Girls' friendships tend to be much more fleeting than those of boys, in part because

What's Most Important to Teens

When teens have to choose one of the three, family is by far more important to them than friends or school.

(percent of teens who cite family, friends, or school as being most important in their lives, in rank order, 1996)

	ranked 1st	ranked 2nd	ranked 3rd
Family	60%	28%	12%
Friends	24	39	37
School	16	34	50

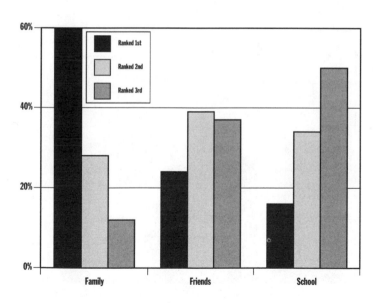

Source: TRU *Teenage Marketing & Lifestyle Study*

Teens Want to Be with Their Friends

Given the choice, teens would prefer to have a guaranteed great time with friends rather than with family.

(percent of teens citing family or friends as the group with whom they would prefer to have a guaranteed great time, by age, 1992)

	family	friends
Total teens	**34%**	**64%**
Aged 12 to 15	40	58
Aged 16 and 17	25	72
Aged 18 and 19	35	64

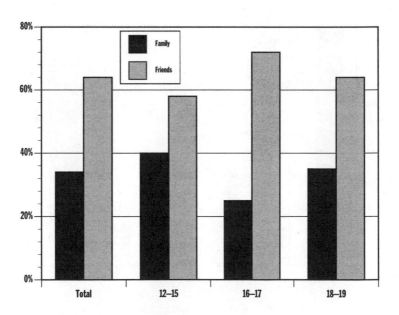

Source: TRU *Teenage Marketing & Lifestyle Study*

girls confide more in each other—making them vulnerable to betrayal. When friends change (as they so often do), there's a gravitational pull toward mom (not dad!), who often is the one safe, stable person in their lives.

As we already found in other measures, minority teens most treasure family. Sixty-seven percent of Latino and African-American teens chose family as the most important part of their lives compared to only 57 percent of white teens.

Other TRU measures have found that 16- and 17-year-olds are most concerned with distancing themselves from their families. Significantly fewer of these "middle-age teens"—who are just beginning to drive and doing the most experimenting in their social lives—named family as being more important than friends. Fifty-two percent of 16- and 17-year-olds chose family as number one in importance compared to 62 percent of 12-to-15-year-olds and 63 percent of 18- and 19-year-olds. As much as teens recognize and value the importance of family in their lives, 16- and 17-year-olds are at the stage where separation from family is natural and desirable.

Friends or Family: A Hypothetical Question

Our data indicate that teens value the role of family in their lives. Most teens also say they enjoy being with their families. But the question is, compared to what? To find the answer, we asked teens: "If you could have a guaranteed great time, whom would you rather have it with, your family or your friends?"

The key phrase here is "guaranteed great time." We are assuring teens of a great experience, be it with friends or with family. Of course, what teens do with friends when they have a great time may be quite different from what they imagine doing with their family. It's not surprising, then, that teens—by a margin of almost two to one—choose friends (64 percent) over family (34 percent). Although teens enjoy spending time with their family, if they have a better offer from friends they will leave their parents at the doorstep. As much as teens love and appreciate their parents, when it comes to socializing, parents take a back seat.

When we share these data with clients, those who are parents of teens nod their heads in agreement. They know they're lucky to get any quality time with their teenage children. They also know the time they spend with their teens will be more enjoyable if their kids haven't turned down another offer to accept (begrudgingly) a family invitation. For many parents, the hardest thing about raising a teenager is that their children's friends replace them early on as the people with whom they most want to spend their time.

Teens aged 16 and 17 have the strongest social ties to friends. These are the most rebellious years, when teens are enjoying new freedoms—staying out later, partying, driving, and dating. The late motivational-research expert, Dr. Burleigh Gardner, described this mid-teen state as "the cutting of the apron string," the time when teens feel compelled to separate from family in almost every part of their lives.

The youngest teens are still somewhat under their parents' wings, which explains why so many say they would prefer to have a good time with their family. In contrast, high school juniors and seniors will go out of their way to avoid spending leisure time with their parents. Recent graduates, however, often discover (and enjoy) their parents from a more adult perspective.

After they have made the initial choice between friends and family, we asked respondents why they chose whom they chose. The overriding reason for those who chose friends was, "I can do things with my friends that there's no way I can do with my family!"

"I wouldn't go out even with my brothers and sisters and let loose at a dance club like I could with my friends," said a 16-year-old girl.

"When we go to the movies, my friends and I look for the cute guys. I would never do that with my parents!" said a 15-year-old girl.

Why Teens Would Rather Be with Friends

Teens who would rather have a great time with friends say the reason is that they can do things with friends that they can't do with family.

(among teens who would prefer having a guaranteed great time with friends, percent citing selected reasons, 1992)

I can do things with my friends
that I can't do with my family.   80%

I spend a lot of time at home with
my family, so when I go out I want
to be with friends.   57

I have more things in common with
my friends than with my family.   50

My friends accept me as I am; they
don't judge me.   39

I like my friends better than my family.   13

Source: TRU *Teenage Marketing & Lifestyle Study*

How Teens Describe
Their Families

**When teens are asked to characterize their families,
most list positive attributes.**

*(percent of teens citing positive or negative
characteristics about their families, 1993)*

Positive

Happy	68%
Loving	63
Supportive	63
Fun	54
Close	45

Negative

Tense	20
At each other's throats	18
Unhappy	12
Cold	6
Abusive	4

Source: TRU *Teenage Marketing & Lifestyle Study*

The other reasons teens give for choosing friends over family revolve around the theme of "I just wanna have fun (with my friends)." Fifty-seven percent of teens say they prefer to be with friends because they already spend so much time with their family. These teens must be counting the time they spend at home sleeping, talking on the phone with friends, or hanging out behind the closed door of their room!

Those who chose to have a great time with their family responded maturely, saying they appreciate the permanency of family in their lives. The parents of family-oriented teens should feel particularly gratified by their response.

"Families provide unconditional love, and that's something you can't sacrifice," said a 17-year-old girl.

"If you get into a fight with friends, that could be the end of that relationship. But if you fight with your family, it gets resolved and it works out," said a 16-year-old girl.

One of our all-time favorite responses to any of our syndicated questions comes from some of those who choose family over friends, explaining, "It's more unusual to have a great time with family!" These teens seem to say, "Hey, having fun with my parents would be pretty weird. Why not, it's only one night!"

In general, marketers should portray teens as having fun with one another. But for family-targeting brands, it is safe to show teens enjoying their parents and other family members. Although the teen years are full of angst and parent–child conflict, teens not only admire and seek advice from their parents, but many also treasure the moments they share.

Parents of younger children might find this fact encouraging, since the parents of teens are always warning them, "Enjoy your children when they're young because when they're teenagers, it's all over." Our data suggest there is still something for parents to look forward to. Despite what many adults fear, most teens not only look up to their parents but feel good about their families.

With these findings in hand, we asked teens in a recent study to describe their families. The results show that teens hold their families in high regard. About 70 percent of responses were positive, while only 30 percent were negative. Further, of the 10 listed characteristics, the five that received the most responses were all positive. Teens are more likely to characterize their families as happy than unhappy, as loving than abusive, as close than cold, as supportive than at each other's throats, and as fun than tense.

Although all five negative responses ranked at the bottom of the list, most of the teens who wrote in alternative responses answered negatively (47 of 73, or nearly two-thirds).

There are few significant differences in family characteristics by gender, age, or race with one exception—the characteristic of fun. African-American teens are more likely than Hispanic or white teens to describe their family as fun. Younger teens are also more likely to say their families are fun. Younger teens, who are less involved in dating and other independent activities than older teens, are more likely to enjoy family outings and activities than teens aged 16 or older.

Whom Do Teens Most Admire?

The question of how to motivate teens is crucial not only for marketers, but also for teachers, counselors, social-service agencies, and other organizations that support young people. Knowing who teens look up to can be a starting point in motivating them. By portraying in advertising the type of people teens (or a teen segment) admire, you can make your advertising more compelling.

To determine whom teens admire, we asked in our syndicated study: "Thinking about somebody whom you really admire—or who even may be a hero to you—which of the following best identifies that person?" Then

Teens Who Say
Their Family Is Fun

African-American teens are most likely to say their family is fun.

(percent of teens saying their family is fun, by ethnicity and age, 1993)

Ethnicity

African Americans	63%
Whites	54
Hispanics	49

Age

Aged 12 to 15	61
Aged 16 and 17	49
Aged 18 and 19	45

Source: TRU *Teenage Marketing & Lifestyle Study*

Whom Do Teens Most Admire?

The largest share of teen boys most admire their father, while the largest share of teen girls say they admire their mother the most.

(percent of teens citing person as the one they most admire, by gender, 1992)

	total	boys	girls
Mother	20%	13%	28%
Father	15	20	10
Sports star	14	23	4
Musical performer/musician	9	9	9
Myself	8	8	8
Celebrity from TV or movies	6	6	6
Other family member	6	6	5
Historical figure	5	6	4
Brother	5	6	4
Teacher	5	3	7
Sister	3	2	4
Business person	2	2	2
Doctor	2	1	2
Leader of social cause	2	1	2
Brave/courageous person	1	1	2
Clergy (i.e., priest, rabbi)	1	1	2
Scientist	1	2	1
Boss	1	1	1
Current political figure	1	1	1

Source: TRU *Teenage Marketing & Lifestyle Study*

we presented them with a list of 20 choices, from mother to historical figure to social leader. Separately, we asked them to identify the specific individual they most admire and explain why. As expected from other TRU research, the results reveal teens' strong admiration and affection for their families. The top two answers are mother and father, respectively.

"My mother. She works full-time and raises a family of four and loves us all and is sweet and understanding," said a 16-year-old girl.

"My dad. He is my best friend," said a 13-year-old boy.

We asked teens this same question in our very first syndicated study in 1983. Then, too, teens most admired their parents. The implications of this finding are challenging to advertisers. As much as teens want separation from their parents, they may reject advertising that denigrates their parents. Humor can be an effective way to straddle this contradiction.

Advertising that shows the importance of parents as role models can be motivating to teens. One such example is a TV ad that was part of Levi's 501 brand's "Got to Be Real" campaign a few years ago. In it, a young Native American teen boy said, "I don't know of any friends who have fathers like mine. He's just one of the greatest guys you can know." His father is shown sitting in the background, smiling subtly but proudly in response to hearing his son's thoughts.

Although parents are admired as much today as they were more than a decade ago, teachers are not. In 1983, teachers were right behind mom and dad as the people teens most admired, but current data show that teachers have fallen out of favor. This same finding emerges when we ask teens whom they would turn to first if they needed personal advice. Again, teachers rank low on this measure, indicating that today's educational system (as represented by teachers) has fallen sharply in teens' estimation over the past 10 years.

Celebrities have replaced teachers as the people teens most admire after mom and dad. Third are sports stars; fourth, musical performers; and

Family Members
as Friends

**Most teens consider at least one family member to be
a friend. Mom is most likely to be that friend.**

*(percent of teens who consider a family member to be a friend,
and the percentage of those who cite specific family members, 1996)*

Family member as friend

Yes	85%
No	13

Family members considered to be friends
(among those who answered yes)

Mom	64%
Cousin	56
Dad	47
Brother	41
Sister	41
Aunt	35
Grandmother	32
Uncle	30
Grandfather	23
Another relative	17
Step-father	6
Step-mother	5

Source: TRU *Teenage Marketing & Lifestyle Study*

fifth, teens themselves. The fact that "myself" scored as high as it did reflects the confidence that a number of teens have in themselves.

Family as Friends

Not only do teens place tremendous value on family, they also view family members as real friends. Family friends can include parents, siblings, cousins (especially true for African Americans), grandparents, and other relatives. In fact, nearly three-fourths of teens consider at least one relative to be a "real friend." On average, respondents consider a total of four relatives to be friends.

Mom is most often considered a friend, and nearly two-thirds of teens who consider any family member a friend name her. A cousin is next, beating out dad. Dad is next, but far behind mom, with fewer than half the teens naming him. Overall, 70 percent of teens say they view at least one parent as a friend. Brother and sister follow, each named by 41 percent of respondents. When brothers and sisters are taken together, nearly two-thirds say they consider a sibling to be a real friend.

Cousins are especially important to African-American teens. Many of these respondents live in close proximity to (or even in the same household with) extended-family members, which enables closer relationships with cousins and others. Twenty-two percent of African-American teens live in a household which includes extended-family members compared to just 10 percent of Caucasian teens. Cousins can make attractive friends because they are often the same age but don't carry the baggage of being a brother or sister (i.e., sharing a room, sibling rivalries, etc.) Female extended-family members are more important to African-American respondents than to Latinos or whites. Significantly more African-American teens say they consider a grandmother or an aunt to be a real friend.

Being of the same gender also facilitates close relationships. Significantly more girls are closer to mothers, sisters, and aunts; significantly more boys are closer to fathers, brothers, and uncles. Even so, more boys name mom than dad as a close friend.

Older teens are more likely to think of a parent as a friend than are "middle-age" teens. While 62 percent of 16- and 17-year-olds consider mom to be a friend, the figure climbs to 71 percent among 18- and 19-year-olds. For "middle-age" teen boys, dad is in the doghouse. While 58 percent of 12-to-15-year-old boys consider dad to be a friend, the figure drops to just 45 percent among 16- and 17-year-old boys.

Significantly fewer minority teens say they consider their father to be a friend. In large part this is so because fewer live with or maintain a relationship with their father. Census data show that 60 percent of African-American children live in a single-parent family, compared to 21 percent of white children.

Advertising that recognizes the importance of family and depicts family members as friends can be moving to teens. Showing sons and daughters confiding in mom and showing African-American teens enjoying the company of cousins can make for relevant, accurate advertising.

"My cousin is my age and she's about my best friend," commented one of our Influencer panelists.

"Mom always gives me advice and she really wants to help, even if she doesn't know what she's talking about," kidded (with some truth) another of TRU's Influencers.

"My dad is a tougher person. You can always complain to mom, but if you complain to dad, he might think you're not 'manly'," shared a 17-year-old boy.

"Mom is a comforting person," simply stated a 13-year-old boy.

Another of our panelists said, "I can relate to my cousin more than to my parents. She's just a couple of years older than me and has recently gone through what I'm starting to go through."

Where Teens Go for Advice

Most teens would go to their friends for advice, but nearly half say they would turn to their mother.

(percent of teens saying they would turn for advice to the persons/services listed, 1993)

Friend	55%
Mother	44
Boyfriend/girlfriend	23
Father	20
Sister	10
Other family member	7
Brother	7
Teacher	4
School counselor	3
Coach	3
Magazine/newspaper	2
Clergy	2
Psychologist/social worker	1
Medical doctor	1
Crisis hotline	1

Source: TRU *Teenage Marketing & Lifestyle Study*

Where Teens Go
for Advice, by Gender

**Teen girls are more likely than teen boys to ask their mother for advice,
while teen boys are more likely than girls to turn to their father.**

*(percent of teens saying they would turn for advice to the
persons/services listed, by gender, 1993)*

	boys	girls
Friend	48%	63%
Mother	41	48
Boyfriend/girlfriend	19	26
Father	30	9
Sister	8	12
Brother	10	3

Source: TRU *Teenage Marketing & Lifestyle Study*

To Whom Do Teens Turn for Advice?

In the marketing of some products, depicting an advice giver in advertising can be effective. This is particularly true for health and beauty aids. To help you decide whom you should picture in an advice-giver role, we ask teens: "Who is the first person you turn to when you need advice about a personal problem?"

By a significant margin, the number-one answer is a friend, mentioned by more than half the teens. Second is mother, followed by girlfriend or boyfriend, and (finally) father.

The nature of the problem determines whom teens turn to for advice. If the problem is, "I need help with algebra," a teen is likely to turn to a competent parent. If the problem is, "I'm thinking about having sex with a particular person," teens are more likely to turn to friends for advice. It is the rare (and fortunate) parents whose teenaged children would come first to them if struggling with the latter issue.

Teens are more likely to turn to their friends for advice for a variety of reasons. The problem may be too controversial or risky to broach with parents, a friend may have recently experienced a similar difficulty, and sometimes it's more comfortable talking with someone who is not an authority figure.

Teenage boys are more likely than girls to go to dad or a brother for advice, while girls are more likely to turn to friends, mom, girlfriends, or sisters. Dad ranks relatively low as an advice giver for several reasons. First, many teens today come from single-parent homes headed by their mother. They don't have a dad close by to turn to for advice. Second, even if teens live with both parents, dad is often less accessible than mom. Finally, in focus groups teens tell us their mother is more interested in their problems and more nurturing in her response than their father.

Nearly 25 percent of teens say they would turn to a boyfriend or girlfriend for advice. If the statistic were calculated only for respondents who have a boyfriend or girlfriend, the percentage would probably double, revealing how important boyfriends and girlfriends are in sharing problems and giving advice.

Adult authority figures outside the family, such as teachers, coaches, counselors, or clergy, all rank low as advice givers. Outside services, such as crisis lines, also rank low among teens. Of course, the only teens who would turn to crisis lines would be those with major problems.

What Teens Talk about with Friends and Family

Teens discuss a myriad of issues with friends. Not surprisingly, the genders differ greatly in what they discuss, with girls enjoying deeper, more intimate conversations than boys. What do teens talk about most? They talk about each other—friends, the opposite sex, and classmates. More than one-third of teens discuss other friends, while 68 percent talk about people of the opposite sex. And, of course, teens love to spend time recounting their weekend adventures: 33 percent talk about "this weekend" or "next weekend."

More serious subjects, such as the future, current events, school, jobs, "deep feelings," college, and "your attitudes," take a back seat to teen gossip of all types. Still, more than one-third say they talk to their friends about "life in general." Teens—especially boys—also exchange information about entertainment—music, movies, TV, sports, video games, computers, and celebrities.

These data show that girls confide in their friends much more than boys do, sharing their thoughts and feelings about deeper, more emotional issues. Significantly more girls than boys talk about dating (including their boyfriends and "who they want to go out with"), other friends, gossip, "secret stuff," "deep feelings," fashion, parents, celebrities, siblings, their "attitude," and even their eating habits.

While girls trade more in emotions with their friends, boys' conversations center more on the rational. Instead of discussing their feelings and hopes, boys talk about interests and activities. Significantly more boys than girls discuss music, movies, TV, sports, current events, jobs, video games, and computers. While girls talk more about romance (i.e., boyfriends and dating), boys talk more about sex.

Knowing what teens talk about with friends is key to portraying them accurately in advertising. Understanding typical teen conversations can help marketers create advertising with which teens can readily identify.

Not surprisingly, teens talk about very different things with their parents than with friends. While girls discuss gossip, boys, and "secret stuff" with friends and boys talk about sex and hobbies, teens talk about school, friends (reluctantly so), the future, college, family, and current events with parents. It's clear that teens much prefer the topics they discuss with friends. It's equally clear that their conversations with friends are more intimate and revealing.

School and grades is the number-one parent–teen conversational topic. In fact, it's the only discussion that more than half the teens hold with their parents. TRU's Influencer panel contends this subject is pervasive in parental talks because it's what parents bring up. Teens' future also is a major topic of discussion: 65 percent talk to their parents about the future, college, and jobs. Daughters talk to their parents about other people in their life more than sons do, while sons talk about events and activities more than daughters do. Significantly more girls than boys talk to their parents about friends, siblings, boyfriends, and "deep feelings." Significantly more boys than girls talk about jobs, current events, sports, movies, and TV shows.

Many products today have a dual teen-and-parent target, relying on mass media for reaching both segments. These data show there are common teen–parent conversations that can be depicted in advertising aimed at a dual target.

Teens value the permanency of family and may even consider some family members to be friends. But family members are often excluded from the circle of friendship when discussions turn to sex, drugs, or drinking.

What Teens Talk about with Their Friends

With their friends, teens talk mostly about friends.

(percent of teens who say the topic is something they talk about with their friends, by gender, 1998)

	total	boys	girls		total	boys	girls
Boyfriend/girlfriend	38%	32%	44%	Current events	19%	22%	16%
				School/grades	18	16	20
Other friends	36	33	39	Jobs	16	18	13
Life in general	35	32	39	Deep feelings	15	9	23
Someone you want to go out with	35	32	38	College	12	11	13
				Fashion	12	7	18
Music	30	34	25	Video games/computers	11	20	1
Sex	27	32	22	Parents	9	5	13
Gossip	26	14	39	Celebrities	7	5	9
The future	25	24	26	Vacations	6	7	6
Next weekend	25	24	26	Brother/sister	4	3	6
Last weekend	23	23	24	Your attitude	4	3	5
Movies/TV shows	21	26	16	Your behavior	3	2	4
Sports	21	33	8	Eating habits	2	1	3
Secret stuff	20	15	26				

Source: TRU *Teenage Marketing & Lifestyle Study*

What Teens Talk about with Their Family

With their family, teens talk mostly about school and grades.

(percent of teens who say the topic is something they talk about with their family, by gender, 1998)

	total	boys	girls		total	boys	girls
School/grades	55%	53%	57%	Movies/TV shows	12%	15%	10%
Other friends	40	33	48	Deep feelings	11	9	13
The future	37	38	36	Music	7	8	7
Life in general	36	35	36	Last weekend	7	8	5
College	34	35	33	Fashion	7	5	9
Jobs	31	35	27	Gossip	6	4	8
Current events	23	26	21	Someone you want			
Brother/sister	18	14	22	to go out with	4	3	6
Sports	17	23	10	Sex	4	3	5
Your attitude	17	16	18	Video games/			
Vacations	16	16	16	computers	4	7	2
Your behavior	16	16	16	Nothing	4	5	3
Boyfriend/				Eating habits	4	3	5
girlfriend	15	11	20	Secret stuff	3	1	5
Next weekend	13	14	12	Celebrities	3	3	4

Source: TRU *Teenage Marketing & Lifestyle Study*

While two-thirds of teens say they can talk with at least one parent about these serious subjects, one-third cannot talk with either parent.

Mom is usually the parent teens can talk to about sex or drugs. Although 35 percent of teens say they can go to both parents with these topics, 26 percent say they can talk only to mom about them while just 4 percent can talk only to dad. Mothers are often more accessible than fathers. And, when teens have a need to "spill it out," they're fairly impulsive about it. Teens say they are more comfortable discussing the intimate details of their lives with mom than with dad because mom is a better listener, more supportive, and at times even helpful.

On the surface these data indicate that teens talk with their parents about the seemingly private parts of their lives, but it's important to realize that the question is worded as "can talk" rather than "have talked." Perception can be different from reality.

Significantly fewer girls than boys say they can talk with their parents about personal issues. Girls are especially reluctant to talk to their fathers about personal topics. Only 27 percent of girls, compared to 43 percent of boys, say they can talk to both parents about these issues. Further, girls are much more likely to go only to mom than are boys (35 versus 17 percent). Only 16 girls of the nearly 1,000 girls in our sample (fewer than 2 percent) say they can go only to dad.

One teenage boy explained, "My dad just lectures, not talks. But he's really good at lectures."

Another boy added, "I would go to my dad, because when he was younger he was more wild and experimented a little more."

A typical teen attitude was voiced by a 17-year-old girl: "My parents don't need to know everything—everything is too much."

And, typical of many girls, a 15-year-old commented, "I would talk to my mom because my dad just isn't that understanding about this kind of stuff."

Which Parent Teens Can Talk to about Serious Issues

Two-thirds of teens can talk to at least one parent about sex, drugs, drinking, or other serious issues. Mom is the one teens are most likely to feel they can talk to.

(percent of teens who can talk to a parent about serious issues such as drugs, sex, and drinking, by which parent they can talk to and gender, 1998)

	total	boys	girls
Yes, total	65%	67%	64%
Both parents	35	43	27
Mom only	26	17	35
Dad only	4	7	2
No, neither parent	32	30	35

Source: TRU *Teenage Marketing & Lifestyle Study*

As predicted from other measures, the "middle-aged teens," ages 16 and 17, are least likely to maintain an open relationship with parents. Latino teens have the most difficulty discussing serious topics with parents. Forty percent of Hispanic teens, compared to 31 percent of both black and white teens, say they are unable to talk to either parent about highly personal subjects such as sex. Culturally, Latino teens may respect their parents in a different sense than do teens of other ethnic backgrounds. This may make it more difficult for them to share personal information about areas in their life their parents may consider taboo.

Social marketers attempting to educate and persuade a teenage audience about issues ranging from cigarette smoking to drugs to sexual abstinence need to incorporate a parent strategy. Because teens hold their parents in such high esteem, tapping into this respect and admiration can be highly effective. Parents need to be given the skills and tools with which to talk to their teenage children about these issues, however.

For product marketers, understanding that teens and parents can talk about personal matters is significant because it means teens and parents can certainly communicate about the far less intimate subject of buying. Marketing efforts that encourage teens to talk to their parents about family purchases—or persuade them to take the initiative as influencers—are viable. But consider the fact that even boys are unlikely to go only to their father to talk about personal matters. Showing girls talking to mom or boys talking to both parents would be the most accurate depiction of these interactions.

What Teens Like to Do with Parents and Friends

The generation gap is narrower today than it once was, with echo-boom teens and their boomer parents sharing common interests. Teens enjoy doing things with their parents such as going on vacation or to restaurants. But there are some activities—such as going to concerts or movies—that teens do not regard as parent–teen time.

What Teens Like and Do Not Like to Do with Their Parents

Teens like spending holidays with their parents, but they don't like going to concerts or movies with them.

(percent of teens citing activity as one they like or do not like doing with their parents, 1997)

Like to do with parents		Do not like to do with parents	
Spend holidays together	90%	Go to concerts	74%
Go to a nice restaurant	86	Go to movies	67
Go on vacations	79	Play video games	63
Eat dinner at home	79	Play on a computer	63
Family parties	68	Play sports	56
Go to church, synagogue	66	Go shopping	54
Watch TV	66	Work on school projects	47
Go out for fast food	64	Have a talk/just talk	43
Watch videos at home	64	Go to sporting events	41
Play board games/cards	60	Go grocery shopping	38
Family outings (zoo, museum)	58	Go out in public	36
Go out in public	57	Family outings (zoo, museum)	35
Go grocery shopping	57	Play board games/cards	33
Have a talk/just talk	51	Watch videos at home	31
Go to sporting events	51	Go out for fast food	30
Work on school projects	45	Watch TV	30
Go shopping	42	Family parties	27
Play sports	35	Go to church, synagogue	25
Go to movies	29	Go on vacations	19
Play on a computer	27	Eat dinner at home	18
Play video games	25	Go to a nice restaurant	11
Go to concerts	16	Spend holidays together	7

Source: TRU *Teenage Marketing & Lifestyle Study*

At least two-thirds of respondents to our syndicated study like to do the following things with their parents: spending holidays together, going to a nice restaurant, going on vacation, eating dinner at home, attending family parties, and going to church or synagogue. These activities are of two types: those which offer teens a free ride (nice restaurants, vacations) and those which reflect teens' genuine desire to be with their family (spending holidays together, eating dinner at home, family parties, going to church or synagogue).

Teens value family dinners and the opportunity they offer for conversation. But teens would much prefer going to a movie with friends than with a parent. Most teens don't want to be seen at a movie or concert with parents. There are surprisingly few differences by age, gender, and ethnicity on this measure. It appears that what teens like to do with their family is fairly universal across the various teen demographic segments. The results of this measure suggest that a variety of parent–teen situations and themes could be shown in ads aimed at a family target, including holiday get-togethers, vacations, and restaurant meals.

What Teens Think about School

For marketers, it's important to understand that teens view school as the ultimate social environment. Schools is where their friends are, and being with friends is by far teens' favorite thing about school. Among teens' top-10 favorite things about school, all but one are extracurricular.

Friends, boyfriend/girlfriend, extracurricular activities, free periods/ recess, and lunch are all more favored than academics. Despite teens' predilection for socializing at school, learning does make the top-10 list of what teens like about school. But no more than 12 percent of the sample liked teachers, classes, grades, and tests. The youngest teens most enjoy the social aspects of school. Significantly more 12-to-15-year-olds than older teens named friends, assemblies/field trips, sports, and seeing their boyfriend/girlfriend as what they like about school.

There are many things teens don't like about school, from classwork to social pressure to simply having to be there. The three things they dislike most are getting up early, tests, and homework. Our data show more than twice as many teens dislike getting up early than don't like peer pressure, grades, teachers, classes, or even the (dreaded) school administration. Teens' passion for sleep can't be underestimated. Teens, in fact, are sleep deprived. Based on their accelerated rate of development, teenagers actually need more sleep than younger children. But they invariably stay up later (they say they can't fall asleep early, nor would their schedules allow them to). Interestingly, some progressive school districts around the country—including those in Minneapolis and Dallas—are pushing high school start times to a later hour to ensure that teens will be awake during first period. Bus schedules are preventing the rest of the country from following this lead because after buses drop off high schoolers, they typically retrace their routes to pick up elementary school students. Pushing back the high school schedule also affects athletics and other extracurricular activities that occur after school.

Grades are the biggest everyday worry of teens. Since grades are based on tests, it's no wonder teens dislike tests so much. Having to study for tests seems to be as distasteful as the tests themselves. When combined, 74 percent of teens cite tests or homework as what they don't like about school.

Although being with friends is teens' favorite thing about school, the pressures surrounding friends and peers can make school unpleasurable and even stressful—at least for some. When combined, 40 percent cite peer pressure, gossip, other students, boyfriend/girlfriend, or friend as something they dislike about school.

Despite what many marketers believe, school scenes are not taboo in advertising to teens. In fact, school is an extremely relevant backdrop for much of teen life. Be careful to concentrate on the aspects of school that teens like most—namely, social aspects. Avoid the dark side of school—tests, homework, classes, and so on—unless you present them with hu-

What Teens Like about School

Most of the things teens like about school are social activities.

(percent of teens citing attribute as one of their three favorite things about school, 1996)

Friends	79%
Assemblies/special days/field days	43
Sports	34
Seeing boyfriend/girlfriend	32
Extracurricular activities	25
Free periods/recess	23
Learning	22
Lunch	20
Being away from home	18
Other students	14
Gossip	12
Teachers	12
Clubs	11
Grades	11
Classes	10
Just being there	9
School administration	3
Tests	3
How long the days are	2
Homework	2
Peer pressure	2
Getting up early	1

Source: TRU *Teenage Marketing & Lifestyle Study*

What Teens Don't Like about School

Teens dislike getting up early and taking tests.

(percent of teens citing attribute as one of their three least favorite things about school, 1996)

Getting up early	52%
Tests	52
Homework	51
How long the days are	27
Peer pressure	25
Classes	24
Gossip	21
School administration	19
Teachers	18
Just being there	14
Grades	14
Being away from home	8
Other students	7
Learning	6
Clubs	5
Assemblies/special days/field days	4
Lunch	4
Sports	3
Extracurricular activities	3
Seeing boyfriend/girlfriend	3
Free periods/recess	2
Friends	1

Source: TRU *Teenage Marketing & Lifestyle Study*

mor. Otherwise, when teens are vegging out in front of the TV watching your ad, one hand on the remote and the other in a bowl of chips, you run the risk of alienating them.

Chapter 11.

Advertising and Promoting to Teens

Much of the work we do at TRU is advertising research, and almost all of it is qualitative. This experience affords us a rich understanding of what advertising means to teenagers, how teens view and interact with advertising, and the type of advertising that is most effective with teens. Understanding how and why teens react the way they do to advertising is an evolving process.

Although we get better at evaluating advertising from a teen perspective each year, we are still surprised at times by teens' reactions to marketing communications. What we learned from a preliminary advertising concept project for Keebler a few years ago is an example of how surprising teens can be. The advertising concepts were created by Keebler's long-standing ad agency, Leo Burnett Co. We've been involved in several Keebler/Burnett advertising projects over the past few years, so we are well aware of the equity the Keebler elves bring to the brand; they comfort moms and attract the attention and imagination of children. Still, we weren't sure what the reaction would be when we showed a Keebler advertising concept, which pictured the elves dancing around packages of chips, to a couple of 16-year-old boys. We were concerned that these older teens might slam the elves. To our (pleasant) surprise, the two boys (one of whom had the voice and attitude of Butt-Head of MTV fame) lit up when the elves appeared, even more than the second graders I had talked to an hour earlier. When I asked them what they thought of the end frame with the dancing elves, the Butt-Head guy said, "If it's a conga line, then that's cool!" (The suggested conga line appeared in a later ad.) The moral of this story: don't try to guess what teens will think is cool in advertising. Check it out!

It's important to recognize right from the start that teens view advertising differently than do adults. To teens, advertising is more than product information (but never forget the importance of providing teens with adequate product information). To teens, advertising is popular culture.

Teens Talk
about Commercials

Most teens talk about commercials, and not always positively.

(percent of teens agreeing strongly or somewhat with the statement, "Sometimes my friends and I will talk about a commercial we either like or hate," by gender, age, race, and ethnicity, 1994)

Total	**80%**
Boys	76
Girls	84
Aged 12 to 15	77
Aged 16 and 17	82
Aged 18 and 19	83
African American	81
Hispanic	86
White	80

Source: TRU *Teenage Marketing & Lifestyle Study*

Just as teenagers discuss the latest episode of "South Park," new movies, or new music videos, they also talk to one another about advertising. Sometimes they praise it; other times, they trash it. Unlike most adults, teens are surrounded every day by hundreds, sometimes thousands, of peers with time on their hands. They spend some of the time with their peers discussing their favorite, and least favorite, commercials.

TRU has developed a quantitative measure that shows the importance of advertising to teens. Based on a series of agree/disagree statements, this measure uncovers teens' involvement with advertising. The findings show that teens are highly involved. Older teens, girls, and African Americans are the most involved with and entertained by advertising.

Our data confirm that advertising is entertaining to teens, which explains why it is such a frequent topic of teen conversation. Eighty percent of teens agree that, "Sometimes my friends and I will talk about a commercial we either really like or hate." Significantly more older teens and girls than younger teens and boys agree with this statement. Significantly more African-American teens than white or Hispanic teens agree.

Being a topic of conversation is not necessarily good. Even if an ad is discussed favorably among teens, it still needs to be clear and persuasive enough to generate sales or shift attitudes. If an ad is received poorly by teens, the negative talk about it may tarnish the image of the brand and result in teen rejection.

Many teens are extremely analytical when discussing advertising, while others react more simply and pointedly. As one 15-year-old girl said, "Advertising that's interesting to watch and makes a statement is the type that catches my attention and might later influence me to buy something."

Equally opinionated is the 16-year-old boy who succinctly commented, "Bad commercials are the ones that are dumb or suck."

Teens want advertising to be entertaining. In fact, three-fourths agree that, "Good advertising can be really entertaining." Surprisingly, the oldest teens are most likely to say they are entertained by advertising, evidence that this feeling is not just youthful enthusiasm for anything that approaches entertainment.

Two-thirds of teens agree that "good advertising helps me make decisions about what to buy," and slightly fewer agree that "good advertising can make me think or feel better about a product or company."

Although entertaining ads can generate interest in a product, teenagers also take cues from other information sources. Nevertheless, the fact that a sizable majority of teens at least somewhat agree that advertising helps in purchase decisions shows that most teens recognize advertising's importance to them as consumers. This finding is confirmed by other measures in our syndicated study. When we ask teens, "What makes a brand cool?" many name advertising. Similarly, when we ask them where they find out about the latest trends, advertising ranks high.

Teens hold high standards for advertising because they have experienced good ads. Most teens think advertisers are not meeting these high standards. Only about two-fifths agree with the statement, "I think advertisers do a good job creating advertising for people my age." With so many brand choices available to consumers, creating compelling and memorable advertising is more important than ever. Because teens can tune out a brand simply because of bad advertising, the stakes for marketers are dramatically high. More than 60 percent of teens agree that "bad advertising can make me think or feel worse about a product or company."

Understanding the risks of exposing teens to advertising that is less than honest, mediocre, or confusing makes clear how critical it is to get it right the first time. By following teens' rules for advertisers, you can greatly increase the odds of developing ads teens embrace rather than reject. Just as teens can be a most unforgiving audience, they can also be the most embracing.

The Rules of Advertising, According to Teens

To marketers, advertising creates awareness, provides product information, communicates brand image, and—they hope—persuades consumers to try (or continue to use) a brand. To teens, advertising is a means of collecting product information and a form of entertainment.

Teens are often skeptical about advertising, quick to reject ads they feel are off target. Because teens are highly segmented demographically and psychographically, different approaches work better with different teen audiences. The challenge for marketers is to create compelling and entertaining advertising that not only attracts most teens, but also does not alienate any single teen segment. Certainly, advertising that is inclusive, reflecting the diversity of today's teenage population, will reach the broadest audience.

In our syndicated study, we ask teenagers to list the dos and don'ts of creating effective teen-directed advertising. We developed this measure by first testing it qualitatively, talking to teens in-depth about advertising in a number of different markets. We showed teens a variety of teen-directed commercials, some excellent and others poor in our opinion. After showing them the ads, we got them talking all the while jotting down their thoughts on an easel pad. The teens were so involved in the discussion that we literally papered the room with sheets from the easel pad in market after market. We combined, condensed, and modified the rules, finally creating a list we could quantify in our syndicated study. Since then, this list has undergone further revisions, based on the original quantitative data and our continued qualitative experiences.

Specifically, we ask our national sample of teens: "Which of the following do you think are the most important rules companies should follow when advertising to teens?" Teens could check up to 5 of the 22 rules included in the question.

Rules for Advertisers

When advertising to teens, honesty is the best policy.
Most teens also say it is important to be funny.

(percent of teens citing rule as one of the five most important rules companies should follow when advertising to teens, 1998)

Be honest	65%
Use humor, make me laugh	52
Be clear	45
Show the product	43
Tell me something important about the product	37
Don't use sex to sell	31
Show situations that are realistic	25
Have a great slogan or jingle	24
Don't talk down to me	22
Don't try too hard to be cool	21
Use great music	21
Show "hot" guys/girls	21
Show people/scenes I can relate to	20
Show people about my age	19
Don't tell me what to do	19
Show me things I've never seen before	14
Don't butcher a song I like	14
Don't make fun of other ads	14
Show celebrities who use the product	8
Show cute animals or babies	6
Be sarcastic	5
Show situations that are fantasy	4

Source: TRU *Teenage Marketing & Lifestyle Study*

Rule One: Be Honest

Unlike children, who often accept anything they hear in advertising, teens are skeptical by nature. They demand truth in advertising—65 percent say honesty is truly the best policy. Commercials that communicate sincerity—that are "antihype"—are refreshing and often embraced by teens.

This rule has become increasingly important to teens over the past few years. Not only do teens appreciate honesty in advertising, they demand it. If teens detect a less-than-honest (or less-than-believable) advertising claim, they tend to reject the product or brand. To teens, exaggeration can seem dishonest, even if done in jest. If what you're telling them is based on fantasy, be clear that you're asking them to suspend their disbelief. Teens can be extremely literal and will reject anything they don't find believable.

More than adults, teens find out about products and advertising from their peers. Word-of-mouth about a dishonest or dumb ad can spread rapidly in teen circles. As one 18-year-old boy said, "I hate it when advertising says one thing but does something else. When we find out the truth, it just makes us mad."

Sprite has been running an extremely successful campaign, which we originally tested in storyboard form. The essence of the campaign, known as "Image Is Nothing," is honesty. One of the original ads, titled "What is Cool?" directly attacked the teen obsession with coolness. It shows a teen obsessing over whether everything he does is cool (with the emphasis on the assumption that everything he does is cool), including what he drinks. Another of the early ads, entitled "What They Will Tell You," confronted the gratuitous use of celebrities and hype to sell products. The spots end with the lines, "Image is Nothing. Thirst is Everything. Obey Your Thirst. Sprite." Teens found this approach refreshing, a product attribute the advertiser had hoped to communicate.

We tell our clients that teens have a highly sensitive "bullshit meter." Not only do they see it coming a mile away, they actively look for it. After all, advertisers have conditioned them to do so. Don't test their ability to detect hype or exaggeration. Instead, respect it. Communicate an air of honesty in your advertising. Teens will appreciate you for it.

Rule Two: Be Funny

No question about it: teens love funny advertising. When examining teens' favorite commercials, their one common characteristic is the use of humor.

Nothing attracts teens to advertising more than humor. Humor is effective because, if done right, it can have nearly universal teen appeal. Other executional elements, such as celebrities or music, may not appeal to all teens and could alienate some. But humor can appeal to almost all, and it can be combined with a variety of teen-favored executional elements to create a synergistic effect. (A celebrity can be shown using an advertised product in a humorous way, for example.) Using humor in advertising is a high-risk, high-reward proposition. It's tough to get it right, but when you do, you broaden the potential audience for your ad.

Humor is not the answer to every advertising campaign. In fact, humor can be counterproductive in communicating certain product attributes. Selling a new high-tech product, for example, might be better done without humor. Reebok's original advertising for its Pump shoe humorously depicted coach Pat Riley and a few basketball players bent down on the basketball floor pumping their Reeboks. But teen athletes take their shoes seriously. They told us they were unsure of the technological soundness of Pumps; their doubts seemed to come from the humorous tone of the commercials.

Reebok's advertising for its next generation of Pumps, the InstaPump, was serious and more "next generation" in tone. It showed the evolution of pump technology. When we tested this campaign among high-school athletes, the teens believed in the technology and appreciated the serious and compelling way Reebok presented this high-ticket item to them. They believed the shoes would fit better and provide stronger ankle support, which would result in increased performance—they would be able to run faster and jump higher.

If humor doesn't make sense in an ad, it's doubly important to be original. If you're not going to leave them laughing, leave them thinking or feeling. Find ways to be perceived as being new and different. Advertisers know they need to set their brands and messages apart from others. Teens appreciate those rare ads that do, that are compelling, entertaining, or provocative in an original way. When we hear teens say, "Wow, that's different! I've never really seen a commercial like that before," we know our client is really onto something (assuming, of course, it's communicating as intended). Work to get teens' attention quickly; their attention span is short. Then, hold their attention throughout the 30 or 60 seconds.

When testing advertising concepts, always ask: Does the idea communicate its intended message? Is the message important and believable? Is the concept age appropriate? Can teens (or the teen target) personally relate to the idea and its execution? And, is the premise new or different? If an advertising concept fails any of these key tests, an advertiser should either change it appropriately or abandon it altogether.

Rule Three: Be Clear

Many media directors struggling with placing an ad that does not communicate its message as immediately as the client would like convince themselves (and sometimes their clients) that teens will get the message through repeated exposure. Media directors talk, after all, about the number (rather than the quality) of impressions. But there are too many alternatives available to teens at the push of a button to expect them to sit through an ad again and again until the message sinks in, no matter how cool or funny it is. As important as it is to entertain teens, clear communication should never take a back seat when advertising to teens.

When exposed to a confusing ad, teens may say, "Yeah, that was cool. But what did it mean?" Teens want to get the message, and they want to get it right away. The key is this: To teens, communication correlates with liking. If teens don't understand the point of a commercial or get lost in its communication, they will dismiss it. Teens are fairly literal; they are not going to work hard to understand what you're saying. Communicate clearly so they get it the first time.

Rules Four and Five: Show and Tell Teens about Your Product

Teens are savvy consumers, and their limited funds are precious to them. Not only do they view advertising as entertainment, they also view it as a source of product information. Teens can become frustrated and tune out advertising that doesn't answer basic product questions. Growing up in a high-tech world, teens are experts at processing information. They are well aware when critical information is lacking. When these two product-centered rules—showing the product and explaining what's important about it—are combined, they become teens' number-two rule (after be honest), reflecting the importance of product information. In TRU qualitative studies, teens have complained, "so many ads never even show the product."

But, what if your brand is in a category driven more by imagery than by physical properties? The answer is to connect your brand, your product, to the advertising. There must be a reason for your brand to be in the ad—and your brand should be the star.

Making the product the star of your ad is probably more important in the video-game category than in most others we regularly research. TRU has conducted much of Nintendo's qualitative copy research over the past several years, working with its advertising agency, Leo Burnett. We've also done qualitative research for other game marketers. No matter how much of a television spot is devoted to showing product shots, we find teens wanting more. Of course, simply showing game footage isn't enough. Typically, game footage alone cannot communicate brand imagery or fully engage teens in a commercial. But in the video-game category, product shots are often the heart of the commercial. How the product is shown and framed (along with the game action itself, of course) is what sets executions apart.

Other Rules

Although other rules don't score as highly as the top five, there is much to learn from them. Many teens think advertisers overemphasize the importance of being cool. As more companies enter the hot teen market, many marketers approach the business by saying, "We're going after teens now. We'd better be cool."

Don't try too hard to be cool. Instead, connect to teens' lifestyles, develop a strategy based on their timeless motivations, or create entertaining advertising. If you don't, teens will see right through you. We included the "don't try to be cool" rule in our quantitative study because of the many times we've heard teens say, after watching a commercial, "Some adult came up with that one just trying to sound cool!"

Don't underestimate teenagers. They are perceptive and draw the line when they feel a copywriter is pushing the coolness button too hard. The problem lies in the difference between what the copywriter thinks is cool to teens and what teens consider cool. It's better to incorporate cool elements only if they enhance the message. Don't try to be cool for the sake of being cool. It almost always backfires.

A great vehicle for connecting with teens is music. Not only is certain music inherently appealing and compelling to teens, it offers two tactical advantages when used appropriately in advertising. First, if teens like a tune or song in an ad, they undoubtedly will pay more attention to the ad. Second, music can signal to teens that an ad is for them. If an ad features a hip-hop, alternative, or metal soundtrack or song, teens know it's for them—and teens crave ownership.

When choosing music for an ad, don't automatically use whatever is the latest and greatest. A catchy original tune, when supported by relevant messages and compelling visuals, can be timeless.

Steer clear of specific musical acts because their popularity among teenagers will probably be short-lived. It's safer to use a style of music that is popular, although there are exceptions. One of our favorite teen ads over the past several years is a Nike execution known as "Instant Karma," featuring the John Lennon song of the same name. When we tested the commercial in focus groups of urban teens, they liked the spot and the song (which plays throughout and comprises the entire audio track), although only a few teens could identify the artist (and even then they named the Beatles rather than solo Lennon). "It's some '60s song, but it's cool and I like it," said one respondent. Nike happened to choose a song which transcends the generation from which it arose. The song worked because it was appropriate for the execution. Remember, the rule is to use great music *that fits.*

Many boomers regard Beatles songs and other music from the 1960s as sacred, disdaining their commercial use. But the only way to expose teens en masse to this great music may be to use it in commercials. My brother Paul, who supports his songwriter/singer career by also working as a music journalist, once asked Yoko Ono during an interview what she thought of Nike using her late husband's music. She was thrilled the music was reaching today's younger generation, regardless of the medium, she told him.

Another example of the flexibility in selecting music for teen-directed advertising is the use by Mountain Dew of the *West Side Story* song "Tonight" in its sky-surfer spot. Who would have thought that a Broadway hit of yesteryear could register with today's teens? But the fact is that the song works because it fits.

If there were a short list of essential rules that must be heeded in any successful teen-directed advertising, "don't talk down" would be on it (along with "be honest," "be clear," and either "be funny" or "be original"). Teens will reject advertising they find patronizing. Remember, teens have a different notion of what is condescending than do middle-aged advertising executives. At the very least, run your copy by a group of teens for a disaster check (not a surprising recommendation from a researcher!). Empathize with teens. Show you understand what's important to them without being condescending. Like adults, teens need to feel respected.

Don't Use Teen Slang

A few years ago, one of our biggest marketing "causes" was to get our clients to minimize their use of teen slang. We've been fairly successful. Before, there was a proliferation of advertising that used teen vernacular in an attempt to signal to teens that a product was for them. But teenspeak usually backfires. If teens feel that an advertiser is trying too hard to be teen, they may reject the advertising as condescending.

In focus groups, we've asked teens about the issue of teen slang in advertising. In one project, each group consisted of three sets of "buddy pairs," each pair representing one school. When we first asked respondents if they thought advertisers should use slang in advertising, most were enthusiastic about the idea. Then we asked each pair to list some of the newest words in use around their school. Although the six teens were from the same general area, they were unfamiliar with several of the words named by their fellow respondents. What's in at one school may not be in at a school across town. After this exercise, the respondents (without prompting from the moderator) recanted their earlier advice, saying, "Well, on second thought, maybe advertisers should not use our language."

Marketers should avoid using all but the most basic slang (e.g., "cool," "sucks, "man") in advertising for a variety reasons:

• Teens want their private language to remain private. They don't want adults to understand or—even worse—use teenspeak.

• Slang words are interpreted differently by different teens depending on geography, ethnicity, etc.

• Not all words appeal equally to all teen demographic segments.

• Language is perhaps the most volatile aspect of teen lifestyle; new words constantly enter the teen vernacular, while old words are just as quickly discarded.

• Slang is extremely faddish and short-lived. What may be in at the time of production may very well be out by the time your ad hits the air. Slang is not essential in creating relevant teen advertising. Instead, look to music, fashion, attitude, activities, and appropriate talent, which are all less risky means of achieving the same objective.

Sex in Advertising

Most teens agree about the top five rules in advertising, but there is less consensus about others. There is little agreement regarding the use of sex in advertising.

Nearly one-third of teens select "don't use sex to sell" as one of the their top five rules for advertisers. Not surprisingly, this is a rule of teen girls. Teen boys, on the other hand, actually advocate the use of sex in advertising.

When teenage boys are asked what they most want to see in advertising, they quickly answer, "girls" (although their vernacular reveals more about what they're actually looking for here). When teenage girls are asked what they think about sex in advertising, a typical response is the one we got from a 16-year-old: "If it's relevant to what they're selling, like condoms, then it's OK." Only 15 percent of girls chose "show sexy guys" as one of their top five rules for advertisers.

Girls want a reason for using sex in advertising. Boys, on the other hand, don't need to see a connection. They just want to see good-looking girls, and the hotter, the better. A sizable 26 percent of boys named "show hot girls" as one of their top five rules for advertisers. If your target is females only, or males and females, be extremely cautious about using sex in advertising. The more sensitive your communication in this area, the safer it will be.

The Four "Essentials"

What do all these rules mean to you? It boils down to four essentials.

1. **Communicate to me!** Teens want clear, honest communication in advertising. Although some media types like to use gross numbers of impressions to justify convoluted communication, saying the message will eventually sink in, don't believe it. Teens want to get your message the first time.

2. **Show me or tell me something about your product!** Teens understand what advertising is for. As much as they want to be entertained by advertising, they also want to get from it a relevant product message. Your brand should be the star of the advertising. If, after watching your ad, teens say "That was cool, but what did it have to do with _____ (your brand)," you blew it.

3. **Give me something to relate to!** Too many advertisers assume teens will find their advertising relevant. We advise our clients to give teens something they can easily relate to on a personal level. Consider music, sports, school scenes (remember, school is the ultimate social environment), parties, boy–girl situations, cool cars, activities, etc.

4. **Entertain me!** It you forget this essential, it doesn't matter how well you did on numbers 1, 2, and 3. You must entertain teens in your ads with humor, outrageousness, intrigue, music, celebrity, and so on.

The Rules for Consumer Promotions

During the past several years, TRU has been involved in evaluating a range of potential teen-targeting promotions, from in-school sampling to major-event marketing. The requests we receive for promotion research have increased noticeably over the past several years. There are two reasons for this: 1) greater marketing efforts targeting teens; and 2) marketers looking for new and different ways (beyond, or in addition to, advertising) to reach teens.

We have probed the attitudes and behavior of teens toward promotions—those they prefer and those in which they have participated. The results have been notably similar, showing that teens prefer simple, easy promotions that offer instant gratification. In one behavioral measurement, we presented teens with six types of consumer promotions and asked them which types they had participated in during the past 30 days. The two most popular were free samples (48 percent participation) and coupons (37 percent). Gift with purchase (27 percent), contests/sweepstakes (22 percent), cash rebates (9 percent), and frequent-buyer clubs (7 percent) followed.

More girls than boys take advantage of free samples, coupons, and gifts with purchases, probably because girls do more shopping than boys. More younger than older teens participate in sampling and contests, while the oldest teens prefer coupons.

Our findings show that promotions requiring too much of teens' time or effort, or those that involve chance, are much less likely to engage them. But if your objective is to create brand awareness or to enhance imagery, the right contest can work regardless of low participation levels. Focus on your gain among those exposed to the promotion rather than on how many actually participate.

To dig deeper into teen response to promotions, we wanted to create a promotion measure similar to our Rules for Advertisers. To begin this

Teen Participation
in Promotions

**Teens prefer promotions that offer free samples,
particularly girls and teens aged 12 to 15.**

*(percent of teens participating in selected types of consumer promotions
during the past 30 days, by gender and age, 1996)*

	total	gender	
		boys	girls
Free sample	48%	40%	55%
Coupon	37	30	44
Free gift with purchase	22	22	21
Contest/sweepstakes	27	24	30
Cash rebate	9	9	9
Frequent-buyer clubs	7	7	7

	age		
	12–15	16–17	18–19
Free sample	51%	44%	43%
Coupon	32	38	47
Free gift with purchase	25	18	19
Contest/sweepstakes	30	23	26
Cash rebate	9	7	12
Frequent-buyer clubs	5	8	9

Source: TRU *Teenage Marketing & Lifestyle Study*

process, we exposed our panel of teen Influencers to a variety of current promotions. We were impressed by the teens' awareness of many of the promotions and by the talk value some of them had created. We did notice, however, that many teens had difficulty differentiating between advertising and promotions. This line has blurred probably because of tightly integrated marketing programs and because so many well-known promotions are heavily advertised in popular teen media.

After talking about some of the promotions, we asked our panelists to generate a list of guidelines for companies wishing to create teen promotions. We then fine-tuned the list before including it as a question in our syndicated study. The results have proved extremely helpful in providing our clients with key criteria for developing promotions and for deciding which elements should be included in promotions.

Not surprisingly, the results parallel those of the behavioral measure. The data show that teens want promotions that are easy to enter, fun to participate in, and instantly gratifying. Perhaps the most important new finding is the importance of winning. Simply put, teens want to win something—almost anything! Rather than enticing teens with a huge grand prize, think smaller. The excitement of winning is such that teens prefer the better odds of winning a small prize than the long odds of winning a big prize. That's why instant-wins, such as under-the-cap promotions for soft-drink brands, are so popular with teens.

Teens want participation to be easy—easy to enter, easy to understand, no proofs of purchase. If there is a top prize, teens endorse money but reject travel. They like college scholarships offers, however.

As is true for advertising, teens demand honesty in promotions. They want marketers to establish credibility while also providing instant gratification. And as with advertising, teens want promotions to be geared toward people their age.

Rules for Promotions and Contests

Teens prefer contests that are easy and fun, with small prizes and many winners.

(percent of teens citing rule as one of the five most important rules companies should follow when promoting to teens, 1998)

It's easy to enter	46%
The contest or promotion is really fun	43
Cash is the grand/top prize	37
You instantly know if you win	37
There are many winners who win smaller prizes	34
There's proof that real people can win	31
The rules are easy to understand	30
It's especially for people your age	28
You don't have to collect proofs of purchase	27
A college scholarship is the grand/top prize	25
You can enter as often as you want	25
You don't have to wait long to get your prize	25
They tell you the odds/chances of winning ahead of time	23
The contest is advertised on your favorite radio station	15
The sponsor is a company you're really into	15
You don't have to enter through the mail	13
The contest has a celebrity spokesperson you really like	13
The contest is advertised on your favorite TV shows	11
There is one big winner who wins a very expensive prize	11
Travel is the grand/top prize	10
The contest is advertised in your favorite magazines	9

Source: TRU *Teenage Marketing & Lifestyle Study*

There are some differences by teen demographic segment. Instant gratification, for example, is more important to boys than girls. Girls are more likely than boys to demand easy-to-understand rules and age appropriateness. Girls also particularly like the idea of college scholarships. Significantly more of the oldest teens want contests that are easy to enter—perhaps because they are busy and there's so much competition for their time.

The essentials of teen-directed promotions are:
1. Keep promotions simple, relevant, and fun.
2. Give teens a real shot at winning by awarding many, albeit smaller prizes.
3. If you're going to offer a grand prize, make it cash or a college scholarship.
4. Establish credibility.
5. Provide instant gratification.

Chapter 12.

Researching Teens

It's probably no surprise that as a researcher I feel it is appropriate and important to devote a whole chapter to the craft of doing teen research. Too often, teen research is done incorrectly. In fact, a notable percentage of our work at TRU is what we call cleanup projects. What often happens is this: a business new to the teen market wisely commissions research to begin to explore the market. The marketer hires the same qualitative consultant (that is, focus group moderator) that handles the brand's adult research. Although this consultant is a known entity and understands the client's business, typically the individual is inexperienced in conducting teen research. Hiring an inexperienced researcher for this often hard-to-handle segment can spell disaster. This chapter is a guide to help you avoid the perils and pitfalls of teen research.

Research is an integral component of the marketing process, and it is particularly important in marketing to teens. Although you were once a teenager yourself, the older you are the more suspect is your ability to predict how teens will react to a marketing concept. Despite our years of researching teens, we continue at times to be surprised by our findings.

Often, clients call and ask for an off-the-cuff evaluation of a marketing idea. When we suggest that they research teens' response rather than rely on our guess of how teens might react, they often say their schedule (or budget) doesn't allow it, that they're comfortable moving ahead on our recommendation. While our batting average in predicting teen reactions probably rises each year, we do not advise clients to proceed with a new piece of advertising or product idea without first checking it out with the target.

Several times, after concluding a presentation at a client's office, we've been asked to evaluate a new advertisement on the spot. Typically, this request takes place in front of an audience that includes the people who developed the strategy, the creatives who executed the strategy, and the client who approved the creative. Although we never say "no" to such invitations, we always preface our remarks by explaining that, despite spending the better part of each week talking to teens and analyzing their reactions to marketing ideas, we still find teens unpredictable. That's why we do research.

With that as a preface, this chapter explains how to conduct teen marketing research, with special emphasis on qualitative research.

First, Set the Objective

Each research project should begin with clear, realistic objectives. As basic as this may sound, some clients ask us to do research without a specific objective. For other clients, the objective sometimes boils down to nothing more than "we want to do research" or "we thought we should do some focus groups." In fact, a highly worthwhile objective is to have brand managers and agency creatives simply listen to (and observe) consumers talking about the brand and/or category. The spark of an idea or a consumer insight often comes when creatives attend focus groups. Unfortunately, creatives do not attend as much research as they should.

Most clients come to us with specific objectives. More often than not, they describe their objectives over the telephone. Once in a while, we receive a formal request for proposal in which the objective for the proposed research is communicated in writing. As with copy strategy, research objectives that are committed to paper are typically well thought out. Writing down the objectives helps bring discipline to this critical stage of the process, making it easier to evaluate whether the objectives are achievable before beginning a project. The objectives should set the direction for your project, focusing on what needs to be and can be accomplished. The objectives determine whether the research should be qualitative (talking to teenagers in depth individually or in small groups), quantitative (asking teens to respond to a survey), or a combination of the two.

Qualitative versus Quantitative

If your objectives begin with words like explore, probe, develop hypotheses, gain an understanding, or brainstorm, then your research should likely be qualitative rather than quantitative. Qualitative research is open-ended and exploratory. It answers the why-questions and provides depth and richness of response.

If your research objectives begin with words such as how many, to determine, to specify, to test, and the like, quantitative research is probably what's called for. While qualitative research develops hypotheses, quantitative research tests them. Qualitative investigation gauges reactions, while quantitative investigation determines the frequency of reactions among teen segments. Qualitative research brainstorms for ideas, while quantitative research measures the appeal of those ideas. Qualitative research directs, while quantitative research specifies.

Qualitative research is more flexible than quantitative research. While quantitative research is based upon a set questionnaire, qualitative research can change in midstream, especially when done by a skilled moderator. When researching teens, flexibility is a valuable tool.

Qualitative research is especially useful when your objective is to enhance, modify, or improve an idea. That's true whether the idea is a new product, a positioning or concept, or advertising. Teens are adept at understanding, reacting to, and offering ideas for improving concepts.

Qualitative research also reveals things that quantitative research cannot. It allows you to observe teens' nonverbal reactions to ideas. It allows group synergy to emerge, which can be critically important in helping you develop or refine ideas. It allows you to probe responses as frequently and deeply as the subject matter or the respondents (or the moderator's skill) allow.

Observing nonverbal reactions is particularly important when researching teens, who often hide their real feelings. The importance of nonverbal response was brought home a few years ago when we tested teen reactions to "warning labels" on RC Cola's teen-targeted Kick citrus soft-drink brand. Although the labels were designed to appear authentic, the label copy was in jest. The two we tested read: "Warning: This product will cause extreme stimulation of the taste buds and will send tremors of satisfaction to your brain" and "Warning: Kick: the hard-core, psycho drink in a bottle."

During the focus-group session, I passed around bottles of Kick with warning labels, asking the teens not to comment about the bottles aloud at first. By their immediate nonverbal reactions, we saw right away that the teens were intrigued by the labels and quickly got the joke, which they enjoyed. But during the in-depth discussion that followed, the teens became overly analytical about the choice of words used in the labels. Their verbal response was less enthusiastic. The nonverbal reactions, however, clearly showed that the labels achieved their objective, creating immediate interest, curiosity, appeal, and age relevance.

Qualitative Research among Teens

Although the backbone of our company is our quantitative, syndicated *Teenage Marketing & Lifestyle Study*, the majority of our business consists of custom research. By far the greatest portion of custom work is qualitative. In fact, as we've often remarked to clients, our syndicated study is probably the most "qualitative" quantitative study that exists because it includes everything from exploratory questions to verbatim responses.

Two primary benefits of qualitative research are directness and flexibility: the ability to get in-depth reactions from consumers with the opportunity to probe and clarify immediately. If you are a first-time youth marketer, just seeing and hearing teenagers can be an eye-opening experience.

Your first decision is which qualitative method to use. The three basic types of qualitative design we use most often are one-on-ones (in-depth interviews with a single respondent), buddy pairs or dyads (interviews with two friends or two teens), and focus groups (we actually mostly do smaller minigroups). We also do triads, larger groups, and various combinations and configurations, depending upon the objectives of the particular project. Your study's objectives should drive the design. While all of the qualitative designs allow you to gain in-depth information, each has its own strengths and weaknesses, as outlined below.

Teen Focus Groups and Minigroups

• **Interaction** Allows synergies among teens to spark new thoughts, ideas, and insights.

• **Subject Matter** Use when subject matter is such that teens will be unlikely to withhold information or temper remarks.

• **Information** Assumes most respondents can say all they need to say about a topic (unaided) in about 8 to 12 minutes in a full focus group or 15 to 20 minutes in a minigroup.

• **Timing** Relatively quick turnaround, depending upon eligibility incidence (the percentage of the population who qualify to participate in the research) and number of groups.

• **Cost** At around $5,000 for a full focus group of 8 to 10 participants and somewhat less for minigroups with four to six respondents, this research is relatively inexpensive on a cost-per-interview basis. The total cost depends on the number of groups, eligibility incidence, and the type of reporting and analysis required.

Teen One-on-Ones

• **Interaction** Most effective when interaction among peers would be inhibiting or counterproductive to a project's objectives.

• **Subject Matter** Especially appropriate when the subject matter is sensitive and teens might not want to talk about it in a group setting. Also appropriate if your research objective is to gauge how well a tested copy, concept, or positioning communicates to teens.

• **Information** Allows greater depth of response. Effective if subject matter is complex or if it will require 20 to 30 minutes to get the needed information from an individual.

• **Timing** Depending on the number of interviews needed, more time may be required than for focus groups.

• **Cost** Typically more expensive per interview than focus groups.

Teen Buddy Pairs

• **Interaction** Particularly suited for products that are used by two people (e.g., a board game or video game). Also effective for communication testing if done cautiously and properly. Can heighten comfort level of young respondents and encourage dialogue.

• **Subject Matter** This extremely flexible configuration can handle almost any subject matter.

• **Information** Allows for great depth of response.

• **Logistics** Sometimes difficult to recruit teens from low-incidence groups, since both friends need to qualify independently.

• **Timing** Similar to one-on-ones, the time needed for buddy-pair inquiry can be longer than that for groups.

• **Cost** Between those of groups and one-on-ones on a cost-per-respondent basis.

Parent–Teen Pairs

• **Interaction** To gain insight into the purchaser–influencer or gatekeeper–initiator dynamic between parents and teens.

• **Subject Matter** Appropriate when the tested product is one the parent purchases, but for which the teen is the predominant influencer or user (e.g., contact lenses, the family computer, a vacation, a family pet).

• **Information** Allows for in-depth understanding of both teens' and parents' perspectives on an issue, with the opportunity to confront them about any conflicts or inconsistencies in their perceptions.

• **Logistics** Research must be scheduled around parents' and teens' schedules.

• **Cost** As with friend pairs, cost per respondent is less than that of one-on-ones but higher than that of groups.

Nontraditional Designs

Qualitative research can go beyond these traditional designs. We sometimes use observational research (observing teens at venues where they congregate or where they use or purchase a product) because it offers unique insights. To paraphrase Yogi Berra, "You can observe a whole lot just by watching." We use observational research to gauge people's attraction to a product or service, how they interact with it, and the dynamics involved in using it or deciding to use it. We also use observational research for answering, "What's new?" or "What's the latest trend?"

Our Kids Research Unlimited division has handled much of the qualitative research for Discovery Zone, the nation's leading chain of indoor playgrounds. To keep its FunCenters fresh and interesting to kids, Discovery Zone experiments with new additions. Rather than just talking to kids who have experienced these innovations, we observe them in the play environment. It's not hard to tell whether kids are having fun when they play. Additionally, our observational research allows us to see the sequence of play, how children interact with other kids in the environment, and how they allocate time among attractions.

We've also tested board games for Parker Brothers through observational research. This works best when the moderator explains the game's rules and gets the players going, then leaves the room during play and observes behind a one-way mirror.

In-store observational research can uncover the parent–teen dynamics of purchase influence, offering ideas for positioning. Observing how teens request items and how parents react to their requests can be enlightening. We've witnessed everything from out-and-out fights between parent and teen to teens sneaking items into shopping carts when mom turns her head. And, of course, we can talk to both parties right at the point of sale, after a decision has been made or a particular dynamic has been observed.

Another nontraditional type of qualitative research is the Immersion Experience. There's no better way to gain an in-depth understanding of consumers than by becoming totally immersed in their culture and lives, even for a short period of time. We've sponsored several teen immersion experiences, titled "Wise Up to Teens!" in which we immerse some of the country's top teen marketers in teenage life for the better part of a day. We expose them to everything from the latest in popular culture to introspective teen-produced videos of teenage life, to an opportunity to interact with and question teen Influencers. We've also done customized Immersion Experiences, designing entire programs around a client's objectives. We have become increasingly enthusiastic about this methodology after realizing that, as moderators, we often gain as much from the experience as our clients.

Immersion Experiences do not always work perfectly. We will never forget the comments of one brand manager, who—along with a colleague—escorted two 12-year-olds on an excursion to a video-game arcade. Despite being equipped (by us) with a guide for observing behavior and asking questions, the brand manager simply couldn't talk to the teens. When he complained that the teens he was with just didn't talk and dismissed the experience accordingly, we decided to add a caveat to all future immersion experiences: adult participants must be able to talk to teens!

Doing research over the Internet is growing in importance. We haven't done much in this area yet, although we have worked on many e-mail projects with members of teen panels we maintain (discussed below). Once on a panel, teens feel committed to responding. One way to get nearly instantaneous, thoughtful responses is to e-mail a question or two to panelists. This method certainly bypasses the natural shyness and peer pressure that exist in face-to-face research. Teens who are quiet in focus groups often open up and offer information and insights when they communicate with a keyboard and a mouse.

The Stages of Qualitative Research: Recruitment

Qualitative research is done in five stages. The first stage, defining the objective, has already been discussed. The second stage is recruiting teens for the study, but first you need to consider sample composition, sample size, market selection (geography), recruiting method, and screening criteria.

• **Sample Composition** First, it's important to recognize that qualitative research does not provide quantitative results. The small sample size in qualitative studies precludes projecting the findings to any population. Still, you should choose qualitative participants carefully to ensure that the sample reflects your target market. If you have no specific teen target (and one objective of your research is to aid in targeting decisions), select a sample composed of different age, gender, ethnic, and geographic segments.

In focus groups, teens are most comfortable when they are with others of the same gender and similar age and background. Recruiting similar teens fosters the bonding of participants, eliciting actionable answers.

Many teens do not feel comfortable with the opposite sex. Consequently, we conduct separate focus groups for boys and girls. If placed in a mixed-gender group, they may feel inhibited and not participate freely. Separating teens by gender will make your research more focused and productive.

Whenever possible, recruit by grade rather than age because grade is a better discriminator of lifestyle. A 14-year-old might be in junior high, middle school, or high school. A 14-year-old in high school will bring different experiences to a group than a 14-year-old in eighth grade. Similarly, when recruiting older teens, an 18-year-old could be in high school, in college, or out of school and in the work force. Strive to keep the grade range in focus groups narrow, including no more than one or two consecutive grades in a single focus group. If you must recruit by age rather than grade, keep the age range narrow, so that members are at most one year apart.

To economize on the number of focus groups for a project, consider eliminating the middle grade group. For example, if your target is 12-to-17-year-olds (or approximately seventh to twelfth grade), conduct focus groups with seventh and eighth graders and with tenth and eleventh graders, but leave out the ninth graders.

As in adult research, it is important not to recruit teen respondents who have already participated in research, except for panel research. Particularly among teens, the responses of experienced participants may be conditioned by their previous experience.

• **Sample Size** Generally, a few focus groups are enough to achieve the objectives of most qualitative research projects. Conducting two to four focus groups of one gender and age segment usually is sufficient. If you do more than that, responses tend to become repetitive.

The size of each focus group will depend on your research objective and the gender of the participants. A large group of girls is typically (but not always) more manageable than a large group of boys, who are more likely to become rowdy and lose focus. Typically, full focus groups are composed of 8 to 10 participants, although we try to dissuade our clients from seating more than seven. Whenever possible, we like to significantly overrecruit our groups, not only to make up for last-minute cancellations, no-shows, and respondents who do not qualify during on-site prescreening, but also to allow us the luxury of choosing the best respondents on-site. Of course, we always pay those we send home as if they had participated; we often also give them some assignment so they feel as if they have made a contribution.

We prefer small groups (known as minigroups) of approximately four to six respondents simply because they are more productive. Even if 8 or 10 would-be participants show up for a focus group, we handpick the more desirable candidates to keep the group as small as the client will allow. To increase the number of respondents in qualitative research, it's better to conduct more small focus groups than add respondents to your scheduled groups. Although fewer individuals take part, each person gets to say more, which is the main idea of qualitative research. A small group also makes it easier for rapport to develop both between moderator and group and among respondents. The downside of a small group is that a few particularly quiet or inarticulate participants can account for one-third to one-half of the group. This makes screening for expressive respondents critically important.

With one-on-ones and pairs, you typically need only a small number of interviews to obtain insights for next-step decision making. Generally, a sample of 12 to 25 interviews is sufficient. The number will vary depending on the specific project objectives and the number of gender and age segments you want to include. Most of the time, patterns begin to emerge after the first five to seven interviews. The remaining interviews tend to confirm those patterns and allow the moderator to probe outlying or emerging issues.

• **Market Selection (geography)** Depending on your project's objectives, try to conduct research in more than one market. This tactic is necessary for assessing regional differences and to diversify your respondents. This approach is particularly important if your objective is to gauge the appeal or personal relevance of an ad or product. Texas teens may find other things appealing or relevant than New York teens. But if the purpose of your research is to learn whether your ad communicates its message (rather than testing for relevance or appeal), then it is less important to include more than one or two markets. Ads that communicate in Dallas should also communicate in Manhattan, unless they contain language or symbols that are regionally specific.

If budget constraints dictate that you conduct only two or three focus groups, you can consider Midwestern teens reflective of the American teen population as a whole. But if your teen target is defined geographically, then your research must, of course, be conducted in that geographic market.

• **Recruiting Method** There are several ways to recruit teenage respondents for qualitative research.

1. Focus-group facilities provide lists of teens from their database of prescreened candidates, segmented by demographics. The best facilities keep notes on respondents, tracking information such as the type of research the teen has previously participated in and whether the teen contributed fully in the research or had a behavior problem. Be careful not to include teens who had behavior problems in a group setting in focus groups, although you may include them in one-on-one interviews. The rowdiest teens may make the most productive one-on-one respondents.

2. You can purchase specialized lists or samples of particular teen segments from traditional list houses or cull them from client databases.

3. Teens can be recruited through random-digit dialing or through the phone book methodology—using telephone directories as a base from which to locate teen respondents.

When a sample is particularly tough to recruit, we often resort to guerrilla tactics, such as placing ads in school newspapers and posting signs where teens, or a particular teen segment, hang out—clubs, parks, athletic facilities, and certain stores. These ads and signs should stress the fee for participating, a fee that should be significant enough to entice "low incidence" teens (such as $50). Be careful: no-show rates are higher for recruits obtained by these methods than for candidates recruited by telephone.

• **Screening Criteria** Potential participants should meet certain criteria before you include them in your study. Not only must they be of the right age and gender, but they must also meet project-specific criteria such as product category involvement or participation in a particular activity. In addition, it is crucial to screen adequately for articulateness to ensure that participants can express themselves in a group or when discussing a sensitive topic with an outsider. The screening technique for articulateness can be almost any open-ended question, such as "What's the best book you've read lately and why?" or "What's the toughest thing about being a student in your school? Why do you say that?"

The teens who pass the articulateness screening are those who do not hesitate to speak up. They express themselves clearly and intelligently. Their answers to the questions are less important than the manner in which they express themselves. At this stage in your project you may be at the mercy of hired recruiters, especially if the type of teen you need for a study is difficult to find. Recruiters hate to drop people who qualify in all aspects but articulateness. But always stand firm on this issue. Make sure recruiters do not invite inarticulate or overly quiet teens, even if it means making another 100 phone calls to find the right people.

While we enjoy a luxurious focus-group facility as much as anyone, when selecting a facility, one criterion is of unique importance: the quality of its recruiting. We keep a detailed log of our experiences, positive and negative, with every facility we use, creating our own rating system that each moderator contributes to after completing research. Because back rooms, rectangular tables, and ubiquitous bowls of M&Ms make Des Moines seem like Tucson, you should keep your own notes on each facility so that you can refer to them later if you ever need to do more research in the market.

It's also important to work closely with focus-group facilities so they clearly understand and properly adhere to the screening questionnaire, which sets out to ensure that each participant is fully qualified. The screening questionnaire probes five areas:

1. Demographics, product usage, or other attributes specific to the study.

2. Parents' occupations. As with adult research, you should avoid recruiting participants from households with members who are employed in advertising, marketing research, or any other capacity within the research industry or your business.

3. Recent participation in other market research projects. We recommend not recruiting someone who has participated in a study in the past 12 months or in more than two studies in the past three years. Experienced respondents may be sensitive to the types of answers desired, producing biased results.

4. Articulateness. Avoid recruiting teens who cannot express themselves coherently in a controlled setting or who are at all reluctant to contribute to a discussion.

5. Trendsetting. For many research projects, it may be most productive to recruit teens who are viewed as the coolest, whose lead is followed by others. By asking trendsetting teens about a product, service, or new concept, you gain insight into what teen opinion leaders think and feel. To put it bluntly, why waste time and money asking teens whose opinions don't matter to their peers to comment on new products or advertising? At TRU, we've developed a model, which we call Teen/Typing, for screening teens in terms of trend adoption. Our screen for Influencers is based on responses to about a dozen key questions, for example.

Another, but more expensive, technique for finding trendsetters is known as pyramidal recruiting. Because of its high cost (up to $800 per respondent for recruiting), most companies use this technique only when developing longitudinal panels, which amortizes the recruiting cost over several projects. To recruit in this way, you should go to the places teens hang out and ask the adults and teens there to recommend trendsetters. Then talk to the trendsetters and ask them to recommend trendsetters. Typically, they recommend others. Talk to those others and ask them to recommend trendsetters. If trendsetters recommend themselves, interview them intensively. You should deem only the most qualified as eligible to participate.

Whether you're recruiting adults or teens for qualitative research, cash is almost always the best incentive, typically around $50. If the research is at a facility that charges a fee for parking, pay extra. If a parent will be driving, pay the parent a little extra, around $15. We usually rely on the local focus-group facility's recommendation on how much to pay, since they know their market best, although we believe in always erring on the high side. Saving a few dollars is short sighted compared to the risk of not filling a group or an interview slot.

It's also important to pay floaters (standby recruits, who substitute for no-shows) about $10 to $20 more than scheduled one-on-one or buddy pair participants because their time commitment is greater than that of a scheduled participant. We usually ask floaters to cover two or three interview sessions.

Finally, talk to the teen's parents, asking permission to include their child in the research (remember, it's the parents who will be driving younger teens to the interview). If you will be asking teens to taste food or beverages, you should get the parents' written permission, specifically asking them whether their children are allergic to any foods. We never reveal a client's identity, but if the subject matter is sensitive, we explain to teens and parents the topic to be discussed. For example, when we did a project for the Partnership for a Drug-Free America on inhalants, we recruited only teens who felt comfortable talking to us about drugs and whose parents had no objection to our discussing the matter with their children.

When participants arrive at the research facility, it's important to re-screen them. The rescreen can reveal changes in a participant's age, product or category involvement, or other factors affecting their eligibility.

Most of the qualitative research we conduct is held at established focus-group facilities, complete with one-way mirrors, microphoned rooms, kitchen facilities, and so on. Typically, focus-group facilities handle recruiting in their local area. Sometimes we conduct focus groups outside facilities, including parks, respondents' homes, schools, stores, camps, restaurants, and community centers.

A one-way mirror offers the least obtrusive method of observing focus groups and other qualitative research. In rooms without one-way mirrors, you can set up a video camera that transmits to a monitor in another room with the observers.

For an increasing number of clients, we are conducting research at venues that are less artificial than traditional focus-group facilities. If a more natural environment adds to the comfort level of respondents and enhances discussion, then nontraditional settings have real merit, as long as everyone feels comfortable and on equal terms. In-home research, for example, should be conducted only with family members or close friends, so that all participants feel equally comfortable in the home. A traditional focus-group facility is a great equalizer. If respondents are strangers to one another, the facility puts them on equal terms.

Friends of mine own and direct one of the country's top boys' summer camps, Camp Kawaga, located in Minocqua, Wisconsin. We conducted a project for them a few years ago, interviewing parents of campers, parents of potential campers, and campers themselves. The findings were helpful in evaluating camp programs and in recruiting campers. We conducted the first two phases of the research by telephone. But when we interviewed the boys themselves, there was no better place than the camp, which allowed the boys to relax and talk candidly. It was especially rewarding to conduct "focus groups" during rest hour, when the boys were lying around on their bunks. No setting could be more natural for them to open up about camp than the cabins they love and share.

The Stages of Qualitative Research: Focus-Group Discussions

The third stage of qualitative research (after setting objectives and recruiting participants) is designing the discussion guide, including any projective exercises that might be used. The guide summarizes the areas to be covered during the discussion or interview, including the topics in the order you plan to address them, the length of time to be spent on each topic, and the issues to be emphasized. The guide becomes a checklist to ensure that each research objective will be fully addressed. It also aids the moderator or interviewer in covering all the important points. It guides the flow of the discussion and ensures that you don't dwell too long on any one topic.

The most effective topic guide resembles a brief outline, listing subjects and key phrases rather than complete sentences or questions. This structure allows the moderator flexibility in phrasing questions. Flexibility, in turn, allows the moderator to respond to unexpected responses or to probe topics that may surface during the discussion.

A guide typically begins with general questions about a research category, then moves on to specific areas of inquiry about your product, brand, or marketing idea. The initial broad discussion allows the moderator to uncover participants' general feelings about a category without biasing them toward a particular product or brand.

As with adult focus groups, the moderator of teen focus groups first explains the ground rules. We start by asking whether anyone has ever participated in a discussion group before. If someone has, we ask that person to explain what's expected. Most of the time, the respondent will use the word "opinion," but if she or he doesn't, we will. As we always do in our focus groups with children, we usually ask teens to quickly define "opinion," making sure that somebody says the words, "it's what you *think* or *feel*."

We also tell them about the one-way mirror (if we're in a focus-group facility), explaining that a couple of our friends are sitting behind the mirror and taking notes because "what you say is very important to us." Stressing the importance of their participation and their opinions makes teens take the task more seriously, which results in a more focused discussion.

Some of our clients are reluctant to tell participants about the one-way mirror, convinced that it will inhibit teens. But if you don't tell teens about it, they will undoubtedly figure it out on their own (especially in a group). Either someone who has taken part in a group before tells everyone else about it at an inopportune moment, or someone sees movement behind the glass. Teens' sudden discovery of the one-way mirror interrupts the flow of the group and can cause them to lose trust in the process and the moderator. When you tell teens about the mirror in the beginning, it becomes a nonissue. Usually, they will wave at the mirror and forget about it a moment later. What's more, we feel we have an ethical responsibility to let respondents know they are being observed and taped.

To reduce the likelihood that any two participants know one another, we never recruit more than one participant from a single school, except for buddy pairs. It is important that all participants be on equal ground. Either everyone knows everyone (as in the case of the Camp Kawaga research), or everyone knows only one other participant (buddy pairs), or no one knows anyone (most common).

Peer pressure operates in every teen community. Even in focus groups where no one knows any one else, there is peer pressure. We address this issue at the beginning of the group discussion. We ask the group (already knowing the answer), "Does anybody here know anybody else?" When everyone sees that the answer is "no," we say, "Well that means none of you will ever see anyone here again. So, there's no reason to care what anybody else thinks!" The teens typically react to this statement by quickly looking around the room, smiling slightly with relief.

This reassurance is an effective segue to our next ground rule (which must be emphasized when working with teens): "We're not here to agree! So if you're the only one who disagrees or has a different opinion, that's great. As long as it's your honest opinion."

Following the explanation of the ground rules is the warm-up, which aids in getting participants comfortable with speaking in front of the group and in bonding the group members. In addition to asking their first names, grade level, and school, we ask teens to share an experience or personal characteristic. One of our favorite warm-ups is: "What have your parents (teacher, boyfriend, girlfriend) recently done that has really pissed you off?"

Regardless of the response, it's important that the moderator verbally or nonverbally shows support for each respondent. Usually, other participants will say, "Yeah, that's happened to me too" or "That would really piss me off, too!" Strangers often quickly grow close by hearing about their common experiences.

To elicit the most actionable and productive focus-group discussion, the moderator should follow five rules:

1. The tone of the discussion should be friendly, open, and fun. Each participant should feel comfortable and respected.

2. Participants should do most of the talking. The moderator's role is to stimulate and guide discussion, not to participate.

3. Teen hierarchy is so strong that even in a group of strangers, leaders will exert themselves. Moderators should not allow one person to dominate the discussion. Similarly, if one or two participants are hesitant to speak up, the moderator should call upon them periodically, asking them to contribute and reinforcing their productive comments.

4. Teens (fortunately!) do not always agree. It's important to hear differing opinions and avoid forcing a consensus. If it appears that some participants are following the crowd, the moderator should play devil's advocate to elicit honest responses.

5. We often ask participants to write down their opinions or ratings on a piece of paper to minimize peer pressure. After they commit their thoughts to paper, teens are more likely to be forthcoming about their feelings. You can use a variety of specialized techniques to elicit honest responses from teens. Some of the ones we use most often are discussed next.

• **Teen Match** We often engage teens in an exercise we call "Teen Match" at the beginning of a focus group. This technique is especially effective in evaluating new concepts or products. In the exercise, we ask teens to name the different teen groups in their school, such as jocks, nerds, skaters, wannabes, preps, etc. The moderator writes the names of the teen types on a chalkboard or easel pad, explaining that they will return to the list later for further discussion. Toward the end of the focus group (after full discussion and evaluation of the test product, service, or concept) the moderator returns to the list, asking the group to match the test product to the teen type to whom it would most appeal. Because affiliation and hierarchy are so important in teens' lives and can shade their opinions about any new idea, this exercise allows you to get a uniquely teen perspective on the status, image, and potential success of the product among teens.

• **Card Sorting for New Concepts and Positionings** When testing new concepts, we often use a card-sorting technique. Card sorting offers a visual as well as physical way to keep young respondents focused. First, the moderator shows the group a series of concepts or positionings on a large board. The concepts should be as complete as possible yet simple, because younger teens in particular have difficulty conceptualizing. Each concept should be as distinct as possible to help respondents discriminate among them. Each should offer a visual reference, concept name, headline, description, and consumer benefit. After the group has viewed the list of concepts, the moderator hands a stack of cards to each participant, each card describing one of the concepts. The moderator asks the participants to sort the deck into two piles, one for the concepts they like and one for the concepts they don't like. Finally, the moderator asks them to stack the cards in each pile in order of likability. This exercise provides an effective springboard for discussing each concept in depth. Depending on the number of concepts tested, one or two usually fall out of favor and another few rise to the top. Then a discussion on how to improve, modify, and combine the best ideas can begin.

• **Product/Brand Sorts** Similar to concept sorts, this technique requires respondents to sort products and brands. A product sort can reveal teens' unique perspectives: how they categorize products; what they believe to be the competitive set; and how they compare products on a wide range of attributes from cool, fun, and age-appropriateness to size, shape, taste, and function.

• **Personification** To best understand brand imagery among teens, we often give respondents pictures of a variety of unfamiliar people. We ask participants to choose the picture of the person who would use each of the tested brands. We also have them describe brands in human terms—age, gender, personality, interests, style, etc.

• **Symbol Boards** In addition to exposing teens to pictures of unfamiliar people, we show them pictures of celebrities, animals, settings, athletic-shoe or apparel brands, cars, and so on, asking them to project their feelings onto the pictures. We say, for example, "If [the tested brand] were an animal, what kind of animal would it be?" Insight springs from the reasons why respondents choose a particular symbol to represent a brand; the actual choice is less important. A respondent who chooses a basset hound to represent a brand may explain her choice by saying that a basset hound is cool or she may say that it is stupid. Either way, the answer is revealing.

• **Word Lists** In this exercise, we give respondents lists of words and phrases and ask them to circle those that best describe the brand in question. Actually supplying teens words is key to doing this successfully. If you simply ask them to offer words without providing a list, respondents have much greater difficulty and the process is far less productive. If you carefully choose the words on the list and offer enough choices, the results should provide a clear picture of how teens feel about a particular brand.

• **Wish Lists** To provide insight into new product development or to enhance existing products or concepts, we often ask respondents to express their opinions with wishes. The rules of the wish list are simple: there are none. When teens are told that anything goes, their natural creativity is engaged to produce new product ideas, modifications, and enhancements.

• **Individual and Team Tasks** Because teens are so affected by peer pressure, even in focus groups, we often assign each participant a task and then ask him or her to present the results of the assignment to the group. In this way, respondents who are reluctant to speak up when sitting around a table are forced to contribute. More often than not, these reticent participants offer valuable insights. In a similar way, pairing teens and forcing them to work with someone they don't know can produce insights that might not emerge through group discussion.

• **Role Playing** Teens (and even children) can effectively participate in role-playing exercises. If one objective of your research is to understand the roles teens play vis-à-vis significant others (parents, siblings, friends, teachers, grandparents, store clerks, celebrity endorsers, etc.), asking participants to take on the significant-other role can provide great insight into the interpersonal dynamics of teenagers and the adults around them.

The Stages of Qualitative Research:
One-on-One, Buddy Pair, and Parent-Teen Pair Interviews

Warm-ups for one-on-one interviews, buddy pairs, and parent-teen pair interviews are just as important as they are for focus groups. Although these respondents don't need to get comfortable with a group, the moderator must establish rapport with the teen. Often the warm-up conversation centers around a teen's recent experience with his or her parents or friends.

During the warm-up, the moderator establishes the tone of the interview. It is important for respondents to feel they are in a friendly, comfortable environment and can talk openly. If the subject matter is delicate, the respondent must feel that the moderator will not pass judgment.

Buddy-pair interviews, that is, interviews with two friends who have been recruited together but independently meet a project's screening criteria, can be highly productive. Having a friend next to him or her increases a teen's comfort level and encourages dialogue. Good friends are also comfortable in disagreeing with each other. In fact, at the start of a buddy-pair interview, we ask the two friends whether they always agree with each other. Of course, they say no. We use this response to emphasize the need for independent thinking and encourage open disagreement. Still, if one objective of the research is to evaluate communication, we always have each respondent commit his or her responses to paper before the discussion, to minimize any bias.

A parent-teen interview is especially helpful in exploring how teens request, influence, or actually purchase a product or classification of products. We usually begin these sessions by warming up with both parties together, then we talk separately to the teen to get his or her perspective on the teen-parent dynamic. We excuse the teen and have a similar discussion with the parent. Then, we bring the teen back in, and, with the parent in the room, discuss and come to an understanding of any contradictions between their perspectives. The most insightful findings often come from discussing the conflicts.

The Stages of Qualitative Research: Debriefing

Debriefing is an important step in a qualitative study. During debriefing, the moderator and all personnel who have observed the focus groups or interviews review the session, focusing on key findings and observations. During this review, you should determine whether all your research objectives were satisfactorily addressed and itemize the relevant insights.

Debriefing is also helpful in providing direction to decision makers who have viewed only one session or only a few of the focus groups.

The debriefing session is an excellent time to discuss the strengths and weaknesses of the stimuli used in the groups. For example, the debriefing discussion may result in the elimination or revision of some less-than-positively received concepts or positionings, confusing storyboards, etc. Moreover, it is an opportunity for both the client and the moderator to review the key findings and decide on the next steps for the remaining groups or interviews. One of the benefits of qualitative research is the ability to quickly change direction, therefore debriefing (formal or informal) should focus on any necessary changes for the remaining interview sessions.

Because it is difficult to take detailed notes of what every respondent says during a focus group, the debriefing is an ideal time to review what teens said as well as what they meant. This helps avoid misinterpreting respondents' intentions. We are also careful during the debriefing not to internalize any client or agency bias.

The Stages of Qualitative Research: Reporting

The fifth and final stage of qualitative research is analyzing the learnings and writing the report. When your interviewing is complete, your project is not. It's rare that everyone who will be involved with the findings is actually present during the research. For some, the only way to find out about the research in-depth is to read the report. And for all, the report serves as a document that summarizes the findings, notes implications, and lays out recommendations. On occasion, the report will serve only as a file filler because decisions have been made during research and finalized during debriefing. In these cases, a report may not be as important, but it is still necessary because, as your company's personnel changes and issues are revisited, the report may be the company's only link to the research findings.

There are alternatives to a comprehensive written report. First, for key management unable to attend the research, we often give a next-day telephone debriefing. Although this method is less formal and less comprehensive than a presentation in person, it's more timely and often more doable.

Another alternative is a one- or two-page topline report that includes key insights, conclusions, and recommendations. Details and verbatim responses that expand upon, add flavor to, support, or document the topline can come later. From a business point of view, clients appreciate the quick topline summation, because it often saves them from writing and issuing a summary themselves.

Regardless of the reporting method, it's always worthwhile to stage a formal presentation of the findings. This gives everyone, including those who were not present at the research, the opportunity to learn the results, discuss implications, ask questions of the researcher, and decide on next steps.

Quantitative Research among Teens

Quantitative research among teens is structurally similar to that among adults, but it needs to be designed with the cognitive and developmental differences between teens (especially young ones) and adults in mind. Here is a brief overview of the basic quantitative methods—mail surveys, telephone interviews, and mall-intercept studies—and their relative advantages and disadvantages in researching teens.

TEEN MAIL SURVEYS

• **Sample** Can be a large, nationally representative sample, although there is less control over the final sample size and composition than with phone or mall-intercept studies. Samples can be purchased from a survey research company.

• **Responsiveness** Teens receive few pieces of mail, so they tend to be more responsive than adults. Cash incentives and follow-up phone calls increase response rates.

• **Stimuli** Mail allows teens to be exposed to visual stimuli, such as pictures of packages, logos, characters, etc.

• **Cost** Relatively inexpensive on a cost-per-interview basis, because long questionnaires can be sent to large numbers of people.

• **Timing** Longer turnaround time than other quantitative methods. Average project length is about eight weeks.

TEEN TELEPHONE SURVEYS

• **Sample** Can be a large, nationally representative sample recruited through random-digit dialing or from a purchased list. As with qualitative research, telephone surveys allow you to eliminate respondents who have participated in research in the past 12 months, unless they are part of a panel. Also, respondents should not live in a household with members who are employed in advertising, market research, or the client's industry.

• **Responsiveness** Generally, teens are willing participants, more cooperative than adults. Still, they have busy schedules, so fieldwork needs to be scheduled accordingly.

• **Stimuli** Telephone surveys do not allow you to expose teens to visual stimuli. Brief concept descriptions, however, can be read to them.

- **Age Appropriateness** Telephone interviewers must be specially trained to work with teens.

- **Cost** Generally less expensive than mall-intercept interviews, depending upon sample size.

- **Timing** Quick turnaround.

Teen Mall-Intercept Surveys

- **Sample** Since mall surveys are conducted only in selected markets, the sample will not be representative of the population as a whole. Still, this method can be an ideal way to set quotas in specific markets. You can recruit respondents at the mall, screen them, and invite them to an in-mall facility to complete the interview. Or, if the questionnaire is brief, you can conduct the interview at the point of interception. You can also prerecruit respondents, which is particularly important for low-incidence segments (for example, teen boys who do the major food shopping for their household and who buy a certain brand of snack chips). Prerecruiting is more expensive, but it gives you more control over the final sample.

- **Responsiveness** Participation tends to be high, since malls are a favorite teen venue. Many teens think intercepts are fun.

- **Stimuli** This quantitative method is the best for exposing teens to visual stimuli, from concept boards to videotapes to food sampling.

- **Age Appropriateness** Appropriate for teens because of the extra control of a face-to-face interview. Also, questionnaires can be presented on computers at mall facilities. Computer questionnaires are often more fun for teens, who are typically more comfortable and more skilled than adults at answering a computerized questionnaire. Computerized questionnaires also allow for skip patterns and rotations. Most importantly, they give teens a certain feeling of anonymity. We've been impressed with the quality—and quantity—of responses we've received from teens answering open-ended questions to which they type in their answers.

• **Cost** Tends to be the most expensive of the three quantitative designs on a cost-per-interview basis.

• **Timing** Depending on mall traffic and the incidence of teen shoppers, this can offer a relatively quick turnaround.

DEVELOPING THE QUESTIONNAIRE

Once you have established the research objective and determined the data-collection method, the next step is to draft a questionnaire specifically designed for teens. If any multivariate analyses will be performed, design the questionnaire with this in mind.

Quantitative questionnaires for teens are similar in design and content to questionnaires for adults, but the questions for teens should be more conversational in tone. Word questions so that teens readily understand them, but avoid condescension. Questions should not be overly inquisitive or too scientific-sounding. Most importantly, they should be fun to answer.

Teens usually do not have difficulty responding to open-ended questions. When probing, however, many prompts of "what else" and "anything else" may overly pressure teens to respond. Usually, one follow-up prompt of "what else" and one "anything else" will suffice, yielding pertinent information and avoiding created responses.

Teens are experienced in working with scaled questions, such as attribute ratings, because of their school experience. These types of questions are most productive if you limit the list to 7 to 10 attributes. When asking teens scaled questions, show the scale to respondents for quick reference. Cards work well in mall-intercept interviews, but in telephone interviews, interviewers should ask respondents to jot down the scale. Make the scale as friendly as possible. Don't bore teens with dull scale descriptors.

Pretest the questionnaire with the youngest respondents to be included in the sample. If the youngest understand a questionnaire, the entire sample should be able to understand it. In pretesting, make sure teens understand the words on the questionnaire, what each question means, and the scales used. Verify the accuracy, logic, and flow of questions and skip patterns. If teens have difficulty with any of these elements, fix them and test again. Don't assume the fix works until it is checked once again with respondents.

In telephone or mall-intercept research, you must train interviewers to handle teenage respondents. They need to understand some basic teen psychology, including that they can never assume a pedantic role. One way to get the right interviewers is to hire young adults who are not far out of their teen years themselves. Twentysomethings often handle teens with attitude better than older adults do.

Finally, validate your interviews. Hire a third-party firm that specializes in validation to confirm that your study was properly administered. We validate up to 20 percent of *each interviewer's* work by phoning the respondent and re-asking key questions. If answers don't match up within reason, throw them out and replace them with new ones. And be sure to validate these as well.

Teen Panels

One method for keeping up with teens that is growing in popularity is to develop your own teen panel. Our company has gained expertise in this area over the past few years. Before embarking on developing your own panel, it's important to carefully consider your objectives and budget. We've found that most of our clients who want a panel often rethink the idea once they consider all the factors. We believe the following are the best reasons for investing in a teen panel of your own:

1. You need to have constant access to a ready, qualified pool of respondents (often a low-incidence group, which is typically expensive to recruit).

2. You need instant reactions to advertising, promotions, merchandising, packaging, and new-product ideas from your target.

3. You are committed to thoroughly understanding your youth target—their lifestyles, attitudes, desires, beliefs, etc.

If the three reasons above describe your needs, also consider the following before deciding to build your panel:

• **Purpose** What are the research objectives you plan to address using your panel? Are these objectives really best answered through a panel?

• **Timeliness** Depending on the panel-building methodology (see below) you use and the number of markets you select, a panel can be developed during a period ranging from a few weeks to about one year. How much time do you have?

• **Budget** Panels are expensive to build and maintain. Establish a reasonable budget. Consider whether you will access your panel frequently enough to justify the cost.

What Kind of Panel?

The size of the panel you need depends on the research objectives you seek to address. Different-sized panels fit different needs. Here are three examples:

• Develop a panel in a few specific markets (strong BDI markets, for example). This type of panel would allow you to get together with your panelists for discussions, which is helpful for developing new teen products. You can meet with panelists individually or in small groups.

• Develop a large, quantitative national panel, representative of your youth target. This type of panel could be used for quantitative evaluations of product ideas. By oversampling in key markets, this panel could also be used for qualitative projects.

• Develop a small, specialized panel spread out geographically. You can send a panel of 30 to 50 teens regular projects to keep you abreast of teen culture. You could correspond with these panelists through the mail, by telephone, or via e-mail (or a combination of the three).

Panel-Building Methodology

Depending on your objectives, budget, and timing, there are different options for how to develop your panel. One of the least-expensive options is something we call a "Building Panel." Over the course of approximately one year, you would build this type of panel from the traditional qualitative (or quantitative) research projects you conduct in your normal course of business.

A faster way to create a panel is what we call the Insta-Panel Audition. We recruit teens to come to a facility and audition them for a panel. In this way, a single-market panel can be created over the course of only one or two nights. Additional markets can be added as desired. To develop a larger, more diversified panel, consider mall (and/or other venues) for intercepts, where teens are screened and undergo complete auditions.

Panel Maintenance

It is important to nurture your panel to keep members involved and active. An ongoing relationship minimizes attrition. We believe in treating panel members like employees, respecting them and paying them well. They will return the favor by being responsive and conscientious.

Conclusion

If your brand does not target teens, you face a daunting task in convincing corporate management that teens are a viable marketing target. You must develop a rationale for investing in this fast-moving segment and persuade upper management that your company can succeed where others have failed. You must convince management that you can sell to teenage America.

Here are three key points to drive home:

1. Teen spending is already huge and the numbers are growing. No doubt about it, teens are a hot market. Their purchasing power, combined with an expanding population, warrant aggressively pursuing this market.

Teen spending is on the rise, and few teens are saddled with the payments that inhibit adult spending, like rent, utilities, and groceries. Teens' considerable income is almost exclusively discretionary. They are consumers with a mission: they want to spend on whatever happens to please them. What a compelling advertising target!

Teens are adept enough at saving money to finance most big-ticket purchases. More than three-fourths of teens have a savings account. Almost all products are well within a teen's reach, including everything from a favorite soft drink to the latest computer software, designer-label clothes, and cell phones.

Even when teens are not buying products themselves, they influence—both passively and aggressively—their parents' buying. Not only do their mothers know what cereal brands to buy for them, parents also seek their teenage children's counsel when buying a family computer or shopping for a stereo or VCR. (Of course, all this buying and requesting shapes teens' future attitudes about your brand.)

Perhaps the most exciting news about the teen market is that the teen population boom is still in its infancy. After 17 years of decline, which ended in 1992, the teenage population is expected to grow each year until 2010, at which time there will be more teens than ever before in the U.S. population. Generation Y is the biggest thing to hit this country since their parents' cohort—the boomers. Those who miss out on Gen Y now will be playing catch up for years to come.

2. Teens can be reached. There are more media vehicles with which to reach teens today than at any time in the past. Although teens' media schedule and preferences differ from those of adults and children, teens have a huge appetite for media. From teen magazines to alternative 'zines and Web sites, from MTV to Fox, the WB, and Channel One, and from place-based media and special events to local radio, media companies are rapidly developing more effective, cost-efficient, and innovative ways to reach the nation's teenagers. Management's old argument that the teen market is too elusive no longer holds water.

3. Teens can be influenced by advertising and marketing. We often tell gun-shy potential teen marketers that trying to understand and appeal to teens is not impossible. Teens are not so enigmatic, so difficult to understand, and so fickle in their likes and dislikes that they cannot be swayed by well-crafted and well-placed advertising and marketing efforts. But teens are also media- and marketing-savvy. They are cynical by nature and bombarded with media messages. You must do your homework if you hope to win them over. First figure out who you are to teens—what they like and dislike about you, and what you really mean to them. Understand the unique perception teenagers have of you, and play to your strengths. Don't try to be something you're not. Teens reject products and advertising that doesn't ring true to them. They revel in the real, the raw, and the honest.

In the past decade, the collective knowledge about teens and the understanding of how to reach them have grown enormously, allowing more companies to create relevant and compelling marketing communications. Many of today's most successful brands are thriving in large part because of their teen efforts. Go ahead, make the case to management. Convince the company leaders to wise up to the power and potential of the teen market. Show them why and how the teen market can grow your business. The rewards of marketing to teens smartly and creatively will be well worth the risk.

Index

16 magazine, 73, 75–76
7-Up, 6
7th Heaven, 79–80

Abercrombie & Fitch, 29, 32
abortion, attitudes toward, 244
Acclaim, 30
Ace of Base, 154
actors as endorsers, 180–183
adidas, 6, 26, 28–29, 32
adult life, hopes and expectations for,
    217–220
adult misconceptions about teens, 223–227
advertising
  and alternative media, 90–93
  and attitudes toward school, 276
  and depictions of advice givers, 267
  and depictions of family members, 264
  and parent-teen relationship, 274
  anti-tobacco, 16, 18, 245, 248
  as a criterion of brand choice, 28
  attitudes toward, 282–285
  direct mail, 90
  humor in, 289–290
  in schools, 91
  in-theater, 90
  involvement with, 67
  place-based, 90–91
  portraying teens in, 197
  rules for, 287–296
  sex used in, 295–296
  slang used in, 294–295
  tied into sports participation, 120
  use of celebrities in, 152–157, 170–183
advice, where to get it, 265–268

African-Americans
  attitude toward advertising, 284
  attitude toward being "cool," 195
  attitude toward family, 253, 258–259
  attitude toward religion, 191
  cable television preferences, 82
  online services, use of, 87
  peer pressure, 191
  popularity of music genres, 161–162
  radio preferences, 71
  social concerns, 240
  sources for finding out about new trends,
    130
age
  activities during the week, 105
  income, 11
  likelihood of buying "teen" products, 48
  looking forward to, 222
  spending, 8
  worries, 231
age aspiration, 46, 204–206
AIDS
  attitudes toward, 237–241, 246
  awareness of, 196
Airwalk, 30, 137
Aiwa, 30
All About You, 73
Alloy, 78
Alternative. *See* Music genres.
alternative media, preferences for, 89
American Eagle, 30
America Online, 85–88
American Passage Marketing Corporation, 92
Amundson High School, 243
Anchor Blue, 30